The Spasmodic Poets

Also by Lori A. Paige

*The Gothic Romance Wave:
A Critical History of the Mass Market Novels, 1960–1993*
(McFarland, 2018)

The Spasmodic Poets
*Appraising a Controversial School
of Victorian Literature*

LORI A. PAIGE

McFarland & Company, Inc., Publishers
Jefferson, North Carolina

This book has undergone peer review.

ISBN (print) 978-1-4766-8296-9
ISBN (ebook) 978-1-4766-4815-6

LIBRARY OF CONGRESS AND BRITISH LIBRARY
CATALOGUING DATA ARE AVAILABLE

Library of Congress Control Number 2022045202

© 2022 Lori A. Paige. All rights reserved

No part of this book may be reproduced or transmitted in any form or by any means, electronic or mechanical, including photocopying or recording, or by any information storage and retrieval system, without permission in writing from the publisher.

Front cover: left to right: Sydney Thompson Dobell, William Aytoun Bust, William Aytoun (wikipedia commons); background image of vintage literary elements (Shutterstock/ Chyrko Olena)

Printed in the United States of America

*McFarland & Company, Inc., Publishers
Box 611, Jefferson, North Carolina 28640
www.mcfarlandpub.com*

This is that same hour
That I have seen before me as a star
Seen from a rushing comet thro' the black
And forward night, which orbs, and orbs, and orbs,
Till that which was a shining spot in space
Flames out between us and the universe,
And burns the heavens with glory.
—Sydney Dobell, *Balder*

Acknowledgments

I would like to thank my colleagues at American International College, particularly Julie Bodnar and Will Steffen of the English Department for their continued professional support, and Nancy Little and Maxine Girard at Shea Library for their invaluable assistance with research and citations.

Table of Contents

Acknowledgments vi

Introduction 1

1. "Some Special Providential Purpose": The Tale of the Spasmodic School   11
2. "Fearless Strains": British Literary Culture at Mid–Century   29
3. "Barbaric Jewelry": Bailey's *Festus* and the Birth of the Spasmodic Ideal   54
4. "With a Halo Crowned": *Gerald, A Life-Drama*, and the Coming of the *Vates*   77
5. "The Unstable Bubble of Inflated Thought": Dobell, Bigg, and the Flowering of High Spasmody   100
6. "All High Poetry Is and Must Be Spasmodic": The Anti-Spasmodic Reaction   124
7. "A Cloud of Poisonous Flies": After the Spasmodics   147

Epilogue: "Vast Displays of Critic Wit": The Future of the Spasmodic School   169

A Spasmodic Timeline   173

Chapter Notes   177

Bibliography   197

Index   205

Introduction

Few literary terms provoke the kind of reaction "Spasmodic poets" does among those who have never heard of them. Non-specialists might express amusement, bewilderment, or outright disbelief (and sometimes all three). This is not surprising. "Spasmodic" has both slang and medical associations that overshadow its literary usage (in fact, a bottle of "Anti-Spasmodic Formula" is currently available in liquid form on Amazon.com). Considering that the name was popularized by a cantankerous (and some might say mean-spirited) periodical reviewer in an attempt to ridicule, one might expect that over the years, some more suitable label would have taken its place. After all, no one still refers to Byron and Shelley as members of "the Satanic School," despite Robert Southey's impassioned efforts. Yet no preferred descriptor has ever emerged. Possibly this is because no other word can fully convey either the flavor or the substance of this fleeting but intriguing episode in literary history.

Few narratives better capture the unique interplay of critical theory, mass media, and public taste, both Victorian and modern, than the tale of the Spasmodics, youthful neo–Romantics who briefly flourished at mid-century but were almost forgotten by 1900. Their ill-fated movement was both an aesthetic and a cultural phenomenon. It is no exaggeration to say that what we now consider "Victorian" poetics was profoundly influenced and in no small part shaped by the unfortunate Spasmodic School's growth, popularity, and (perhaps inevitable) decline.

Admittedly, it would be difficult to proclaim the Spasmodics' artistic preeminence among the better-known Victorian authors, although the fine quality of a few of their later works might come as a surprise to some. This is especially true since the rare studies that accord the Spasmodics more than a superficial mention often present the excesses of selected lines from a Spasmodic work or two only to exemplify a dying Romantic impulse desperately floundering beneath the staid march of

Introduction

Victorian letters. It is remarkably easy to open any "Spasmodic" volume at random and find passages that stand out as embarrassingly histrionic, even by Victorian standards, such as this passage from Dobell's *Balder*: "I do stand / Blood-hot from head to heel but cool within. / Blood-wet and steaming blood from every pore / Incarnadine, but retching at those mouths / The red surcharge that killed me." Some Spasmodic images are so bizarre that they are indistinguishable from conscious parody, such as Bailey's "God tore the glory from the sun's broad brow, / And flung the flaming scalp off flat to Hell." Others are unintentionally humorous, such as Smith's "He is to us / But a rich odor,—a faint music-swell."

The neglect of these works is not entirely unjustified: the significance of the Spasmodics to their original Victorian audience, as well as to literary history, rests less with the poems themselves than with the movement's chronological position. From approximately 1850 to 1860, the Spasmodics' shadow fell across virtually every serious discussion of Victorian poetics. Many mid-nineteenth century writers were associated with the Spasmodic School in one way or another, either as adherents (willing or not) or as outspoken detractors. Some critics, like Clough, expressed both admiration and hostility toward them in equal measure; the controversy surrounding their work informed and influenced (often disadvantageously) periodical reviewers' estimates of the three major Victorian poets. Tennyson and both Brownings were compared to and even occasionally identified with the School, and Arnold's seminal 1853 Preface has been identified as a response to, or more accurately a rejection of, Spasmodic theories and practices. It is no exaggeration to claim that without giving thorough attention to the artistic context which produced many admittedly superior poets, we cannot thoroughly understand their works.

Modern Victorianists who are familiar with the Spasmodics usually come to them via two main critical thoroughfares, Lionel Trilling's *Matthew Arnold* of 1939 (republished as a mass-market paperback in 1955) and Jerome Buckley's 1951 *The Victorian Temper* (along with the vast number of subsequent works that cite or gloss either or both of these seminal studies). Trilling's abbreviated treatment is typical of modern assessments of the Spasmodics. He alludes to something almost progressive in their fragmented artistic treatment of a fragmented contemporary world, but stops short of acknowledging, much less praising, this potentially radical approach:

Introduction

As laid down [in *Firmilian*] the Spasmodic principle was a simple one: "The office of poetry is to exhibit the passions in that state of excitement which distinguishes one from the other." "Passion," indeed, was all: bombast, formlessness, the straining of metaphorical language to its limit were the result of this preoccupation.... The Spasmodics saw something of the complexity of modern life, but saw it without a coherent idea and responded to multitudinousness with the multitudinousness of a literary method which paid more attention to parts than to their integration.[1]

Though Buckley's analysis is more extensive than Trilling's, he reaches essentially the same conclusion, though for him their implosion resulted from their shared inability to master a suitably traditional literary form, that of the epic:

Inflamed by borrowed passions and their own ranting emotion, the Spasmodics yielded to a titanic egotism.... Godlike, they sought to create worlds in their own image; theirs was a thoroughly subjective art peopled by men of sensibility, heroes very like themselves.... More consistently than their greater contemporaries, they dreamed of a Victorian epic ample enough to embrace the manifold aspiration of the nineteenth century. Yet none possessed an architectonic sense at all commensurate to his high vision; and none would submit to the formal discipline requisite for the proportioning of an epic structure ... obsessed with their lofty ambitions, they remained minor poets failing in a major key.[2]

These two studies, both classics of scholarship, characterized the Spasmodics as misguided dilettantes who roused a great deal of critical discussion in their own time, worth salvaging from deserved obscurity mainly because of Arnold's *Preface*, Tennyson's *Maud*, and a wave of anti–Browning criticism of the 1850s. Though Buckley seems to appreciate the advantages of studying lesser-known poets in their original context, he declines to speculate on the popular forces that shaped and then promoted such poets. Instead, he uses them as means to an end, of interest only as foils to more successful poets and poetic theory. Buckley presents their work as a confused (and confusing) jumble of the philosophy and artistic methodologies espoused by Carlyle, Byron, Goethe, and Shelley, with a dash of Keatsian sensuousness thrown in for shock value.[3] For Trilling, the Spasmodics embodied the kind of crass intellectualism manqué that Arnold spent his entire life railing against. He notes their origins in the "dissenting lower or middle classes" and attributes their brief popularity to their "intense yet pious" attitudes and the "respectable Satanism" that titillated an undiscerning public (as the scandalous escapades of Byron, founder of Southey's putative "Satanic School" once had).[4] Neither Trilling nor Buckley disputes that they

Introduction

attracted a large number of readers and earned the (sometimes grudging) respect of Arthur Hugh Clough, John Ruskin, and George Eliot,[5] among other respected commentators, nor that their contributions had a significant effect on the critical discourse of the day. Both imply, at the very least, that Arnold's contribution to posterity in the form of his literary output and the formation of the canon might look very different had the Spasmodics not attracted his attention (and his scorn).

Over the next few decades, the productions of the Spasmodic School's leading figures attracted little critical attention. After the 1960s, as traditional methods of critical analysis like formalism and historicism began to fade, the Spasmodics languished as well, consigned to the well of inferior poets and outdated ephemera. Scholars still encountered them while researching other mid–Victorian figures such as Clough, Swinburne, or Charlotte Brontë, who exchanged a number of illuminating letters[6] with the Spasmodic poet Sydney Dobell. They sometimes surfaced during discussions of the Romantic movement and Victorian attitudes toward Byron, Shelley, and Keats, and they often merited at least one endnote or index entry in any in-depth study of Tennyson or the Brownings (especially with respect to *Aurora Leigh*, which has often, and not inaccurately, been identified as a Spasmodic production). Yale University Press released Mark A. Weinstein's *William Edmondstoune Aytoun and the Spasmodic Controversy* in 1968, but its focus was on Aytoun's anti–Spasmodic crusade rather than on the school or its proponents. In 1992, Martha Westwater explored *The Spasmodic Career of Sydney Dobell* and attempted to rehabilitate Dobell's reputation by identifying proto-feminist elements in his works. By then, however, their works had ceased to be anthologized and the movement was excluded from British literary chronologies. Fate had bequeathed the Spasmodics to a few specialists and a handful of unpublished dissertations.

Then came the millennium. Now, with an entire century between us and the Victorians, the critical sands have shifted again. The growth of contextual studies has yielded a vast supply of forgotten minor writers whose texts have been denied what scholars call the "privileging" accorded to others. Redressing and restoring these omissions can offer a more complete perspective on the original time period (and perhaps, by refraction, our own). Despite, or perhaps because of, their public shaming and dramatic fall from grace, interest in the Spasmodics has revived. As a product of the relatively new field of mass-produced entertainment, their public reception provides a useful index of popular Victorian taste

Introduction

in poetry and social politics: the battle that erupted in the periodical press after *Firmilian* in some ways resembles a modern internet-based flame war in analog form. Their legacy is especially meaningful with respect to Victorian critical theory and the development of what we now call the Victorian canon.

Scholars now accept that any group of works chosen for study or interpretation is, at best, a selection guided by the informed tastes of one or more selectors or, at worst, a politically determined act of deliberate exclusion. Certainly this is also true of those selections traditionally culled from the Victorian period, the prolific nature of which requires a substantial degree of winnowing (for which Matthew Arnold, who disdained working-class poets like the Spasmodics, provided a heavy guiding hand). What might be touted either implicitly or explicitly as a representative sampling of, say, Victorian poetry might be more accurately acknowledged as an academic reconstruction reflecting some degree of (perhaps benign) bias. Inevitably, certain authors will appear ubiquitous, others will be underrepresented, and a good many others will simply be omitted without comment or apology. Into the third category will probably fall many names that the average Victorian reader would be puzzled not to find in the first.

Science fiction fans often refer to a concept called "Sturgeon's Law," which inelegantly but insightfully states that "ninety percent of everything is crap."[7] Theodore Sturgeon was referring to modern paperback novels, but the idea could certainly apply to nineteenth-century literature. Much Victorian poetry is of a lamentable quality and scarcely deserves reconsideration. Some of this material was unread or perhaps even unpublished in its day, and might be said merely to reflect, rather than to have influenced, cultural aesthetic standards. The omission of such poems from critical studies can scarcely be questioned. Other kinds of works, however, present greater difficulties. What should we make of those poems which have not stood the proverbial test of time, but were popular successes, widely read and imitated, upon their original publication? The Spasmodics, who were not only casualties but catalysts of nineteenth-century canon formation, fall into this category. Inquiries into the subsequent exclusionary practices of critics, scholars, and publishers, not to mention increasing awareness of class and gender issues in the works of Arnold, Trilling, and Buckley (among many others who occupied privileged positions in society, academia, and publishing), have rediscovered authors like Alexander Smith and Sydney Dobell. It now seems clear that they were rebuffed (some might

Introduction

say destroyed) as much for their lack of social standing as for a lack of innate talent (which they certainly possessed).

Thankfully, the acknowledgment of the Spasmodics' influence and importance has provided fresh avenues for academic discourse. The poems themselves have, somewhat surprisingly, proven amenable to feminist, Marxist, neohistoricist, and gender-based approaches; a recent article title, "Alexander Smith and the Bisexual Poetics of *A Life-Drama*,"[8] indicates just one of many innovative paths forged by a new generation of Victorianists. Research has extended the Spasmodics' circle of influence far beyond Arnold, Tennyson, and the Brownings; echoes of their themes and techniques can also be found in Swinburne and the Decadents as well as the works of American poets like Emily Dickinson and Walt Whitman. Best of all, digital tools like Project Gutenberg will preserve their works well into a future Dobell, Smith, and their circle could never have imagined.

The new academic attention to cultural studies has provided the Spasmodics with another niche. By looking beyond the (sometimes punitive) scrutiny of traditional academic close reading and repositioning it within the context of early mass-consumerism and popular entertainment, scholars can assess the Spasmodics' contribution with the same fairness others have applied to, for example, gothic tales and sensation novels (both of which certainly contain many Spasmodic qualities). This practice has, in effect, liberated the poetry and has also revealed unexpected literary quality in some cases. The expansion of Victorian literary studies from England proper into other parts of the British Isles has also increased interest in the Spasmodic movement, which had strong ties to both Glasgow and Edinburgh. Alexander Smith, in particular, has commanded recent attention as an observer of the conditions unique to nineteenth-century Scotland. Simon Berry's detailed and sensitive biography *Applauding Thunder* (2013) attempts to restore Smith to his rightful place in Scottish literary history.

Another area of interest has been the role played by the Victorian periodical press in the Spasmodics' dramatic rise and fall. Smith and Dobell in particular might accurately be called both the products and victims of an expanding publishing marketplace and the commercialization of culture. Briefly caught in the Spasmodic critical net, Tennyson nearly drowned in its harsh currents as well. With the benefit of a hindsight the Victorian critics obviously did not have, we can discuss the changing conception of the poet, both in the poet's own eyes and in the critics', in the context of emerging modern methods of criticism

Introduction

as expressed in the periodicals of the day. An important contrast exists between the eponymous protagonist of Dobell's *Balder*, a poet who wants most of all "Power like a god's and wielded as a god," and what we would now call the modernistic pessimism of Arnold's narrators. If the Spasmodics were the creation of the commercial press, they were also its victims: the praise initially heaped upon these very young men gave them an inflated sense of their own powers and allowed them to drift toward aesthetic dogmatism. Just as abruptly they were denounced by equally imperious critics who used the press to hound them into obscurity (one review of Alexander Smith's *Poems* brutally recommended that Smith's bared buttocks be whipped, schoolboy style).

The Spasmodics and their supporters saw the role of the Victorian poet in distinctly Carlylean terms; he should be nothing less than a *vates*, a prophet for his own age, defining not only the purpose of art but influencing the course of society. In this context, the Spasmodic poets may be fruitfully compared to the better-known Pre-Raphaelites, since for a time various authors were called "Spasmodic" by their detractors in the same way that "Pre-Raphaelite" came to describe works and artists which were not official members of Rossetti's Brotherhood.[9] Of course, in one sense, a comparison with the Pre-Raphaelites is not entirely appropriate: except for a single collaborative volume of poems by Smith and Dobell, the Spasmodics did not share their work with each other, did not prepare a written manifesto, and did not sponsor a forum like *The Germ*. They did not choose the term "Spasmodic" to express a coherent, and to some appealing, direction; it was bestowed upon them by hostile reviewers, and the insult stuck like a burr.

On the other hand, a comparison is illuminating (and not just because Rossetti was an admirer of Dobell[10]). Chronologically, the two are not far apart, since the Brotherhood was formed in 1848, and Bailey's *Festus* (regarded as the first "Spasmodic" poem, though the term did not yet exist in that context) received its most important critical notice in 1850 in *Blackwood's*, a pivotal periodical in the Spasmodic debate. Both the Brotherhood and the Spasmodics were groups of extremely young men rebelling against what they perceived as rigidity and emotionlessness in early Victorian aesthetics. Their youth is worth noting, as all wished to shape the poetics of their own generation by making use of the Romantic trends of the previous one. Both were ridiculed for practically the same poetic faults, generally related to an infusion of extreme Romanticism, and consequently both influenced the structure of subsequent literary productions. The main point

Introduction

of departure, in fact, is that Pre-Raphaelitism attracted a second set of disciples, such as Morris and Swinburne, and thus gained a chance to mature; the Spasmodics found no new followers after the periodical press, led by *Blackwood's*, had humiliated them, and poets accused of being Spasmodic, as both Browning and Tennyson were, embarrassedly shook off the association. The Romantic impulse, both in poetic content and towards the priestly poet/prophet or *vates*, is not to be found again until the Pre-Raphaelite movement, and in near-parodic form among its declension, Aestheticism.

Ultimately, the Romantic turn of Victorian poetry hoped for by the Spasmodics, which they hoped would meld Byronic fire with (arguably idiosyncratic) Christian devotion, never came about. In its place stood the mournful introspection of poems like "Dover Beach" (1867), in which Arnold's speaker laments the "melancholy, long, withdrawing roar" of faith from a more innocent and trusting world. Ironically, the barrenness he mourns is one Arnold himself had helped to bring about through his stern and thorough rejection of Spasmodic aesthetics. By the end of the tumultuous 1850s, his intellectually conservative vision for British poetry had emerged triumphant. It is tempting to wonder, though, if he recalled the dramatic clash between the Spasmodics' exuberant Romanticism and his own staid Victorianism when he depicted the epic struggle on that darkling plain.

Dobell, Smith, and their circle had hoped to change literature and their readers' lives on a grand scale. In one sense, they succeeded, as the critical backlash against their works in no small way helped to form, for good or for ill, the Victorian canon that inspires our scholarship. In another sense, they were able to transcend the constraints of their time and place and occasionally reach into modern literary sensibility. Their tormented protagonists explore the conflict between raw individualism and a hypocritical society, an approach that would become commonplace, even expected, in the century that followed theirs. Balder's homicidal psychopathy would have raised few eyebrows after the collective trauma of World War I.

Modern scholars inhabit a secular, technologically driven world Victorians would hardly recognize; yet most of us can easily relate to the Spasmodics' struggle for social and artistic acceptance, the momentary taste of sweet success, and the soul-shaking disappointment that followed. Though their literary careers ended in disappointment, they would probably be gratified to know that even in the twenty-first century, they have not been and should not be forgotten.

Introduction

What follows is an attempt to document, in the appropriate social context, the trajectory of the Spasmodic School in both its original incarnation and in subsequent appraisals. This study examines the various personalities and aesthetic principles that fashioned the movement without championing any particular critical stance or verdict. Ultimately, the quality and appeal of the Spasmodic output remains a matter of personal taste, though the movement's struggle appeals to literary, cultural, and above all human interest. The scholarly apparatus contained within cites a number of competing interpretations, approaches, and judgments for readers with varying degrees of expertise in the many facets of the Victorian world to explore and build on.

1

"Some Special Providential Purpose"

The Tale of the Spasmodic School

The story of the Spasmodics could easily form the basis of a sentimental Victorian novel or even an introspective epic poem in the emotionally charged (some might say overwrought) style they favored. The plot would center on the struggles of a passionate neo–Romantic poet, championed by an earnest progressive literary mentor but persecuted by a hidden enemy who attacked with an unusual but rapier-sharp weapon. Hounded by pitiless conservative critics and ultimately betrayed by a fickle reading public, he would die young, ridiculed and embarrassed. His artistic promise would remain tragically unfulfilled, his legacy tainted by the echoes of his public humiliation.

With a few minor adjustments, this hypothetical tale could accurately chart the spectacular arc of the so-called School's two principal figures, Sydney Dobell and Alexander Smith, who burst onto the scene in the early 1850s and enjoyed a brief but ultimately disillusioning brush with literary celebrity. The pair had been the discovery of George Gilfillan, a Presbyterian clergyman who moonlighted as a kind of literary agent. Born in 1813, Gilfillan spent his youth immersed in Romantic poetry, especially that of Byron and Burns. Largely self-educated, he bypassed the public-school curriculum steeped in Latin grammar and Ancient Greek textual analysis, so crucial in forming the tastes and standards of men like Arthur Hugh Clough and Matthew Arnold. Despite his extremely modest origins as the eleventh child of a Secessionist Highland minister,[1] Gilfillan managed to attend the University of Glasgow and obtain a parish of his own in Dundee. There, he advocated tirelessly for the poor and disenfranchised while maintaining his love for and belief in the transformative nature of what we now call Romantic poetry.

The Spasmodic Poets

Gilfillan became a frequent contributor to various periodicals as well as a mentor to aspiring authors from all walks of life, but especially those whose social class or circumstances excluded them from university training or professional references. Unlike Arnold, whose class-conscious snobbery and misogyny is openly displayed in both his criticism and his private letters, Gilfillan welcomed and promoted the work of tradesmen, self-taught members of the lower middle class, and women. Eager writers (many of them Scottish) deluged him with manuscripts of all sorts,[2] hoping not only for constructive feedback but publicity. Among those whose works he reviewed in print were several poets who would later be tagged as "spasmodic," including John Stanyan Bigg and Gerald Massey. In fact, a more accurate name for this particular grouping of poets might be "The Gilfillan School." What these men had in common went beyond ardent Romantic twists of phrase and a mutual love of Byron and P.J. Bailey's proto–Spasmodic epic, *Festus*. All of them were working-class men who were committed to mid–Victorian reformist ideals such as Chartism, Corn Law repeal, and other populist causes.

Like so many others, Smith and Dobell submitted their poetry to Gilfillan in hopes of having their talent recognized and their poetry published. When Gilfillan read their work, he was both impressed and excited. His enthusiasm was not unjustified, even if it may have been overstated. In championing their cause and their verse, Gilfillan also emphasized their humble economic circumstances and their admirable work ethic as they (like Gilfillan himself) combined a passion for writing and self-improvement with the necessities of industrial toil. Gilfillan's efforts were earnest, but in some ways misguided. His fulsome praise probably sounded naïve and short-sighted even in his own day, especially to his more privileged, and in most cases Classically trained, colleagues. In the majority of cases, his encouragement did not translate into lasting professional advantage for his protégés. With respect to his two most notable discoveries, Smith and Dobell, it demonstrably caused them lasting harm. However, in the early years of the 1850s, the future seemed bright for all three.

Of the two, Sydney Thompson Dobell seemed better positioned to take his place among the *literati* of the day. Born in Kent in 1824, Dobell was recognized as a precocious child with a flair for language and a passion for reading. His grandfather had founded an idiosyncratic religious sect that discouraged excessive contact with the outside world, so Sydney was educated at home with the expectation that he would one day lead the flock. His unusual childhood helped shape him into the

1. "Some Special Providential Purpose"

idiosyncratic poet he was to become. "[T]he child's remarkable precocity naturally suggested the thought that he might be elected for some special Providential purpose," Richard Garnett noted in 1898. "The combined feeling of isolation and superiority thus generated did much to mould the boy's character, and contributed alike to the strength and weakness of his poetry. His education was private, and the want of all opportunity of measuring himself with others produced a false estimate of his own powers, which misguided him in their application when he came to write his principal work."[3] Dobell had already supplied a few modest contributions to various periodicals when he sought Gilfillan's opinion. The frothy praise he received in response probably struck the earnest but indulged young man as no more than his due, and in no time his first epic poem, *The Roman*, was published under the palindromic pseudonym Sydney Yendys.

The Roman dramatized the adventures of a freedom-fighting monk during the struggle for Italian independence. The poem had enormous appeal for an audience intrigued by news accounts of Giuseppe Mazzini's revolutionary activities. As Garnett dryly notes, no doubt thinking of Dobell's next major work, this first effort "is not merely a vigorous, but a thoroughly sane performance."[4] Dobell also joined Gilfillan in writing for *The Palladium*, an Edinburgh-based journal that lasted only from July 1850 to February 1851. Later remembered as a "magazine written mainly by members of the 'Spasmodic' school"[5] as well as a "mutual admiration society among the writers,"[6] *The Palladium* has secured a special place in literary history precisely because of one of Dobell's contributions—in this case a prose work, which has arguably become his best-known and most-quoted work. In September 1850, Dobell wrote an article entitled "Currer Bell," in which he reviewed a group of late–1840s novels by (he theorized) a single author using three different pen names. The titles of these novels, which had already attained a respectable measure of success by 1850 and would go on to secure exponential levels of fame, were *The Tenant of Wildfell Hall*, *Shirley*, *Jane Eyre*, and *Wuthering Heights*.

"Currer Bell" was not Dobell's' first encounter with the famous literary family of Haworth. It is almost certain that Dobell was the anonymous reviewer of the "Bell brothers'" *Poems* in the July 1846 issue of *The Athenaeum*.[7] In this essay, he singles out the poems of Ellis Bell, or Emily Brontë, as inherently superior to those of "Currer" (Charlotte) and "Acton" (Anne), a point of view supported by virtually all modern critics. Curiously, he does not refer to this earlier review in his piece on

The Spasmodic Poets

the "Bell" novels, and he now seems to believe that all three pen names belonged to Charlotte. Despite this error, his critical judgment on the relative merits of "Currer" and William Makepeace Thackeray proved strikingly prescient: "Thackeray has yet written nothing which will survive its age," Dobell wrote.[8] "Currer Bell has given us one work, at least, which will endure with the prose literature of our language. That work is *Jane Eyre*." He was not the only reviewer to speculate that all three works were the product of the female imagination.[9] However, he was among the first, at least in a major Victorian publication, to express a conviction that the author's gender strengthened the works' artistry and message. For these reasons, Dobell has earned a citation in nearly every modern study of the Brontë novels.

Though he was less admiring of *Wuthering Heights*, he praised it sufficiently[10] that the last surviving Brontë sister, Charlotte, sent him a new edition of the book along with a letter confirming his suspicions that the "Bells" were women, though they were also three separate entities. This initiated a lively correspondence between the two, in which they discussed not only literary theory in general but the controversy surrounding Dobell's most "Spasmodic" poem, *Balder*. Not surprisingly, the character of Balder reminded Charlotte of her sister Emily's enduring and equally Byronic creation, Heathcliff. She also (correctly, as it turns out) predicted that both critics and the public would be horrified by Balder's ruthless, even murderous egoism.

To his credit, and in stark contrast to other prominent male Victorian authors, Dobell, like Gilfillan, seems to harbor no resentment toward women writers on account of their gender. His respectful and serious literary discussions with Charlotte Brontë contrast starkly with the sexist rebuff she received from the poet Robert Southey when she sent him some of her youthful verses in 1837[11] and Matthew Arnold's ill-considered (as well as ill-mannered) remark about Brontë's last novel, *Villette*. "Miss Brontë has written a hideous undelightful convulsed constricted novel," the notoriously misogynistic Arnold groused in 1853, after he had met the author at a literary gathering hosted by Elizabeth Gaskell. "It is one of the most utterly disagreeable books I have ever read—and having seen her makes it more so."[12]

Soon after Gilfillan had helped launch Dobell's career, he happened upon another promising supplicant. Alexander Smith, born in 1829, was twenty-one when he wrote to Gilfillan; since the age of ten he had traced patterns on muslin for ten hours a day in a Glasgow factory, composing verse in his head and on scrap paper while he worked.[13] Deeply

1. "Some Special Providential Purpose"

impressed with the young man's talent, Gilfillan introduced him to the public in *The Eclectic Review*. Gilfillan urged Smith to expand his original poetic fragments into a book-length epic poem, which eventually became 1853's *A Life-Drama*. The poem followed the personal and artistic travails of Walter, a privileged young poet who seeks, and ultimately finds, both love and literary fame. Its structure was, unsurprisingly, a bit loose and its metaphors frequently (even embarrassingly) purple. Two plot points invited controversy and even moral censure: one in which Walter accosts a prostitute on a city bridge (though he requests nothing beyond angst-riddled conversation) and another in which he either seduces or sexually assaults the object of his affections, Violet. In addition, as Linda Hughes has pointed out, the poem contains surprisingly progressive suggestions of homosexual attraction between Walter and a deceased poet-friend as well as an interlude describing an interracial relationship.[14] These transgressions were explained away, with some nervousness even on the part of Gilfillan, as the naïve author's unintentional echoes of the Byronism and Gothic Orientalism that had been fashionable a few decades earlier.

Despite (or perhaps because of) these scandalous elements, the reading public responded even more enthusiastically to this work than they had to *The Roman*, apparently charmed by both Gilfillan's warmly proselytizing style and the earnest dedication of the hopeful poet. This work, which attempted to organize all of Smith's miscellaneous verse into a long verse narrative, sold well and inspired a number of flattering reviews. Even Clough, with all his years of formal education and his close friendship with Matthew Arnold, found himself mesmerized by the democratic symbolism[15] of Smith's efforts; writing for the *North American Review*, he touted the youthful laborer's talents and political views at the expense of Arnold's poetic artistry, much to Arnold's outrage. Strong sales enabled Smith to leave the muslin factory and transition into the professional middle class. Eagerly marketed and lauded in the periodical press as exciting new poetic voices, Dobell and Smith found themselves celebrated as revolutionary artists and even prophets ushering in a new world order, perhaps Shelley's fabled "unacknowledged legislators" made flesh.

By the end of 1853, Gilfillan's fanciful rhetoric and fervent endorsement made him a kind of Spasmodic kingmaker. Unfortunately, his zeal[16] also set the youthful Spasmodics up for a terrible fall. No sooner had their promising spark caught fire than it flamed out in spectacular fashion. While public reception had been initially positive, and the early Spasmodic works much read and immensely admired, a long drop waited on the other side of this critical precipice. Critics who favored a more Classical (in the sense of Greco-Roman) approach to poetry, like Matthew Arnold, expressed distaste and even horror for this new, highly emotional and sometimes grotesque subjective style; his strong reaction even prompted a quarrel with his friend Arthur Hugh Clough, who had publicly championed Smith's poetry over Arnold's. Arnold's 1853 Preface to his collection of poems, as well as his removal of "Empedocles on Etna" (which places an arguably Byronic protagonist in a Hellenic setting) from the volume, was a direct response to both Smith's success and Clough's approval. The two critics' argument over the merits of Alexander Smith might serve as a metaphor for the Spasmodics' downfall: despite Clough's initial enthusiasm, within the space of a few months, he soured on Smith and recanted his support of *A Life-Drama*. "If you haven't read A.S. [Alexander Smith]," he advised his fiancée in a letter, "don't trouble yourself; 'tis hardly worth the while."[17] Perhaps to his own detriment as a poet,[18] he reaffirmed the Classical principles in which he and Arnold had been trained.

The implosion of Gilfillan's circle was the result of two mortal blows that came in quick succession during the spring of 1854. The first was the publication of what is now considered the quintessential Spasmodic poem, Sydney Dobell's *Balder*. This poem, with a hero we would today call a malignant narcissist and an implied act of infanticide, not to mention a good deal of pompously overwrought verse, exhausted the patience and goodwill of readers who had enjoyed *The Roman*'s rebellious spirit and tolerated *A Life-Drama*'s excesses. Thanks to Smith's association with Dobell and Gilfillan, his debut volume was caught in the deadly crossfire. A series of increasingly scathing reviews skewered the two young poets' social pretensions and aesthetic crudeness.

The second, which delivered the *coup de grace* to the fledgling Spasmodic movement, came from Edinburgh via the well-respected and ubiquitously popular *Blackwood's Magazine*. While Gilfillan and his protégés scribbled away, they were blissfully unaware that an unseen nemesis was preparing an attack. Unlike an antagonist in a lurid Victorian novel, this enemy would not use a pistol, poison, or a dagger—at least not in a literal sense. Instead, his weapon of choice would be something far more accurate, piercing his target straight through the heart. Depending on one's perspective, William Edmondstoune Aytoun is either the black-hearted villain or the high-minded, intellectually responsible hero of the story. Either way, there can be no doubt

1. "Some Special Providential Purpose"

that he both named and demolished the so-called Spasmodic School. Ironically, in destroying the Spasmodics he gave them an enduring identity; Aytoun himself might well be forgotten today if not for his connection to Gilfillan, Smith, and Dobell. His first attack on what he called "The Spasmodic School" came in the form of a mock review in the March 1854 issue of *Blackwood's*. To his surprise (and perhaps disgust), readers assumed the imaginary subject of the review, a bizarre poem called "Firmilian," was real and clamored to read more. To oblige them, Aytoun extended his whimsical fragments into a book-length epic, much as Smith had done the year before, and presented it as a stand-alone volume.

Forty-one years old in 1854, Aytoun was already an established lawyer, educator, critic, and an author of both prose and poetry when he published *Firmilian: A Spasmodic Tragedy*. He was also fiercely conservative in both his literary and political views, especially with regard to social class and position.[19] There can be little doubt that one aspect of the Spasmodic controversy irked Aytoun (and perhaps Arnold, whose Preface Aytoun praised in his article "The Two Arnolds") even more than their supposed lack of technical skill and decorum—the prospect of working-class writers, self-taught rather than formally educated at one of the major universities, presuming to appraise the human condition and speak for (or perhaps against) their betters. It also seems clear that the real target of Aytoun's wrath was not the Spasmodic poets themselves, but the man he considered their reckless pied piper, George Gilfillan. In fact, Aytoun expressed his contempt for Gilfillan's presumptive encomiums, as well as the idea of the poet as social prophet, in one of his mock review's most biting comments when he singled out his fictional Spasmodic poet "T. Percy Jones" as "that long-expected phenomenon, the coming Poet." This is language lifted almost verbatim from one of Gilfillan's effusive reviews; Gilfillan himself even appears in the poem as the doddering (and doomed) Apollodorus, who mistakes the cry of a costermonger for the song of a born wordsmith. Attentive readers would have recognized this name as the pseudonym Gilfillan used when promoting his new discoveries.

Aytoun's broad, arguably crude (at times even sophomoric) humor often strikes modern readers as excessive, condescending, and unnecessarily callous. However, in its time it was regarded as devastatingly accurate and riotously entertaining. Hoots of laughter from every corner drove the newly designated "Spasmodics" from public view and all but extinguished their literary prospects. Gilfillan was no longer taken

The Spasmodic Poets

seriously, though he continued to publish literary criticism as well as champion marginalized Scottish writers.[20] Smith and Dobell continued to write, notably collaborating on a book of poems about the Crimean War in 1855 (a work Aytoun also savaged in *Blackwood's*). The following year, Dobell tried again with *England in Time of War*, while Smith married and turned to prose with the encouragement (and perhaps at the suggestion) of Dobell, who noted that "[Smith] will find prose more lucrative than poetry, and he has the power, I believe, to do great things in it."[21] Unfortunately, Smith's Spasmodic infamy followed him, generating at least one entirely spurious charge of plagiarism and almost costing him his post as Secretary at the University of Edinburgh due to the supposed "immorality" in *A Life-Drama*; Dobell, then living in Scotland as well, intervened to save him.[22]

Eventually, Smith wrote two novels, *Alfred Hagart's Household* and a sequel, *Miss Oona McQuarrie*, and had embarked on a third when he died of typhus at the age of 37. His circle remembered him as a devoted husband and father as well as a cherished and loyal friend. His book of essays, *Last Leaves*, confirms this judgment. In one of the selections, "Sydney Dobell" Smith praises the recently deceased Aytoun,[23] who had nearly destroyed his life and career, as "a brilliant poet and wit" and defends Dobell's talents, so unjustly derided. "[T]here is nothing more curious than the fluctuation of literary reputations," he notes with a touch of sadness.[24] "In the interest of Sydney Dobell, I move for a new trial in the courts of criticism." The reappraisal never came about; the mature works of both men were either snubbed or mocked. Though plagued by ill health, Dobell struggled on until 1874, ironically and tragically beset by epileptic spasms that made writing nearly impossible. Four years later, Gilfillan died as well. By the end of the century, they and their retroactively designated Spasmodic colleagues were nearly forgotten except as the object of scholarly derision or (perhaps worse) condescending pity.

Though the label "Spasmodic" became current in 1854 after the publication of *Firmilian*, there is no exact point in time when the movement began. In fact, it is safe to say that no actual movement, at least in the usual sense of the word, ever existed. However, Philip James Bailey's *Festus*, first published in 1839, is commonly (and retrospectively) identified as the harbinger of the themes and techniques that would come to be accepted as "Spasmodic." The "school" was eventually expanded to include not only *A Life-Drama* and *Balder* but also *Gerald*, written in 1842 by John Westland Marston, an editor who had published some of

1. "Some Special Providential Purpose"

Dobell's poems in *The National Magazine.* J. Stanyan Bigg, whose name clearly inspired Aytoun's "T. Percy Jones," had published *Night and the Soul: A Dramatic Poem* in 1854, just in time to be swept up in the *Firmilian* debacle. Other frequently encountered Spasmodic satellites include Richard Hengist "Orion" Horne and two poets who, like Smith, were members of the laboring class, Gerald Massey and Ebenezer Jones. Additional "members" have come and gone as scholars and critics sift and re-evaluate various Victorian authors. Robert Browning and Tennyson's *Maud* usually merit at least a passing reference in most modern discussions of Spasmody; Mrs. Browning's *Aurora Leigh* is clearly similar in form and content to *A Life-Drama*. The poem's early feminism apparently redeemed it for modern critics, as it is still widely anthologized and studied. Jerome Buckley famously suggested that Emily Brontë might have taken inspiration not only from Byron, but also from early "Spasmodic" works like *Festus* and *Gerald*, both published before her death in 1848.[25] Dobell's praise of *Wuthering Heights* and his creation of the Heathcliff-like anti-hero, Balder, prompt an interesting question. Was "Ellis Bell" an early Spasmodic who worked in prose?

For the most part, what were singled out as "Spasmodic" characteristics in poets and poetry by the Victorian critics are still useful markers today. For example, we can still recognize (and express affectionate amusement for) the overwrought bombast and strained rhetoric of the poetic voice, the oddly forced imagery and metaphors, and the loose organization of each piece, all of which were targeted by Aytoun, Arnold, and others. Most of all, perhaps, we can identify the self-absorbed megalomaniac self-absorbed poet-hero who occupies the central place in all Spasmodic poems. Though he bears some resemblance to characters like Manfred and Heathcliff (and perhaps even the vampire Lord Ruthven), it is important to note that he is not merely a Byronic hero but a Byronic poet. In fact, we are now in a position to see that every Spasmodic element was in fact an expansion of a particular attribute of what we now call, as the Victorians did not, the Romantic impulse. The Spasmodic School represented one possible direction Victorian poesy might take; had it been successful, J.F.A. Pyre would not have been able to seriously assert in 1909 that "the decadence of modern poetry began from Keats."[26] The culmination of this supposed decadence came in the modern era, when solipsism became not only tolerated but desirable in a protagonist. By a curious strike of misfortune, the Spasmodics were simultaneously both behind and ahead of literary fashion.

As a literary term, "Spasmodic" was likely introduced by Thomas

The Spasmodic Poets

Carlyle. In "Goethe's Works" (1832), Carlyle complains of "spasmodic Byronism, bellowing till its windpipe is cracked" and in "Sir Walter Scott" (1836) he expresses disgust with "Werterism, Byronism, and other Sentimentalism tearful or spasmodic" which had disfigured British literature in his day.[27] During the following decade, "spasmodic" obviously gained some currency, and appears in R.H. Horne's *A New Spirit of the Age* as a point of comparison between the poetic dramas of Robert Browning and J.W. Marston (both of whom, along with Horne, were eventually designated "Spasmodic poets"). Another recognizable use of "spasmodic" as it would be used in 1854 and after occurs in Charles Kingsley's 1853 article "Thoughts on Byron and Shelley." Reviving Carlyle's original application, Kingsley expands it to describe the neo–Romantic movement of the 1850s by jeering at "such spasmodic melodies as seem to those small minds to be imitations of Shelley's nightingale notes" and describing "a spasmodic, vague, extravagant, effeminate, school of poetry, which has been too often hastily and unfairly fathered upon Byron."[28]

By 1855, the label was ubiquitous enough that George Brimley could describe Tennyson's poetry as containing "a touch of that exaggeration which belongs to the 'spasmodic school'; he also refers to the apparent glibness of fellow critics who bandy about such epithets as 'morbid,' 'hysterical,' 'spasmodic,' which may mean one thing or another, according to the sense, discrimination, and sympathy of the man who applies them."[29] Brimley even wonders if it might even be applied to Shakespeare, given the apparent over-enthusiasm of some critics in bandying the label about:

> Why, good sir or madam, does not Shakspeare [sic] let Juliet and her Romeo adorn Verona with troops of little Juliets and Romeos, to do as their papa and mamma did before them? Why does not Cordelia live to comfort Lear in his old age, restored to true appreciation of his daughters? Why does Ophelia drown in a ditch; and Hamlet, after murdering Polonius, die by chance medley? Why are not Othello's eyes opened before, instead of after his fatal deed, and he and Desdemona allowed to spend the rest of their days in peace and mutual trust? Is it, think you, because Shakspeare belongs to the hysterical, morbid, spasmodic school, and likes the violent excitement of melodramatic incident? We should be sorry to stake much upon the reception any of these poetic issues would meet with from certain critics, if they now for the first time came up for judgment.[30]

Apparently, at least as far as Brimley is concerned, accusations of Spasmody had become not only commonplace but subjective enough to seem nearly meaningless.

1. "Some Special Providential Purpose"

In the Victorian era, as now, the term "Spasmodic" had a predominantly medical association, referring to various physical tics and palsies, but also fits of (sometimes psychosomatic) emotional turmoil.[31] Aytoun's choice of the sobriquet was even more accurate than perhaps even he realized, since the Spasmodics did not shy from describing intense bodily reactions,[32] either metaphorical or physical, in response to erotic, psychological, and philosophical stimuli. In fact, Dobell's theories of poetry specifically call for somatic arousal through patterns of verse,[33] similar to the way a person might find himself instinctively moving in response to music. With their frequent themes of madness and artistic torture, Dobell and his fellow Spasmodics unwittingly anticipated the literary future (not to mention some of Tennyson and Robert Browning's most acclaimed works). Both their experimental forms and their attention to subjective experience would not have seemed the least bit remarkable, much less offensive, a hundred years later.

Kirstie Blair has demonstrated that "Spasmodic" also carried an additional connotation in the early nineteenth century: that of a shameful "effeminacy," which the Spasmodics deliberately incorporated as a "radical poetics" that attempted to challenge some of the "key attributes of mid–Victorian manliness."[34] The first Spasmodic poem, *Festus*, had originally been praised for its "manly taste,"[35] suggesting that the implications of genderized poetics were never far from the minds of nineteenth-century reviewers. Interestingly, the now-familiar concept of "muscular Christianity," so central to understanding Victorian ideals of masculinity, also has identifiable ties to the Spasmodic School. Though coined in 1852, the phrase was popularized in a review of Charles Kingsley's 1857 novel *Two Years Ago*,[36] which features the character of Elsley Vavasour, widely identified as the lampooning of the typical Spasmodic poet.[37] With his epicene manners and outrageous attire, Vavasour is a Byronic anachronism as well an anticipation of Oscar Wilde and the Decadents of the 1890s. He is also a fraud and a threat to a social order predicated on sober English manliness.

The corpus of "Spasmodic" texts is actually quite small, although the poems themselves can be voluminous; these works, along with the poetic theories of Sydney Dobell, the only Spasmodic who attempted to explain his methods in essay form,[38] help us understand Victorian attitudes toward Romanticism in general and the later English Romantics in particular. In the early nineteenth century, Wordsworth (who had died in 1850, the same year Dobell published his first long poem, *The Roman*), Coleridge, Byron, Shelley and Keats were not grouped together

The Spasmodic Poets

as they are in modern literary chronologies and educational curricula. The term "Romantic Poetry" was not used in England in its current sense until after the 1871 translation of Hippolyte Taine's *History of English Literature*. Rather, critics preferred to group poets in terms of "schools" or movements and to place a well-known poet at the head of such a group. A few aimed to titillate, as when Robert Southey classed Byron and Shelley as members of the "Satanic School." Others seemed merely condescending, such as *Blackwood's* grouping of Hazlitt, Hunt, and Keats as the "Cockney School," with the attendant suggestion of urban loutishness. In this context, the term "Spasmodic School," with its implication of physical infirmity (if not outright effeminacy) and its application to poets who were primarily of working-class origins, conveys an equally patronizing aura.

This may have been intentional. Early Victorian critics had viewed the poems of Shelley and Byron as at least partially political, but gradually the concept of what we now call English Romanticism had mellowed into a synonym for airy sensuousness and a vague, non-threatening mysticism. Many of the so-called Spasmodics published verse that was at least potentially subversive; Ebenezer Jones and Gerald Massey were both outspoken sympathizers with the Chartist movement, and Dobell's *The Roman* unabashedly embraced the topic of Italian liberation. By focusing on the Spasmodics' supposed emotional excess, socially conservative critics like Aytoun and Arnold neutralized any potential radical messaging in their poetry. Whether this was deliberate or the effect of subconscious class bias is impossible to determine.

Whatever they were called, these earlier poets fascinated the rapidly expanding reading public of Victorian Britain, who spent the first decades of the nineteenth century actively debating their artistic and personal merits. Shelley and Keats found new respect and popularity, while admiration for Byron rapidly cooled. His poems were now subject to new and more probing analyses than had been attempted in his own time. More often than not, they were found wanting both in form and substance (interestingly, and with good reason, many of the criticisms levelled at them were almost identical to those soon to be hurled at the Spasmodics). Though he eventually softened toward Goethe, Carlyle never regained his admiration for Byron. His letter to Macvey Napier of April 28, 1832, asks, "What was he, in short, but a huge *sulky Dandy* ... he taught me nothing that I had not again to forget."[39] Victorian distaste for Byron's libertinism also increased as the image of the Regency fop/dilettante poet lost its charm in a more moralistic and serious age.

1. "Some Special Providential Purpose"

In contrast, Byronic passion did not abate so completely for the Spasmodics; Sydney Dobell recorded the fact that he knew every line of *Manfred* by heart. He and his fellow Spasmodics showed no interest in the innovations of Wordsworth or the theories of Coleridge except as they influenced the later Romantic poets of whom they were so fond. From Keats they took sensuality and a passion for opulent detail, from Shelley mysticism, and from Byron an overpowering individualism shading into misanthropy. Perhaps the overriding "Romantic" characteristic adopted by the Spasmodics was that of complete subjectivity, both in terms of subject matter and presentation. All Spasmodic poetry revolves around a central heroic figure, who is usually Byronic to various degrees, and depicts outside events only as filtered through his enlarged, even prophetic, sensibilities. Spasmodic poetry aimed to exult personal experience—not of men who shared their own lower-middle-class origins, but rather that of a poet who enjoyed an economic freedom their creators did not. The major conflict every Spasmodic poem addressed was the struggle of the idiosyncratic consciousness for liberation, if not supremacy, in an industrialized environment.

Gradually emerging from discussions of poetic relevance was an extensive consideration of what attributes would constitute the ideal Victorian poet. That such a man (and it would have to be a man, not a woman) would appear to lead his age both morally and artistically is taken as inevitable in countless review essays in almost every literary periodical of the period. John Sterling's 1842 assessment, inserted in his review of Tennyson's *Poems*, is fairly typical:

> What poetry might be in our time and land, if a man of the highest powers and most complete cultivation exercised the art among us, will be hard to say until after the fact of such a man's existence. Waiting for this desirable event, we may at least see that poetry ... must wear a new form, and probably comprise elements hardly found in our recent writings, and impossible in former ones.[40]

The first Spasmodic productions, like the first productions of Tennyson, were published during this ongoing dialogue. George Gilfillan must have taken the debate both seriously and personally; his promotion of Dobell and especially Smith is tinged with evangelical urgency. After *Firmilian* and Matthew Arnold's 1853 Preface, many critics not only opposed, but actively ridiculed Gilfillan and his Spasmodic protégés in the guise of restoring Classical balance and decorum to poetry. This chastening tone is best exemplified in the review of Alexander Smith's *Poems* mentioned earlier, who suggested that Smith's

The Spasmodic Poets

"pantaloons" be peeled back and the "paternal scourge" applied for his audacity.[41] The Spasmodics' transgressions were depicted not simply as aesthetic blunders, but social overreach that offended Victorian paternalism itself. After all, Arnold and his anti–Romantic partisans were interested in "improving" the working and middle classes; their instructors could obviously not come from their own working-class rank, but would have to be university men, trained in Classical languages and convinced of the rightness of the class-based British (often specifically English) patriarchy.

The outcome of the debate assured that the latter voice would become stereotypically Victorian, the figurative whipping chastening not only Smith but the imagination of an entire culture. What Welby called the "spasmodic assaults" on what was now "the established order" of both society and art are left to eccentric figures like Swinburne (who, not coincidentally, has been reclaimed in recent years as a later and more gifted incarnation of a Spasmodic poet).[42] Those who became the serious poets of the age, for their contemporaries and for us, would have bristled at the mere adjective. Criticism in the style of George Gilfillan was banished from the attentions of serious Victorians, along with any genuine hope of a Romantic revival suited to Victorian social or artistic needs. By the end of the decade, the weariness had grown oppressive, and the naïve expectation of a literary prophet, couched in populist Christian language, was painfully abandoned.

The collapse of the Spasmodics' reputation as serious and even important poets can be traced through their systematic exclusion from the Victorian canon. Obviously, the degree to which a poet or group of poets is remembered by subsequent generations is largely dependent upon the availability of the works in question, either through anthologies or modern editions. Since the Spasmodics have been denied the latter, the anthologizing process takes on special significance, and indeed their gradual disappearance from late nineteenth century poetry anthologies reflects the overall pattern of their systematic exclusion from critical consideration.

Of the three major Spasmodic poets, Dobell, Smith, and Bailey, Dobell has fared the best among the English anthologists, and the common assertion that he was the most talented member of the ill-fated school may be as much due to his greater representation as to any intrinsic superiority in the selections themselves. In Dobell's own lifetime, the Reverend Robert A. Willmott included two of Dobell's lyrics, as well as two of Bailey's, in his *Poets of the Nineteenth Century* (1857).[43] Dobell

1. "Some Special Providential Purpose"

is also the only Spasmodic included in Thomas Humphrey Ward's *The English Poets: Selections*, for which Matthew Arnold (Ward's uncle by marriage) composed the general introduction and which was necessarily intended to follow Arnold's critical tenets in making those selections. Perhaps the largest assortment of Spasmodic poetry, exceeding even that found in either of Arthur Quiller-Couch's *Oxford Books*, is that of Edmund Clarence Stedman in his *A Victorian Anthology 1837–1895* (1895), which presented no less than eleven Dobell poems, five excerpts from Bailey's *Festus* and five by Alexander Smith. Alfred H. Miles' *Poets and Poetry of the Nineteenth Century* (1907) and Burton Egbert Stevenson's *Home Book of Verse, American and English* (1912) likewise contain Spasmodic poems, though they are allotted considerably less space. Alexander Smith has on the whole fared better as a Scottish poet, for a handful of his poems, especially "Barbara," "Squire Maurice," and especially "Glasgow" have been reproduced in at least five well-known compilations of Scottish poetry, including Lindsay and Mackie's *Book of Scottish Verse* (1983).

At first glance, the number of anthologies reproducing Spasmodic poets might seem adequate to ensure future investigations into the School. However, it would be misleading to ignore the significantly larger number of anthologies in which they are shunned. None of the many editions of Palgrave's *Golden Treasury* (the first of which appeared in 1861), for example, include a single Spasmodic poet. This in itself is not startling, since Palgrave was guided in his choices by Tennyson, who had ample reason to resent the Spasmodics after *Maud* was roundly denounced as a production of their ilk. Yet Palgrave's anthology proved extremely influential in shaping readers' poetic tastes, and even Quiller-Couch acknowledged his indebtedness to what was sometimes thought of as "a critical canon" in its own right.[44] Nor are the Spasmodics found in any of Untermeyer's compilations, which played an analogous role in forming American tastes. It is worth recalling that the development of a broad market for anthologies was roughly concurrent with the development of the Victorian canon as we know it today, which was in large part a response to a need for standardized curriculums in higher education.[45] Anthologies intended for scholastic purposes, which like Ward's would have been dependent on the criteria developed by educator-critics like Arnold, began to compete with anthologies intended for leisure or family-time reading, as the title of Stevenson's *Home-Book* suggests. The latter class of readers considered the Spasmodics acceptable as entertainment and light popular philosophizing;

The Spasmodic Poets

the academic set did not. Henry S. Pancost's *Standard English Poems* (1899), the title of which suggests that it too aspired to set just that standard, contains no Spasmodic works, and for all the Scottish volumes containing one or two of Alexander Smith's short lyrics, he is not represented in the *Oxford Book of Scottish Verse* (1966).

On the other hand, the Spasmodics did merit a mention in W. Davenport Adams' *Dictionary of English Literature* in 1880, which declares that they "have been admirably ridiculed by Professor Aytoun in his *Firmilian*,"[46] and Dobell is included in C. Lewis Hind's *One Hundred Second-Best Poems*, which, according to Riding, would probably have been enough to imply that he was really fodder for a "second best reader" and to damage his reputation accordingly.[47] This may well have been true, for today, Spasmodic works are seldom reproduced in modern texts, with the exception of those like Donald Gray's *Victorian Literature: Poetry*, which are concerned with completeness and therefore supply a few brief excerpts from the three major Spasmodic dramas with a disclaimer regarding their quality. Except for a few introductory comments by the editors of such volumes, the popularity and widespread fame of the Spasmodics in their own time could scarcely be inferred.

W.H. Auden's introduction to his volume of nineteenth century minor poets (which includes one of Dobell's short poems with no critical commentary or notes) gives a few criteria to distinguish a major poet as opposed to a minor. According to Auden, one cannot be simplistic and merely say "that a major poet writes better than a minor," since it is possible that "the major poet [may eventually] write more bad poems than the minor."[48] Rather, the major poet will be distinguished by evincing a wide range of subject matter, an original vision and style, and a mastery of verse technique which will make the chronology of the major poet's work clear to the careful reader, in other words showing significant intellectual maturity gained over the course of his career.

All of these observations are useful in reconsidering the artistic importance of the Spasmodics, who faltered mainly in the first and third requirements but who genuinely believed they were purveying an original and important vision in an inspired manner. That they were in actuality somewhat derivative and pedestrian does prevent them from assuming major status, but renders them significant in a different capacity. After all, a major poetic voice fulfilling Auden's requirements might well prove too singular to accurately represent the temperament of his age or the more mundane concerns that would have affected millions of his less articulate contemporaries. On the other hand, the

1. "Some Special Providential Purpose"

Spasmodics, with their somewhat transparent philosophy and their naïve trust in a deterministic world order, represent a particular historical moment to an extent a major poet could not. The Spasmodics changed the course of literature mostly through their existence, rather than the power of their words; ironically enough it is for this reason that the Spasmodic phenomenon can be regarded as both product and precursor of a number of the literary and social trends of the early Victorian era.

In hindsight, it is clear that the Spasmodic controversy largely centered around the desirability of preserving Romantic ideals in the Victorian age, and that the Spasmodic debate was actually a contest between two schools of criticism rather than poetry. At the climax of *Firmilian*, the Gilfillanesque character, Apollodorus, is crushed by a falling body hurled from the top of an imposing and perhaps subconsciously phallic tower. The Spasmodic poets, young and inexperienced as well as informally educated members of the lower middle or working class, can be seen as victims who suffered a similar fate. When they are viewed in this light, Aytoun's triumphant campaign to drive them from the literary profession and enforce Matthew Arnold's criteria seems less heroic than Weinstein and others have portrayed it. As the *Firmilian* debacle died down, a few commentators seemed to realize they had gone too far. Coventry Patmore, who authored the well-known poem "The Angel in the House" in 1854, attempted to analyze the movement with belated regret for the harsh treatment they had received in the periodical press with his essay "Poetry—The Spasmodists" (1858). Ruskin observed, too, in the "Claude and Poussin" section of *Modern Painters V* (1860) that "spasmodic" was really just another word for "passionate": "The word, though an ugly one, is quite accurate, the most spasmodic books in the world being Solomon's Song, Job, and Isaiah."[49] The apologists arrived too late, however. Literary fashion and audience interests had moved on.

Spasmodicism might best be described as the trunk of a spreading literary tree, rooted in Romanticism and eventually branching out into Aestheticism and Decadence. The serious, Classically-based poetic system Aytoun and Arnold preferred proved unsustainable; Arnold himself attempted a poetic drama in the Greek style, *Merope*. After its failure, he drifted away from writing poetry in favor of prose. Aytoun's poetic efforts found only modest success and all but *Firmilian* sank into relative oblivion. By the late 1860s, poetry itself was losing its place as the predominant form of social commentary and aesthetic discourse. The Victorian novel, penny dreadful and triple-decker alike, had begun

The Spasmodic Poets

to assume that role, while "serious" poetry increasingly distanced itself from mundane issues and contemporary injustices. This gulf widened for another half-century, until the self-satisfied didacticism of the Aytoun and Gilfillan camps alike would disappear in a cloud of toxic mustard gas.

2

"Fearless Strains"

British Literary Culture at Mid-Century

The Spasmodics and their works were products of early Victorian middle-class expansion as much as literary experimentation. A variety of social trends contributed to the development and progression of the Spasmodic phenomenon, among them increased literacy and the role of periodicals, evangelical religious fervor, the cult of self-help and the related admiration for working-class poets. Likewise, it is not unreasonable to interpret their downfall, spearheaded by a group of university-educated men intent on reforming public taste, as a conservative backlash. Innumerable scholarly studies have focused on each and all of these cultural movements, but they are worth revisiting, in an admittedly generalized manner, in order to contextualize and reassess the Spasmodic movement.

Of the major Spasmodic poets, only Bailey was of the leisured upper-middle class, taking a law degree but choosing not to practice (Marston, a peripheral figure, followed a similar course). Dobell and Bigg were born into merchant families, while Alexander Smith, Ebenezer Jones, and Gerald Massey were all factory hands with literary aspirations. Only Bailey and Marston received university degrees; the others had limited schooling or, like George Gilfillan, the Spasmodic mentor, were mainly self-taught. Dobell, as we have seen, was educated at home according to the peculiar guidelines of the eccentric religious sect founded by his grandfather. There can be little question that the Spasmodics' outsider status affected both their poetic techniques and their critical reception. For one thing, their literary knowledge was approximately twenty years out of date, since at the time the only affordable volumes of poetry for men of their means were reprints of eighteenth-century and early Romantic works including those of the Graveyard School.[1] This would certainly account for their apparent regression to the Byronic style which had already gone out of fashion in most artistic circles, referred to as a supposed "immaturity" of style. As Arnold remarked of Alexander Smith in a letter to Clough, "I have not read him—I shrink from what is so intensely immature."[2] To the disgust of some with more elitist views, Smith and the other Spasmodics had attempted to compose serious poems without the sort of rhetorical training university men like Arnold would have taken for granted, and Arnold himself seemed vaguely aware of this difference when he told Clough in the same letter that, despite admittedly "remarkable" things in Smith, "I think at the same time he will not go far."

If class-consciousness prevented objectivity in Oxbridge circles, however, it probably had precisely the opposite effect on the British reading public. Put in simple terms, literary pursuits of varying degrees of sophistication soon became common to the general populace, with printed materials more accessible than ever before. What Altick calls "culture-at-home publications" were best-sellers at mid-century, and guides like *Chambers' Information for the People* were turned out at impressive rates throughout the 1830s and following.[3] Innovations in printing had made news-sheets and religious tracts common fodder for the literate city-dweller, and working-men's institutes and factory schools were steadily increasing potential consumers of printed materials.[4] Altick estimates that there were between five and six million active readers in England by 1855, and according to Houghton some 25,000 journals were published over the course of the Victorian era, almost all intended for middle-class consumption.[5] Some four million poems appeared in local Victorian newspapers alone.[6] Even less affordable magazines might sell tens of thousands of one issue, while the cheaper papers and journals might have sold hundreds of thousands.[7] These types of publications were read by the young Spasmodics, all of whom began submitting poems to journals in early adolescence; eventually the same pages became the vehicle by which they were introduced to the public.

If Spasmodic technique and themes do not seem particularly satisfying in the highest intellectual sense today, it must be recalled at once that the kind of material favored by England's mass readership in the 1850s would have seemed even less so. Almost everyone has heard of "penny dreadfuls," also called "penny-bloods," which became popular in the 1840s and continued to sell well for several decades (and are still part of twenty-first-century popular culture). These were cheap, ill-written tales of sentiment, true crime, and quasi-Gothic adventures, with all three elements occasionally combined for true sensationalism,[8]

2. "Fearless Strains"

and were a common source of entertainment for workers even while on the job.[9] More specialized in form, but similar in theme and explicit detail, were cheap Gothics and true-crime novels.[10] Less studied than the penny dreadfuls, but ubiquitous at the time, was the broadsheet. Aimed at working-class consumers, the broadsheet was often an illustrated account of a particularly ghastly murder or a public execution. Such sheets often sold in the millions, and those who made their living through their production were not averse to inventing lurid accounts to boost revenue, somewhat in the vein of modern supermarket tabloids.[11] Even the most factual accounts were strongly laced with theatrical dialogue supposedly taken from the mouths of the participants and portentous events spiced with editorial embellishments. A good many accounts of particularly heinous murders end with the hand of God literally intruding upon an assemblage of people, who may be, for example, about to execute an innocent defendant, to point out the guilty party.[12] One such broadsheet from the first half of the nineteenth century[13] depicts a father beheading his own child. In the graphic illustration accompanying the text, the head rests on a wooden table with the body lying nearby amid pools of blood. This example of public taste is worth remembering in contrast to the outcries of *Balder*'s more genteel readers, who were horrified and morally incensed even though Dobell's poem does not provide a single detail about the infanticide which presumably takes place. It is tempting to speculate on the success the Spasmodics might have won had they turned their hands to the writing of penny dreadfuls or what came to be known in the 1860s as sensation novels.

Both the verbiage and illustration of the broadsheets, the cheap newspapers, and the penny novels of the time may be said to have been flavored by the melodramatic conventions common both to the stage and to literature, though the influence of mid-nineteenth century melodrama on the literary productions of the time (most certainly including those of the Spasmodics) has too often been overlooked. This, too, is largely a class issue, since the highbrows shunned melodrama in favor of subtler creations that were considered more profound. Melodrama was, however, a common and accepted convention for the masses, and melodramatic gestures, speeches, and sentiments were the standard motif in most forms of popular art. Acting handbooks for the theater illustrated the wildly expansive, but nonetheless stylized, gestures used to convey particular emotional extremes.[14] These same gestures are found in the illustrations accompanying both news items and fictions, and

The Spasmodic Poets

they have their verbal counterpart in certain Spasmodic outbursts, for example Balder's infamous "Ah! ah! ah! ah! ah! ah! ah! ah! ah! ah!/By Satan!"[15] Ludicrous as this line may seem in a supposedly serious poem, in context it functions as a recognizable melodramatic gesture, and it is of course important to remember that *Balder*, as well as the other Spasmodic works, was written in the form of a poetic drama, and that reading aloud to a circle of friends or family, in dramatic fashion, was ordinary practice.[16] Tellingly, none of *Balder*'s contemporary reviewers paid this line, which seems so peculiar today, any particular attention, but focused instead on the moral depravity of Balder himself. It appears that the emotional excess of Spasmodic poetry, so jarring to later readers, would have been accepted by the contemporary middle-class, which made up its primary audience, as a normal and even expected method of heightening dramatic tension. Compared to the characters in some of the dramas they had seen on stage, Balder and Walter might seem restrained.

While the majority of lower- and middle-class readers entertained themselves with penny Gothics and tales of true crime, some readers with more erudite tastes also dabbled in poetry, considering this a more intellectual pursuit which might lead to personal and thus social betterment. Even working men took the reading of poetry seriously, and the Spasmodic poets were among their chosen favorites: Altick relates an anecdote involving two colliers who were drawn together by a mutual admiration of *Festus* and subsequently embarked on an examination of Wordsworth.[17] As *Blackwood's* observed while reviewing Smith's *Poems*, "There are homes in England almost as common as hothouses, where fine criticism is nightly conversation.... The demand for excellence in authorship exceeds the supply."[18] The intense involvement of so many readers of poetry naturally created both the commercial market alluded to by the reviewer and a kind of cult intent on discovering and rewarding poetic genius.[19] Since the Wordsworthian strain of Romanticism in particular had established that poetry might issue from even the lowliest mouth, readers were prepared to lionize even the most unlikely poet, such as a farm-laborer like Stephen Duck,[20] to whom Southey paid tribute in an 1831 volume of working-class poets, or a factory hand like Gerald Massey or Alexander Smith.

If a work's moral content appealed to the public, a good deal of technical ineptness might be forgiven. The popularity of *Festus* and Dobell's early effort *The Roman* illustrate this, as did the career of another author who outstripped the Spasmodics in popularity, yet was

2. "Fearless Strains"

almost universally regarded by critics as an utterly inept craftsman even in his own time. Martin Farqhuar Tupper, who like Bailey was called to the bar but never practiced law, published his *Proverbial Philosophy* in 1838, and for the next twenty-five years managed to sell no less than five thousand copies a year.[21] Tupper has long been acknowledged as a rather baffling phenomenon in the history of middle-class taste; as *The Cambridge History* drolly observes, this work which "earned for [Tupper] the title of 'The People's Poet Laureate'" is no less than "incredible rubbish" which "myriads of people thought might be poetry in the beginning of the second third of the nineteenth century."[22] The same work notes, however, that it was the middle and lower middle classes which raised it to the heights it attained. From the first, critics had despised it and even used it as a kind of touchstone: the *Saturday Review* composed its reviews "for the amusement of people who do not read Tupper themselves and like to look down upon people who do ... it [was] inconceivable that anyone who reads Tupper should ever look at the *Saturday Review*."[23]

Unlike the Spasmodic poems, *Proverbial Philosophy* has no characters, but like many of them it has no unifying dramatic structure and could be rearranged without detriment to the sense. Instead, it is an unabashedly dogmatic collection of authorial pronouncements, in strikingly unimaginative hexameter, on a variety of ethical topics which might concern the average British Protestant. The entire concept of the book, as well as its phenomenal sales, seems to reflect the predominant middle-class mores of mid-century. Its popularity makes it useful as a sociological document rather than a work of literature. In his study of Tupper's appeal to the British middle class, Ralf Buchman suggests that while post–Reform Bill cultural and economic standards were almost entirely in this industrious group's control, a kind of herd mentality, rather than a push towards individualism, resulted. Morality became less a question of social benefit than a matter of accepting and enforcing instilled notions that had served one's father and grandfather well and were therefore not to be questioned or re-evaluated. Obviously, Buchman is generalizing, but Tupper seems to have gone out of his way to be congenial to his public's taste, declaring his political stance "Conservative-Liberal"[24] and breezily ignoring even the possibility of rational objections to Christianity's validity. Rather than refute specific scientific theories which discredited Creationist doctrine, Tupper concentrated on sentimentalizing the positive effects of faith ("Of Faith," 2nd Series) and insisting on the need to indoctrinate the very young into Protestant ritual, such as family prayer-sessions ("Of Education," 1st Series). In form, as well, Tupper was sensitive to the requirements of his intended audience. Buchman regards the currency of the proverb as a natural corollary to such moral smugness since it offered both succinctness and venerability. The public's delight with Tupper's "proverbs" was therefore predetermined; some even memorized long sections of the book[25] and used it as a guide to life in much the way they used the less easily understood Bible.

Although their moral earnestness and intellectual naiveté may have led them into the absurdities and dogmatism of Tupper on occasion, there can be little question that early Victorians were dynamic, inquisitive, and earnestly concerned with mental improvement. The Spasmodics were nurtured by the same tradition in which they would eventually write, one aspect of which might be labelled popular ethical philosophy. Great numbers of poets rushed to publish the results of their own meditations, from the young Robert Browning down to another short-lived sensation, a lace-worker rather appropriately named Ragg.[26] The initial popularity of Bailey, Dobell, and Smith seems likewise to have been the result of a peculiar combination of originality and blandness: while their flashy images and heroes filled with feeling captivated a public eager to discover profundity even where little existed, these poets were not, at least until *Balder*, forward enough to challenge accepted moral norms. Spasmodic works dealt with potentially explosive issues such as religion, gender roles, and even the physical expression of sexuality. Yet their treatments of such topics is always apolitical and even banal, their emotions theatrical rather than deeply affecting. When they shocked their readers, they did so by accident. Smith's Walter relinquishes his radical agnosticism to become a country squire while his creator was still afflicted with poverty, for example, and Dobell would one day lament that his greatest fear was to be "morally misunderstood." In essence, the Spasmodics were effigies of Byron without Byron's libertinism or satirical dimension, and when they did exceed the banality of melodrama, as *Balder* attempted to do, both readers and critics turned away in disgust and apprehension.[27]

Victorian society's need for poetic counsel did not, of course, exist in a vacuum, with readers using verse alone as a source for intellectual instruction or self-help. Although they may have read widely, they were still dependent upon more formally educated minds to aid in forming opinions. Therefore, an important guiding force in literary culture was, increasingly throughout the nineteenth century, the periodical press.

2. "Fearless Strains"

Its expansion correlates, not surprisingly, to that of literary criticism as a profession. For the first time, literary critics directed the tastes not of a handful of scholars or colleagues, but the public at large. Like the poets, they were instructors and guardians to a trusting populace, and most of them took this role seriously. A book review, for example, might serve merely as an excuse for a reviewer to expound morally. Dogmatism and the assumption of a prophetic mantle became standard, even though reviewers themselves were often narrowly educated and largely ignorant of the ideas they commented upon.[28] They tended to attack rather than reconsider their own bias. Here the Spasmodic movement also reflects historical change. Dobell and Smith, in particular, were creations of the periodicals. They were introduced and popularized in the pages of the magazines, and their poetry was widely disseminated thanks to the common practice of printing long excerpts, or even complete poems, alongside a review (whether flattering or not; then, as now, controversy tended to stimulate sales).

Yet the Spasmodic phenomenon does not only reflect the popular taste of the time. Its roots also took hold in particularly rich critical soil. Reveling in its newfound supremacy, the periodical press began to move beyond merely reviewing books and commenting on current publishing trends, ultimately developing methodologies that inform critical practice to this day. By the 1850s, what we now call the Romantic movement was approximately thirty years past; the next distinct cultural phase, namely the High Victorianism which would retrospectively characterize the entire century as smugly repressive and shamelessly hypocritical, lay some thirty years ahead. Society was changing rapidly, along with literature and the role of criticism. Commentators like F.D. Maurice attempted to place English Romanticism into historical and critical perspective and, at the same time, to prescribe the ideal direction for the new Victorian poetry. The periodicals' fervid spirit of inquiry stimulated intellectual exertion and aesthetic experimentation alike. The creation of the Spasmodic School, as well as the critical and public reception of the Spasmodic poets' works, owes much to these theoretical discussions. Romantic enough to fill the lingering void left by the waning spell of Byron, yet Victorian enough to uphold shifting middle-class notions of hierarchy, the Spasmodics were for a time accepted as exemplifying the highest order of poets, of necessity devoted to cultural scrutiny, and expressing the particular concerns of the age for posterity.

While the term "Romantic" would not have been available in its current sense to critics during the Spasmodic period, the word did occur, usually in lower case. It was used in the first quarter of the nineteenth century simply to distinguish works of the Classical period from those of the Middle Ages and Renaissance; none of the major critics of the period employ it in the manner we do now.[29] Instead, as we have seen, literary historians of the time preferred to group poets as the members of movements and to assign a conceptual generalization to each. The best-known examples of this type of classification are Byron's "Satanic School," the "Cockney School" of Hunt and Keats, and the "Lake School." While not as encompassing as "Romantic" would be, all three names reinforced literary as well as social divisions. While "Lake School" eventually lost its hostile overtones, it was originally intended to imply narrow parochialism, and the latter two names were intended to abuse and insult by casting, respectively, moral and intellectual aspersions on the poets in question; "Spasmodic School" was intended to follow the same pattern.

A distinct political undercurrent also clung to these jibes; the French Revolution was still a fresh memory to Jeffrey, Southey, and Lockhart, and their terminologies were born of a political conservatism which revolutionary-minded young poets (many of them associated with Chartism and other working-class movements) seemed to challenge. Only as political tempers mellowed and fears faded did critics begin to characterize the Romantics as preoccupied with personal feelings rather than radical individualism, leading to charges of "effeminacy" and socially irresponsible content. For example, outraged at what he considered public apathy toward the issues of mid-century Britain, Charles Kingsley called the reading public of 1853 "a mesmerizing, table-turning, spirit-rapping, Spiritualizing, Romanizing generation, who read Shelley in secret, and delight in his bad taste, mysticism, extravagance, and vague and pompous sentimentalism. The age is an effeminate one.... Shelley's nature is utterly womanish."[30] The shift in sentiment, not to mention pervasive misogyny, had a direct effect on the reception and the naming of the "Spasmodic School." By the time Aytoun popularized the term in 1854, it was used exclusively to vilify lapses in aesthetic, rather than political, judgment. And, as we have seen, the term "Spasmodic" itself suggested delicacy and physical weakness unbecoming in a male author. Aytoun's own fictional poet, "T. Percy Jones," promotes himself almost entirely as an advocate of subjective, rather than democratic, expression.

The major Romantic poets, with the exception of Wordsworth, were all dead by 1835; nonetheless, for almost two decades they dictated

2. "Fearless Strains"

the tastes of both the educated reading public and the prominent intellectuals who helped shape that taste. Newman, Keble, and J.S. Mill all upheld the true aim of poetry as expressing the inner content of the soul[31]; in "What Is Poetry?" (1833), Mill went so far as to declare that the "Poetry of a poet is Feeling itself."[32] Discussions of the technical aspects of poetry were also naturally affected by this dichotomy. Though a few dissenters continued to prefer the Classical style, some critics decided to redefine the true nature of literary quality so that the Romantic poets they admired might be better regarded.[33] Theories of composition now favored the short, personal song or lyric, strongly infused with a Wordsworthian "common language" at the expense of formality.

Long subjective poems, such as *The Prelude*, replaced attempts at epics; as early as July 1828, *The Athenaeum* was lamenting, in a feature article called "On the Decline of Epic Poetry," the loss of this "sacred medium of moral instruction."[34] The Romantics' humanity and supposedly unfettered style were elevated above the aridity of Dryden, Pope, and other eighteenth-century formalists, who had emphasized decorum of style at the expense of feeling and declamation. An article in the September 1834 *Blackwood's* accused Dryden of being "the only powerful poet of whom it can be said that he never drew a tear," and Mill concurred that "vulgarest of all ... is that which confounds poetry with metrical composition," thus definitively valuing one over the other.[35] Kingsley, writing in 1853, considered this shift in artistic emphasis an ominous development for English poetry. Complaining that poetry is "dying down among us year by year, although the age is becoming year by year more marvelous and inspiring," he identifies a "false principle" in the decision made by the earlier anti–Classical poets that "established canons of poetry were to be discarded as artificial" as well as their insistence that the poet should "be his own law" in terms of form and subject matter.[36]

Another unsigned article, which is probably Kingsley's as well, "Keats and His School" (1848), also targets such "daring rejection of all conventionalities save those of the writer's own sect" as an impediment to understanding, and hence reproducing, quality in poetry.[37] It should be obvious that the Spasmodic style of poetry could never have come about if not for the advent of this looser, less disciplined style of composition; as even the most cursory reading will show, Spasmodic works are filled with strained, even inappropriate imagery and a deliberate lack of attention to the formalities of scansion and episodic unity. One passage from "Keats and His School" is striking, since it prefigures many

The Spasmodic Poets

passages found in the torrent of Spasmodic condemnation which would appear six years later. Criticizing the "juvenile" Keatsian imitator who "picks up rhymes as they come, like pebbles in the road, presenting you always with something pretty, however incongruous"[38] in an attempt to dazzle with shimmering quantity rather than artistic purpose, the article might well be speaking of Dobell, Smith, or Bailey. The overall lack of coherence also lamented in the essay would be another charge frequently levelled at the Spasmodics, whose loosely designed poetic dramas skip from episode to episode as well as from locale to locale (sometimes unspecified, though one memorable stage-direction in *Festus* sets the scene "Everywhere") without establishing adequate connections between each.

These anti–Classical trends in early nineteenth-century poetry reflect a growing preference among poetry's general readership for emotional, rather than rational, aesthetic modes even after the great Romantic poems had drifted from public attention. This attitude, again, has great implications for the Spasmodic poets, and so is worth considering in detail. One obvious observation is that it coincides with the late eighteenth-century growth of objective scientific thought. The progress made during the "Age of Reason" challenged the traditionally superstitious world view which had spawned both the Graveyard School and the Gothic novel and continued to affect the beliefs of the masses. This conflict had gradually come to preoccupy the Victorians, as the more empirical state of mind demanded by continual scientific progress vied with the sentimentality they cherished and the religious faith they struggled to maintain. Victorian interest in classifying and rating the more spiritually secure poets of the century's first decades may well have originated in their desire to co-opt at least some of that earlier confidence, now increasingly elusive, in a universal Truth and a metaphysical Order.

After their downfall, the Spasmodics were ridiculed as affecting wisdom beyond their years and, even more offensively, pummeling their readers with bombastic pronouncements generated by this false understanding. Yet, in retrospect, they seem no more overconfident than a good many of their contemporaries (Tupper being a case in point). In *The Victorian Frame of Mind*, Houghton suggests that the oft-noted Victorian tendency towards dogmatism and posturing is actually the result of the age's thinkers grasping for opinions and rhetorical positions that would relieve their epidemic intellectual insecurity,[39] and certainly this disorientation of sensibility was very much alive at the time of the first

2. "Fearless Strains"

Spasmodic productions. D. Masson's 1853 review of Alexander Smith's *Poems* and E.S. Dallas' *Poetics* in 1853 contrasted two possible intellectual stances in terms of their respective approaches to sorting out the mysteries of the world:

> On the one hand, the intellect of man may brood over [the universe] inquiringly, striving to penetrate beneath it, to understand the system of laws by which its multitudinous atoms are held together, to master the mystery of its pulsations and sequences. This is the mood of the man of science. On the other hand, the intellect of man may brood over it creatively, careless how it is held together, or whether it is held together at all.... This is the mood of the poet ... who walks amid Nature's appearances ... starting at every step, as it were, a flock of white-winged phantasies that fly and flutter into the heaven of the future.[40]

Even though their direct social commentary is scarce (with the possible exception of that found in Dobell's early work *The Roman*), the Spasmodics' awareness of and manner of addressing this particular issue may account for their congeniality to the average Victorian mind, for passages discounting the scientific, in favor of the sentimental, approach are numerous. For example, *Balder* presents a character named Dr. Paul, a physician who generally has difficulty appreciating his friend's poetic productions. At a crucial moment, Paul says of himself and his fellow empiricists:

> I call us the gnomes
> Of science, miners who scarce see the light
> Working within the bowels of the world
> Of beauty.

If the criticism of the empirical temperament here seems merely implicit, Dobell eventually reassures his readers, as Balder the poet challenges one of Paul's objective medical diagnoses, that in fact "love is more than science."[41] It is of no small consequence that W.E. Aytoun's Spasmodic parody, *Firmilian*, burlesques just this speech by putting it in the mouth of the title character (the quintessential Spasmodic poet) to deride the scientific point of view as antithetical to his purposes as a neo–Romantic and narrow-sighted to boot. Spotting a particularly beautiful site on the mountainside, he declares that men "of science"

> overlook the outward face of things;
> Seek no sensation from the rude design
> Of outward beauty; but fulfil their task
> Like moles, who loathe the gust of upper air,
> And burrow underneath![42]

The Spasmodic Poets

By implication, the Spasmodics' insistence on intuitive, rather than pragmatic, knowledge is one of the core faults which trivializes their poetry for more progressive thinkers. It may also have class implications, since university-educated males, at least, would be expected to abjure superstition in favor of a more robust and rationally informed intellectualism. The virulence of Aytoun's denunciation of the Romantic sensibility, like Arnold's occasionally bitter exasperation with the British public[43] suggests how stubbornly that public clung to the comforting but unscientific creeds held over from simpler times.

The gradual elevation of these aspects of what we now consider the Romantic propensity had not, of course, come about wholesale. The development of Victorian criticism had precipitated reassessments of the poets who been part of the original movement. "Thoughts on Byron and Shelley" and "Keats and His School" were only two of many articles which were, from the first decades of the nineteenth century, actively debating the relative merits of Wordsworth, Shelley, and Keats. Arnold, with his insistence on seriousness and sincerity as the basis for great poetry, did not join in singing the praises of the rediscovered Romantic aesthetic. While some reviewers happily employed previously neglected poets like Shelley and Keats as standards to measure more recent contributions, a steady number remained unimpressed. Though Arnold is often portrayed as standing alone in his distaste, R.G. Cox[44] has successfully demonstrated that he was, in fact, merely giving more coherent expression to complaints against the Romantic impulse which had been voiced, albeit less elegantly, in several periodicals beginning some thirty years before "The Function of Criticism" appeared in 1863.

These early Victorian reviewers, Cox suggests, concentrated mainly on two main failures they regarded as endemic to Romantic poetry. First, the Romantic poets were, many felt, guilty of investing their works with little deep or philosophical thought and imbuing them with no clear intellectual purpose. Second, the better-known poems of Keats, Shelley, and their imitators appeared to lack relevance to modern life. Such poems were thought to be overly mystical and sensuous to the point of absurdity, or, in the case of Byron, so self-contained in their passion as to be ultimately impotent. The lack of a sufficiently important or universal subject, particularly in Wordsworth's case, was another frequent allegation by earnest critics against poetry that was, they felt, simply not saying enough that was timely and significant.

The case of Byron was of particular concern to those seriously interested in poetry's future. Within a few years of his death the almost

2. "Fearless Strains"

rabid popularity of Byron, as well as critical estimation of his poetry, had begun to decline seriously.[45] During Tennyson's undergraduate years, a formal debate was even arranged, as Arthur Henry Hallam and two other Cambridge delegates challenged an Oxford group to uphold the relative worth of Byron over Shelley. The Oxford group won the day, but the Cambridge Apostles, harboring in their circle the future Laureate, were fated to triumph by surer, albeit more gradual, means. Looking back in 1896, George Saintsbury went so far as to declare that any "enchantment" one found in "Byron's bastard and second-hand Romanticism" would instantly evaporate once one encountered "sight or sound of real poetry" such as that of Wordsworth, Shelley, Coleridge, or Keats.[46] Browning and Swinburne were among the poets who suffered the same disillusionment with their former idol.

Largely, complaints against Byron took two forms: one remonstrated against his poetic style, and the other expressed distaste for the effect his works might have on impressionable readers. Thomas Carlyle became an especially fierce denunciator on both counts. In his younger days, Carlyle had been among Byron's most ardent admirers. His reaction upon hearing of the poet's death is reminiscent of the youthful Tennyson's morosely inscribing "Byron is dead" on a piece of sandstone. Writing to Jane Welsh, his future wife, on May 19, 1824, Carlyle laments that this news "came down upon my heart like a mass of lead; … as if I had lost a Brother! Oh God! … There is a blank in your heart and a blank in mine, since this man passed away." In less than five years, however, his attitude had reversed. "Goethe" (1828) calls Byron's listless gloom and "artless" posturing "old & trite," and expressed the hope that Byron would be the last poet of his kind. "Burns," published in *The Edinburgh Review* that same year, denigrates Byron's "scowling, and teeth-gnashing, and other sulphurous humour" as closer to "the brawling of a player in some paltry tragedy" than an example of serious art with important social implications.[47]

Carlyle's most sustained critique came in *Sartor Resartus* (1833), in which his protagonist struggles to free himself of Byronic self-absorption. This, perhaps, was the aspect of Byron's poetry which aroused Carlyle's strongest disapproval: Byronic heroes like Manfred or Lara not only endure, but actually take pride in and even cultivate their aloofness from ordinary, lesser men. Their lives are lived within their own consciousness, rather than among their fellow mortals, and individual, subjective feeling is paramount. Teufelsdröckh might as well be speaking directly to Manfred or a number of other Byronic heroes

The Spasmodic Poets

when he delivers his edict to stop "fretting and fuming, and lamenting and self-tormenting," and instead famously advocates, "Close thy *Byron*; open thy *Goethe*."

It was perhaps inevitable that the Carlylian ideal of Work and subordination of the individual ego to the common social organism[48] would find widespread favor. As England's feudal social structure gave way to one organized around middle-class economics, and as the land became peppered with both slums and newly affluent middle-class households, the old aristocratic indiscretions, such as heavy drinking, promiscuity, and a lack of social conscience, were increasingly looked upon, at least publicly, as morally distasteful and irresponsible. Likewise, the conception of the heroic had narrowed considerably, partly due to modern economic realities; as Kingsley wryly notes, "Byron's Corsairs and Laras have been, on the whole, impossible during the thirty years' peace; and piracy and profligacy are at all times, and especially now-adays, expensive amusements, and often require a good private fortune—rare among poets."[49] Nor did Byron's satiric poems find more favor than those featuring egotistical heroes, for these were too strong for the hypocrites scattered among the earnest.[50] In short, a demand for more realistic poetry, portraying a more "common" or Wordsworthian hero, and promoting community betterment, had rendered the Byronic hero a mere relic of a lost literary innocence that most likely could not, and in the minds of many should not, be recaptured.

The Spasmodic poets would have suffered this loss acutely, insofar as they were willing to relinquish Byron at all. P.J. Bailey, in retrospect considered the first Spasmodic, had grown up near Newstead Abbey, the Byron estate, had seen the dead lord lying in state, and naturally perpetuated the Byronic mystique in his writings; he and Sydney Dobell had memorized, respectively, *Childe Harold* and *Manfred*.[51] It was really no accident that the Spasmodics recreated many of his supposed faults, such as excessive introspection at the expense of community involvement and the lack of a unified poetic plan. Yet none of the Spasmodics ever repudiated Byron as Carlyle and Swinburne did. For them, Byron's slippage from literary fashion was less a fact to be lamented than one that could be, if not actively reversed, ignored.

On two points, the neo–Romantics and the anti–Romantics are strangely united. One is the continuing need for a hero in the Carlylean sense. The growing dissatisfaction with Byron as a role model did not, of course, indicate that the Victorians were outgrowing the need for idols altogether. Byron, as much as any of his protagonists, had towered

2. "Fearless Strains"

over English letters like Colossus, and had enabled his readers to share his enlarged stature even as they regarded it with growing skepticism. The loss of this Byronic ideal left a blank in many hearts besides Carlyle's. Even he, having proven Byron's inadequacy to serve as the hero he required, could only remedy Teufelsdröckh's psychic dilemma by finding him a more appropriate hero, Goethe, a strategy Kingsley likewise urged.[52] Henry Taylor attributed Byron's decline in public esteem to readers' "satiated appetite" for Byronic adventures rather than an overall change in taste, since, as far as he could tell, former admirers had not yet "transferred their admiration to any worthier object."[53] Nowhere does Taylor suggest that poet-worship itself is not a worthwhile pursuit, or that the poet may be excused from his presumed duty to educate the public. Arnold, too, was reluctant to dismiss Byron, and refrained from lamenting his influence on English poetry. In his Preface to *Poetry of Byron*, he championed Byron as one of the two major voices of the age, the other being Wordsworth, and in "Haworth Churchyard," written upon the death of Charlotte Brontë, Arnold pays tribute to Emily Brontë by portraying her as a kind of female Byron (the Brontë sisters, not coincidentally, fascinated Spasmodics like Dobell and Swinburne, both of whom greatly admired *Wuthering Heights*). The sentiment expressed is nostalgia rather than ridicule or condescension.

Some, who shared the preferences of Kingsley and Arnold and were disgruntled with the Romantic Poets and their allegedly mystical preoccupations, found relief in the more sober and purposeful work of Henry Taylor, whose Preface to *Philip von Artevelde* (1834) was central to nineteenth-century poetical taste and poetic theory. This poetic drama earned high praise both for its aesthetic and moral merits and for the system of poetics set forth in its Preface. Taylor's drama was praised by *The Edinburgh Review* for its emphasis on intellectual soundness over mere sensuousness, and the *Athenaeum* lauded the author's coherence, lack of obscurity, and all-around good sense in eschewing bombast and emotionalism.[54] In his Preface, Taylor had much to say about the Romantic poets' inadequacies, suggesting that the Romantics are suited mainly for "very young readers," mainly because youths presumably share their disdain for common sense and reason. This failing is evident in the Romantics' deficiency in selecting proper subjects for their poems. Neither were they intellectually demanding enough, either on themselves or on their readers, who, Taylor hopefully observes, are beginning to return to the sounder poetry of earlier eras. In many cases, a surplus of dazzling images was employed to mask, for the benefit of both reader and writer, a sorry poverty of original thought. Byron, especially, might have been "the greatest poet of his age" had he united true philosophy to the fiery feeling which was unfortunately founded on "contracting self-love."[55]

Although *A Life Drama* and *Balder* were not to appear for nearly twenty years, Taylor's indictment of post–Romantic poetry, particularly that which was Byronic in tone, anticipated many reviewers' reactions to the supposed superficiality of the Spasmodics:

> The poetry of the day ... consists of little more than a poetical diction, an arrangement of words implying a sensitive state of mind, and therefore more or less calculated to excite corresponding associations, though, for the most part, not pertinently to any matter in hand; a diction which addresses itself to the sentient, not the percipient, properties of the mind, and displays merely symbols or types of feelings, which might exist with equal force in a being the most barren of understanding....[56]

Taylor articulated almost perfectly what many had come to believe the proper direction of poetry must be. His edicts to teach while entertaining, to expound without passion or extravagance, were taken seriously by reviewers and helped bring about one of the most uninspiring and soporific periods in English poetry. The amazing success of the first Spasmodic poem, P.J. Bailey's *Festus*, was in Gosse's opinion due to the public's boredom with what he unenthusiastically dubbed "the school of good sense."[57]

More passionate lovers of poetry continued to search for other role models. For one group, which would eventually include Sydney Dobell, Tennyson became a possible replacement for Byron; when Dobell, already published himself, met Tennyson at a gathering, he supposedly called their introduction, much to the Laureate's embarrassment, "the crowning honour of [his] life."[58] Another heroic figure co-opted by the Victorians in the wake of Byron's decline was John Keats. His *Poems*, almost completely neglected for twenty years, had been reprinted in 1840, and Keats' fame and appeal grew steadily afterwards. As might be expected, given the loss of the political dimension in criticism of what we now call the Romantic poets, the least political of these came to be widely considered the quintessential example of such poetry, hence the debate, in print, concerning the propriety of designating a "school" of Keats. Since the Victorians were becoming increasingly insistent that their ideal poet should address the social concerns of the age, further critical tension sprang from the adoption of Keats as a model. Despite the numerous flaws of theme and technique which had already been

2. "Fearless Strains"

discovered and expounded upon in Byron's poetry, his work nonetheless seemed comparatively free of the escapist and, to some, irresponsibly ethereal flavor found in Shelley[59] and Keats.

As "Keats and His School" notes, Keats' influence on the age had proved "deeper, and consequently less obvious" than was at first perceived. Tennyson himself, for example, was "in many respects, what Keats himself might have become, had he lived among the Cambridge 'Apostles' rather than among London 'Cockneys.'"[60] The poets' transference of loyalty would later be portrayed by Gosse as a logical progression of Victorian hero-worship: while Tennyson and Browning "had gaped at Byron and respected Wordsworth" and "had been dazzled by Shelley," ultimately each "had given his heart to Keats."[61] Their fervid admiration led reviewers to notice and admire Keats; presently, regard for Keats' work spread among the general reading public as well, who found him sentimentally appealing. George Gilfillan touted Dobell and his working-class discovery, Alexander Smith, as poets of the prophetic dimensions required, worthy successors to Shelley and especially Keats. Many serious readers, including A.H. Clough, were eager to believe in his assessment.

Just as those who had found new admiration for the lyrical sensuality of earlier decades rushed forward to praise Keats, those whose tastes more closely approximated Arnold's did not hesitate to blame his influence for the weaknesses they found in contemporary poetry. As late as 1907, J.F.A. Pyre blamed Keats for the "decadence of modern poetry"[62] in spite of the more solid Romantic contributions made by Coleridge, a trend which had started with the article "Keats and His School." The faults pointed out in that piece are said to be equally applicable to the "school" of Keats' modern imitators, of whom Tennyson is the most promising precisely because of his relative freedom from immoderation. To be "overlaid by conceits" like Keats, on the other hand, is no less than dangerous to any "mind not inveterately disciplined in the Dryden and Pope school of taste." Such a mind is in constant "danger of being carried away" into aesthetic preoccupations at the expense of more practical mental exercises.[63] On this point in particular, "Thoughts on Byron and Shelley" is equally cautionary, claiming that the real "mischief" of an aesthete like Shelley is his ability to make "the unrest and unhealth of sensitive young men" fashionable, hence rendering them idle and introspective, for years at a stretch. Such men, it claims, must be critically evaluated not only as poets, but also as "teachers." He does not hesitate to assert that, as teachers, "both have done harm."[64]

The Spasmodic Poets

As Kingsley's comment demonstrates, the second point on which both ideological camps concurred was that so much responsibility should be put on the poet as social critic and moral example. The number of critics and readers who were prepared to take this possibility entirely for granted represents yet another Victorian adaption of Romantic theory, in this case the idea of the poet as supreme commentator and teacher, a kind of cultural interpreter who could perceive a divine plan for society and convey it, through poetry, to his fellow men. The attribution of near-mythical status might have been, as with Victorian dogmatism, an exorbitant reaction to an unsettling Utilitarian disdain for poetry as mere rhetorical entertainment. Cultural insecurity, again, prompted lovers of literature, including critics in both camps, to make grandiose claims for the poet's importance rather than mounting a quiet but less reassuring defense.[65] The original conception of the Romantic poet as a kind of mystic "seer" had now expanded to include a new type of poet, a kind of urbane *vates*. He was expected to effect, via his powerful and divinely inspired imagination, a renewal of spiritual awareness and thus of public virtue.

Because of the tacit acceptance of this principle among reviewers, the productions of both new and established poets were scrutinized with intense concern for their ethical content. By the mid-nineteenth century, the social uses and the aesthetic value of poetry were considered virtually inseparable. To the good fortune of the burgeoning Spasmodics, a poet who had captured the public imagination could be nominated to such status without having proven technical virtuosity; in fact, some imperfections in style might even endear him to his less-gifted public. One review of Alexander Smith's *Poems* revels in just this feeling of kinship with a great soul who had risen from among the masses:

> Verily, Alexander Smith, thou hast limned the poet's outline greatly to our mind: a many-sided man is he, with thoughts that wander abroad all over the universe of God, and large-souled sympathies with all the brotherhood of men.[66]

Not even Arnold was exempt from the yearning for a modern prophet. In spite of his ostensible rejection of the Romantic impulse as a proper direction for English literature, his essays on greatness in poetry and his attempts to refine the taste of the reading public (particularly that sector composed of the newly literate mercantile class) demonstrate his essential adherence to the same concept; he differs only in his

2. "Fearless Strains"

choice of poets as suitable moral leaders.[67] Like other critics of the time, Arnold slipped comfortably into the new parlance which centered on the revived concept of the *vates*, or poet/prophet who took his inspiration from above, and comfortably combined quasi-religious with analytical vocabularies.

Despite laudable appreciation for the great poets who preceded them, serious Victorian readers also longed for the appearance of a poet who would directly address the unique concerns, and incorporate the particular advances of their age, in his art. The anxiety with which all awaited this event is expressed both in the periodicals' constant fear that poetry is dying and in their willingness to hail a variety of young men as the poet they sought. P.J. Bailey was one such example. *Festus*, first published in 1839, became immensely popular, if Horne's spirited defense in *A New Spirit of the Age* is any indication, precisely because of its rejection of Taylor's theories and return to unapologetically emotional content. Even Tennyson was caught up in the Bailey frenzy, declaring that he felt himself to be a mere "wren beating about a hedgerow, [while] the author of *Festus* was like an eagle soaring to the sun."[68] The poem was reprinted twelve times in England and no less than thirty times in America, and lovers of *Festus* even created a compendium of their favorite passages. Bailey was not, of course, the only new poet to be trumpeted as the authentic voice of the age. Due largely to the partisanship and enthusiastic reviews of George Gilfillan in *The Eclectic Review*, Alexander Smith and Sydney Dobell were raised to similar prominence.

Because they address almost all the early Victorians' concerns regarding the state of poetry at the time, and because they are themselves the foundation of much of the eventual critical reaction against the Spasmodics, Gilfillan's original reviews are worth looking at in detail. Though it may seem unorthodox to examine the reviews before extending the same attention to the poems themselves, it is important to remember that the idea of a "School" consisting of young poets who were not personally acquainted would probably not have come about if not for Gilfillan's championing of all three during a set chronological period. Even more importantly, encountering the reviews in advance of the actual poems would, in fact, have been the experience of a majority of Victorian readers. In most cases, copious extracts of the first Spasmodic poems were presented to the public via the periodical notices; in Smith's case, the poems were still in manuscript at the time of Gilfillan's review and would therefore have been unavailable in any case.

The Spasmodic Poets

Though reviews for Dobell's youthful effort, *The Roman*, published under the name "Sydney Yendys" in April 1850, were not quite as enthusiastic as Gilfillan's, they were not unlike his in tone and in the issues they addressed. *The Literary Gazette*, for example, praised the epic nature of the poem, which was over three thousand lines long, as "a notable literary effort in these times,"[69] perhaps recalling the decline of epic lamented in *The Athenaeum* years before. *The Athenaeum* itself spoke of poetry in extravagantly cosmic terms, noting that for each great poem or "calm star that keeps its orbit in harmony with all the other worlds, we have a hundred comets that streak and disappear"; in the face of such literary transience, a work like Dobell's, "which indicates a return to the completeness of poetic art [is] welcome." *The Athenaeum*, like the *Literary Gazette*, did mildly point out a few stylistic problems in the poem, such as Dobell's overabundance of opulent but at times strained imagery and his tendency to become incoherent and bombastic. It is interesting to note that these are virtually the same flaws eventually, albeit much less patiently, directed at *Balder*. Still, in spite of these immaturities in technique, the reviewer declares that Dobell possess no less than "the sure pledges of high and lasting excellence."[70]

In contrast, Gilfillan was not content to merely look forward to the eventual fruition of such promise. Instead, he begins his own review by restating, in rhetorically extreme form, the position taken by pessimistic critics like Kingsley regarding poetry's supposed decline. According to Gilfillan, the cry too often heard in contemporary reviews is that "poetry is declining—poetry is being extinguished—poetry is extinct. To talk of poetry now is eccentricity—to write it is absurdity."[71] Gilfillan himself, on the other hand, is determined to remain hopeful on poetry's behalf. For one thing, the reading public is not as indifferent to quality as some critics have supposed. In fact, rather than "call[ing] the men of the age swine," men of letters should concentrate on "cast[ing] down the pearls":

> We have often imaged to ourselves the rapture with which a poet, of proper proportion and due culture, if writing in his age's spirit, would be received in an age when the works of Coleridge, and Wordsworth, and Keats, are so widely read and thoroughly appreciated. He would find it "all ear."[72]

Clearly, Gilfillan regards the newfound popularity of the Romantic poets as evidence that his educated contemporaries have finally developed a taste discriminating enough to recognize and reward true poetic quality. It also indicates that Gilfillan considered the characteristics

2. "Fearless Strains"

of the poets named as closer to what his age required than, for example, Taylor or any other later poet, though any poet attempting to capture "the age's spirit" would logically benefit from an understanding of its particular issues both political and aesthetic. What Gilfillan proposes is that his modern ideal conjoin the obvious advantages of being alive and informed with selected attributes of the Romantic poets, having first modified those attributes to better suit that changed moral climate of the mid-nineteenth century. "Byron's energy," for example, should be "better controlled," "Shelley's earnestness" should be "better instructed," and "Keats' sensibility" should be "guarded and armed." The poet must also be both "genius and artist" and "have sung over to himself the deep controversies of his age, and sought to reduce them into an [sic] unique and intelligible harmony." Most of all, however, he should "have a distinct mission and message, savouring of the prophetic."[73] Carlyle would have agreed.

This last point is especially important to Gilfillan, and was of special importance to Dobell also, accounting in large part for the later misunderstanding concerning the authorial intent behind *Balder*. Gilfillan, a clergyman, is calling for no less than a "near and glorious resurrection" of poetry, and insists that his ideal poet see his "mission" in evangelical terms also. Wordsworth and Coleridge, unlike the other Romantic poets he mentions, are found to be appropriate models just as they are, because the two have a "Christianized" view of, respectively, Nature and philosophy. As might be expected, Romantic poetry's emphasis on the mystical and spiritual, as opposed to the almost clinical pragmatism of the "school of good sense," accounts more for Gilfillan's enthusiasm than its subject matter or artistic style. After all, Gilfillan asserts, poetry originally developed from prayer, and his ideal poet must make full use of the interconnectedness of the two. He must accept wholeheartedly that Christianity "as rightly understood" (by Gilfillan, at least, and not by orthodox Anglican authorities) is both "the root and the flower of all truth" and thus the only possible inspiration, and end, for poetry. Perhaps more importantly, his ideal poet must not hesitate to make this fact known, and should without apology "sing his fearless strains to the world." He should recognize the gift of poetry as a sacred calling, as Gilfillan excitedly designates it: "He should have a high idea of his art—counting it a lower inspiration, a sacred trust, a minor grace—a plant from a seed originally dropped out of the paradise of God!"

Having set out and explained these far-reaching criteria, Gilfillan proceeds to consider several likely candidates from the current crop of published poets, since a man adequately versed in the concerns of the day must already be engaged in writing about them. After dismissing Macaulay, Tennyson ("neutralized so far as great future achievements are concerned"), Emerson, both Brownings, and, somewhat prophetically, Aytoun, he concludes that, undoubtedly, P.J. Bailey and "Yendys" are the two best contenders for "the vacant laurel," thus making the first tentative (though of course unnamed) Spasmodic grouping. Yet Bailey, while eminently possessed of "genius," and concerned with metaphysical matters, unhappily has "little aptitude to teach." Dobell, on the other hand, seems positively born to instruct. To emphasize the young man's suitability to assume this prophetic role, Gilfillan introduces him in pseudo-mythical tones of awe. While Bailey's qualifications as the "coming poet" are being debated, "a young voice has suddenly been uplifted from a provincial town in England, crying 'Hear me—I also am a poet; I aspire, too, to prove myself worthy of being a teacher.'" Assuring his readers that "some of the most fastidious of critical journals" share his enthusiasm,[74] Gilfillan proceeds to quote several long passages from *The Roman* and praise the young author's "masculine health, maturity, and Christianity" as opposed to the more effeminate "mystic school" of years past (presumably Shelley's) and compares the stamina of his verse to Byron's.[75] Dobell would thus appear to have demonstrated, and in the refined form suggested, the Romantic and vatic traits Gilfillan has just finished prescribing.

It is tempting to wonder if, in the interests of becoming Dobell's mentor, Gilfillan manufactured many of his ideal poet's requirements based upon Romantic tendencies already apparent in *The Roman*. Certainly his assertions concerning the poem's "maturity" are suspect considering not only the poem's obvious lack thereof but also the other "fastidious" periodicals' attempts to point out and then excuse many transgressions of form based on Dobell's youth and inexperience. Gilfillan's almost laughable bombast seems less incongruous once one recognizes the element of self-congratulation. Discovering the poet of the century, or at least convincing others that he had done so, might after all be considered an accomplishment second only to actually assuming the laurel. On the other hand, Gilfillan may have quite honestly revealed his particular taste in poetry when he declared, at the outset of his review, that he found "a grandeur about passion when carried to excess"; in Spasmodic poetry he would not have had to wrestle with many subtleties of expression in that regard. In any case, Gilfillan

2. "Fearless Strains"

employs an astrological metaphor similar to *The Athenaeum*'s to convince his readers of Dobell's cosmic proportions, then slips in a Biblical allusion to reassure them that their literary savior and prophet had arrived to resolve any intellectual crises they are suffering. Dobell, more than any other of the "rising 'Sons of the Morning'" is destined to

> "fill his crescent-sphere": revive the power and glory of song; give voice to a great dumb struggle in the mind of the age; rescue the lyre from the camp of the Philistines [and make] the names "of poet and of prophet." ... the same.

Dobell, perhaps recalling his insular religious sect's high hopes for him, felt deeply flattered and encouraged by this established critic's patronage. He soon set to work on a multi-volume Christian poetic drama, the first part of which became *Balder*.

Three years later, in November 1853, Gilfillan published a notice of another discovery, and another serious candidate for poet of the age. He welcomed Alexander Smith to the company of the anointed in almost identical terminology. "Well is his uprise often compared to that of a new star arising in the midnight," Gilfillan declares in his review of Smith's unpublished manuscript (constituting a unique critical approach in itself), virtually defining the *vates*: "He is a new messenger and mediator between the Infinite and the race of man, continually an instructor to his kind." With "the mellowing, softening, and spiritualizing moonlight of his new genius" Smith has "lifted up his daring rod to the heavens, and extracted new and splendid imagination from their unfading fires."[76] By the time this review (with its unfortunate, though not entirely inappropriate, phallic references) appeared, the Spasmodic circle, though still nameless, had expanded, for Gilfillan adds Smith to a group now consisting of Dobell (still referred to as Yendys), Bailey, and J.S. Bigg. These four are portrayed as actively engaged in spreading their own "poetic and religious creed," and, if anything, Smith is "even more Christian."[77]

There can be little doubt that the attention, often negative, given the Spasmodics by other periodical contributors was more a reaction to Gilfillan's inflated praise than to the admittedly grave shortcomings in the poems themselves. Though Gilfillan was apparently not mistaken regarding his audience's desire for both heroes and prophets, and helped both *The Roman* and *A Life-Drama* attain considerable commercial success and at least temporary critical acclaim, he was somewhat premature; consequently, Dobell and Smith suffered a humiliating loss of prestige. In a review of Arnold's *Poems* written at about the same

The Spasmodic Poets

time, Aytoun denounced Gilfillan for leading young poets astray, and parodied his inflated rhetoric by quoting from a fictional article on the recently discovered "Tunks," obviously intended to represent Smith.

"Tunks" would have been better served, Aytoun declares, by remaining in "trade" (factory work) instead of being led astray by promises of artistic accomplishment and (implicitly) social promotion:

> "Tunks may not, like Byron, possess the hypochondriacal brilliancy of a blasted firework.... He does not pretend to the spontaneous combustion of our friend Gander Rednag [Yendys/Dobell]." ... He has, however, according to Guffaw [Gilfillan], a genius like a "meteor-standard of the Andes." [By such false encouragement] a very excellent young man, who might have gained a competency by following his paternal trade, is [placed] in imminent peril ... by the folly of an unscrupulous scribbler [and] the poisoned chalice of Guffaw.... There are no bounds to the credulity of a poet of one-and-twenty.[78]

Without doubt, some of Aytoun's vitriol toward Gilfillan, his fellow Scot, stemmed from political and religious disagreements. Yet his concern for the futures of naïve young poets, instantly plunged from obscurity into fame, proved justified. Given the zealous tone of Gilfillan's idolatry, it is no wonder that Dobell and Smith developed an overconfident attitude regarding their supposedly prophetic roles and became less concerned with polishing their craft than in living up to Gilfillan's extravagant expectations. The casual, and to many morally distasteful, audacity of *Balder* eventually represented to Aytoun and his fellow skeptics a worst-case scenario made real. Though his pity for "Guffaw's" victims may seem ironic, considering his primary responsibility for their subsequent and lasting embarrassment, there is no reason to suppose that Aytoun regarded his campaign to drive the Spasmodics from the literary profession as heroic. Rather, he appeared to regard it an ethical and an aesthetic necessity. To that extent, at least, he would not have seen himself as self-serving in the manner of Gilfillan, and he probably viewed his eventual triumph over his excitable rival's entourage with a sense of intellectual complacency, if not actual relief.

As the clash between Aytoun and Gilfillan demonstrates, the Spasmodic poets were the ultimate products, as well as the victims, of a critical game of one-upmanship that had lasted half a century and had taken an eccentric turn into quasi-religious proselytizing. The debate was, in some ways, a final effort to sustain the Romantic impulse in England, both in content and in the concept of the priestly poet-*cum*-prophet or *vates*. Such conviction in such a man's supremacy among humankind,

2. *"Fearless Strains"*

surpassing even Shelley's secular idea of poets as "unacknowledged legislators of the world," is a testament to the Victorians' continuing fascination with, and often subconscious wish to return to, the passion and faith of their pre–Industrial forebears.

As the nineteenth century moved into its second half, greater understanding of literary methods, theories, and historical judgment created a space for genuine academic appraisal even of iconoclastic and experimental poetry.[79] The earlier abuses of anonymous periodical reviewers, which had deeply wounded authors like Browning, Tennyson, and Charlotte Brontë, slowly gave way to a more professional, objective, and scholarly style that aided in the formation of a recognizable, and educationally useful, English canon. The stronger Victorian talents were eventually rehabilitated and appreciated. Unfortunately, the Spasmodics were not among this select group.

The Spasmodics' age was said to be more "intent upon self-glorification" than any other before it.[80] As long as they were prepared to contribute to that goal, they were applauded and promoted. Once they seemed ready to move to a more autonomous plane, where they could experiment with conventional forms of expression as well as theme, their laurels were snatched away. Shaky though their technical skill may have been, the ripening of their powers of ironic social commentary may ultimately have caused their ruin. The Victorian world, it seems, was not quite ready to embrace poetic subjectivity, much less anarchy. Nonetheless, an engrossing literary drama was about to play out on the mid-century stage.

3

"Barbaric Jewelry"

Bailey's Festus
and the Birth of the Spasmodic Ideal

In his volume of biographical reminiscences, Edmund Gosse referred to Philip James Bailey as one of two "representatives of what poetry was in these islands before the commencement of the Victorian era." More specifically, he named Bailey as the last vestige of the outmoded Romantic impulse or "mystical enthusiasm" that Henry Taylor's Preface had done its best to quell. Bailey really was an artifact, for he was both the first and last Spasmodic. Born on April 22, 1816 (just one day after Charlotte Brontë), Bailey lived to reach the age of 86. By the time he died in 1902, not only Queen Victoria but even the younger Dobell, Smith, and Bigg were long deceased and their works almost completely forgotten.

Bailey's longevity was, ironically, his critical undoing. All his life, he projected an image of aesthetic sensibility and sagacity: "Superbly handsome in physique and countenance," *Chambers' Cyclopaedia of English Literature* admiringly noted in 1901, "he rivalled Tennyson in the art of looking like a poet."[1] His "manly taste" was singled out for special praise in contrast to the more delicate poetic musings of the Romantics.[2] Arthur Hugh Clough, who would briefly fall under the Spasmodic spell in 1853, also felt the tug of Bailey's vatic magnetism.[3] Yet, although he retained even "in extreme old age all the faculties of the mind,"[4] he never equaled his earliest critics' expectations. Nor could he be venerated as a promising talent who might have achieved great things if not for a premature death. Instead, he survived to see his *Festus* slip from near-canonical status to ridicule, and his once-lauded poetic powers almost universally derided. Unwilling to relinquish his role as oracle, he continued to cultivate the appearance of one even after his literary fame had waned. In the manner of the poet of "Kubla Khan,"

3. "Barbaric Jewelry"

with his "flashing eyes" and "floating hair," Bailey maintained a "rapt sensitiveness" of features[5] framed by "a cloud of voluminous white hair and curled silver beard," causing him to resemble "a sort of prophet or bard."[6] Sadly, he had taken these extreme measures in vain. Once considered a possible spokesman for everything that was vital about his Age, he was eventually invoked to illustrate its absurdities, as in Robert Birley's curt assessment: "That men like Tennyson admired [*Festus*] is evidence of the weakness of the civilization of the nineteenth century, evidence, perhaps, of its coming dissolution."[7] *Chambers' Cyclopaedia* saw things differently, rating (as did many others) "Bailey's place in Victorian literature ... not far below Tennyson and Browning" and expressing "certain" hope that "a critic will soon arise ... to do for him what Addison did for Milton."[8] Yet, more than a century after his death, this has not happened and now seems unlikely in the extreme.

In fairness to Bailey's contemporary admirers, of course, Birley should have noted that even they seemed to regard their poet as idiosyncratic and difficult. *Chambers'* characterized his style, with charming Victorian vigor, as "volcanic" and "incandescent ... shaped by the powerfully wielded hammer of his imagination on the iron anvil of his thought," but at the same time also admitted that "his imagination outsoared his technique."[9] Though his first volume's "vogue was almost Byronic,"[10] Bailey's post–*Festus* career was fraught with disappointment and embarrassment. His 1850 volume, *The Angel World*, struck readers as even more shapeless, mystical, and cryptic than *Festus* had been. It sold poorly, apparently having alienated the public, and in 1854 Bailey found himself pilloried with the other "Spasmodics" despite his protests. His next volume, *The Mystic*, was published in 1855 after the Spasmodic controversy had fully erupted. Probably as a result of complaints about Spasmodic shapelessness, Bailey decided to construct this work on the opposite principle of rigid formality, but the result was so controlled as to appear stilted and inanimate, and it did not attract a following either.

Embittered, Bailey conceived a plan to force these later works on his readers by inserting long sections of his later poems, almost verbatim, into *Festus* as newer editions were called for. As a result, the original poem became more unreadable and diffuse, something of "an impossible sausage," with each reprint, as *The Cambridge History of English Literature* remarked; readers who could get through it in any of its many versions "must be possessed of a singular prowess or of a still more singular indifference and insensibility."[11] Bailey was increasingly regarded as something of a huckster and a fraud. Weygandt's pitying tone in 1936 is representative:

> Poet and prophet Bailey tried to be, but he was neither. His attempts to justify God's ways to man, to create a liberal and reconciling Christian philosophy to give the world an optimistic creed that would content it with modernity, are to-day but Victorian twaddle, tiresome and almost unreadable.... He is a poor craftsman in verse and no prophet at all.[12]

Certainly it is possible to condescend to Bailey, as Weygandt does, and to marvel (or snicker) at his deluded egotism. Yet his early optimism regarding his artistic future is understandable when considered in context.

Festus had first appeared, albeit in a much shorter form, in 1839, and by the time its Jubilee edition was published in 1889 it had exhausted twenty-two printings, half of which were pirated, in England and no less than thirty in the United States.[13] Lovers of *Festus*, called "Festonians," even created a compendium of their favorite passages. The poem's enthusiastic audience was composed of both evangelical and erudite readers, so Pickering, Bailey's publisher, made a point of using favorable reviews from both sources to advertise his product and encourage even greater circulation and publicity.[14] As a result of this well-engineered promotion, Bailey was able to count among his admirers Thackeray, Tennyson, Bulwer-Lytton, Walter Savage Landor, and both Brownings. Even Arnold, later to become virulently anti–Spasmodic, commended Bailey's talents to Clough in an 1848 letter by calling him one of "the most promising English verse-writers" of the time.[15] Bailey also acquired George Gilfillan as his champion. By 1850, the same year in which he discovered Sydney Dobell's *The Roman*, Gilfillan was touting *Festus*, which had actually been released eleven years earlier, as a "phenomenon" and calling it "a new comet in an old sky."[16] Bailey's reputation as a leading poet seemed assured by the time he turned thirty.

Biographically, Bailey had much in common with Dobell, seven years his junior. As would be the case with Dobell, Bailey's father was a member of an unconventional religious sect which abjured a Calvinist theology in favor of one which more closely resembled Unitarianism. Unlike the isolationist Dobell family, however, the Baileys maintained an enquiring and liberal outlook which helped shape the Universalist doctrine favored by the poet in *Festus*. As far as literary matters were concerned, Bailey's father, again like John Dobell and many other men

3. "Barbaric Jewelry"

of their generation, was an ardent admirer of Byron who set his son to memorizing *Childe Harold* and even took him to view their idol's body in Nottingham. The elder Bailey, who had once owned and edited a newspaper,[17] encouraged his son to write and publish as had Dobell's, and was willing to support the young man financially as he did so. Though Philip studied law at Glasgow University, poetry remained his only profession from the age of twenty until the end of his long life. *Festus* was first published anonymously in 1839.

Although Bailey is now habitually identified as the first of the Spasmodics, the association originally rankled him. In a letter of 1893, he proclaimed his objections and defended *Festus* as a poem with a markedly different agenda than those composed with "crude and hasty treatment" by the fame-seeking scribblers he believed the later Spasmodics to be. His work, he maintained, had been intended to perform the more philosophical function of spiritual enlightenment, and had been composed for no such self-aggrandizing purpose as Smith's and Dobell's. He had "no sympathy with their works specially, nor with their ways," and, sharing his protagonist's immodesty, boldly declared

> as is obvious to any one who has only read even the preface to the recent Jubilee edition of *Festus*, that no more orderly and methodical poem is to be found in the whole range of English literature ... nor, considering the extent of its compass, more fitly compacted as a whole ... we may suppose added under the final heading of the prefatory analysis above alluded to, a special differentiation of the work which follows, in its spiritual teachings and conclusions, from those insisted upon by the majority of writers who have advisedly chosen the illustration of such themes....[18]

Even though this syntactically convoluted and astonishingly confident assessment of the poem sounds uncomfortably similar to the burlesque preface in which "T. Percy Jones" defends *Firmilian*, Hugh Walker, for one, sympathized with Bailey and resisted accepting a Spasmodic classification for *Festus* because "we must grant that the work is far too laboriously hammered out to be fairly described as 'spasmodic.'"[19] In light of these arguments it may be worth examining in more detail the reasons for attributing the school's paternity to Bailey.

In retrospect, it can hardly be denied that *Festus* set an example for other poets eager for impassioned models. The ideas it expressed about the superior leadership potential of the poet himself pushed earlier Romantic speculation to an extreme metaphorically expressed in Festus's coronation scene, and this aspect of *Festus* in particular was to become a staple of later poetic dramas like *A Life-Drama*, *Balder*, and

The Spasmodic Poets

Night and the Soul. The fact that Bailey's technique proved congenial to George Gilfillan, the Spasmodic mentor, further suggests his conceptual affinity to the other works Gilfillan so rigorously promoted. In letters, Gilfillan recommended *Festus* as a model to both Smith and Dobell as they commenced work on their own poetic dramas. Thus, although Gilfillan seems never to have been in personal contact with Bailey, the Spasmodic association was established early on. By 1876, William Michael Rossetti could state without fear of contradiction that

> It is apparent that Mr. Bailey had a good deal to do with the genesis of the Spasmodic School; *Festus*, with its yearnings of unsubstantial passion, and of thought adventuring into boundless space, and boxing the compass of speculation, must have pioneered Smith into the staggering fervours of the *Life-Drama*, and Dobell into the magniloquent hysteria of *Balder*.[20]

Rossetti's point is sound, and identifies exactly those aspects of *Festus* which formed the basis of Spasmodic poetics. With regard to Bailey's protests, the intent and execution of a work must be considered as two separate variables; the tendency of early Victorians to confuse the two probably accounted for much of *Festus*'s popularity to begin with. Not only was Bailey obviously mistaken about his work's clarity and conciseness, he was avoiding the obvious. Whatever his own opinion of later Spasmodic works, the unapologetic eccentricity of *Festus*'s style, hero, and theme (what *The Cambridge History* calls, with some ambivalence, the "strangeness"[21] that distinguishes a poetic phenomenon, whatever its intrinsic value) really had made a detectable impression on their authors and, inevitably, their content. Ironically, in his later years Bailey "was sometimes present at Westland Marston's symposia, where Rossetti, Swinburne, 'Orion' Horne, and other celebrities were wont to meet."[22] All of these names would have been familiar to anyone acquainted with the Spasmodic School; every one of them had some connection to the label at one point or another in their careers. Presumably these four men, at least, found their ideas perfectly compatible and worth discussing in depth.

Although *Festus* was in some ways an unexpected and perhaps to some an inexplicable phenomenon, a good many of its supposed unorthodoxies are readily accounted for when the poem is looked at in relation to a few works which contributed to its genesis. Some, like Goethe's *Faust*, provided obvious inspiration; others bear a less apparent resemblance, but were equally or perhaps even more consequential to its development. One such work was recognized even by Bailey's

3. "Barbaric Jewelry"

contemporaries as what might be called a negative example, serving as a model for Bailey to work against. In a chapter of *A New Spirit of the Age* (1844) entitled "Henry Taylor and the Author of *Festus*," Richard "Orion" Horne, sometimes referred to as a minor Spasmodic himself, celebrated Bailey's poetic bravado and originality in contrast to the emotionless boredom of *Philip van Artevelde*, Taylor's model poetic drama. Echoing Bailey's own beliefs, Horne stressed the need for imagistic, mystical poetry to provide a "fair entrance-porch for Heaven" and a point of contact with God via "the finite maker who devoutly conceives these things." The latter is, of course, the poet whom God has endowed with "genius" for precisely this purpose.[23] Horne described *Festus* as no less than "a call to arms" for a successful attack against extreme poetic rationalism, and was ecstatic to find that, at last, in its pages, "Sound sense's throne is sinking!"[24]

Indeed, *Festus*'s flagrant hyper-Romanticism primarily accounted for its popularity. Its puzzling structure, consisting of longwinded discourses between somewhat wooden characters, haphazard collections of scenes, and little or no coherent storyline or dramatic conflict, seem to have invigorated, rather than impeded, the poem's original readers, who found again in Bailey the large-scale passions of Byron and the languid mysticism of Shelley. The hymn-writer James Montgomery praised it for the disorientation, so close to emotional ecstasy, it produced: reading it, he claimed in terms that again recall "Kubla Khan," made a man feel that he "has eaten of the insane root that takes the reason prisoner" but it emulated the fruit of "the tree of knowledge of good and evil" in its beneficial spiritual effects.[25] Many other readers were equally eager to quaff Bailey's intoxicating elixir in large draughts.

Bailey was especially fortunate in publishing his poem, with its obvious parallel to *Faust* both in title and subject-matter, during a surge of interest in Goethe, who had died in 1832 and whose works were being energetically discussed and translated, not to mention promoted by Carlyle, an idol to all the Spasmodics, throughout the remainder of that decade.[26] For this reason alone it would have been natural for Bailey to have fastened upon Goethe's version rather than Marlowe's as his model, but it is significant that these two retellings were the products of nearly opposite intellectual climates. By softening the original Faustian themes and presenting a less theologically extreme interpretation of the original tale, Bailey was able to appeal to a Victorian middle class eager to move beyond dour Calvinism. In the poem, *Chambers'* notes, "deity is more humane and humanity more divine. It adumbrates a prophetic

The Spasmodic Poets

ideal of a divine humanity which will ultimately transmute all evil into all good." As a result, its "heroically youthful optimism ... falls like a snowflake on the feverish lips of the modern pessimist."[27] It is easy to see why this brand of what we would today call feel-good New Age philosophy would attract a newly literate, theologically curious, and perhaps existentially anxious public.

As Bailey's more literate readers might have known, Marlowe's version depicts a Renaissance scholar who attempts to transcend the superstition of the medieval world in favor of worldly experience and empirical investigation, while Goethe's Romantic perspective advocates mysticism over the empirical tenets of the waning Age of Reason. Bailey's Clara serves roughly the same purpose as Goethe's Gretchen, reminding the protagonist that his journey must lead him back to an indulgent God who forgives him and smiles on his audacity; significantly, there is no parallel female figure in Marlowe and a return to modest faith is never presented as an aesthetically compelling alternative for his doomed Faustus. The Romantic poet Goethe's version was also Miltonic in a sense that evidently appealed to Bailey. It can be no coincidence that Milton's Satan had fascinated the Romantics, and Goethe's Faust had himself assumed some of that character's dynamic qualities. The early Victorians apparently could still identify with Faust (more comfortably, perhaps, than with Satan) as a radical individualist with aspirations for not only understanding the principles of the cosmos, but for ordering them as well.

Festus is indebted to Goethe's poem for its theme and several specific features, such as the opening Prologue in Heaven, several scenes in which Festus and Lucifer fly through the night, and some lines which appear to be near-translations of the original German.[28] Another recognizable source is Byron's *Cain* (1821), also a product of the Romantic preoccupation with Satan. Bailey's love of Byron would have virtually compelled him to follow his idol's model, and it is certainly true that Festus more closely resembles Cain or Manfred than he does Goethe's middle-aged scholar. Bailey's depiction of various Angels and the courtly debates in Heaven perhaps inevitably suggest Milton and Goethe, but the language of these scenes was inspired by *Cain*. For example, Bailey's Prologue opens with an ecstatic chorus of Seraphim and Cherubim praising God in alternate choruses:

> SERAPHIM. God! God! God!
> As flames in skies
> We burn and rise

3. "Barbaric Jewelry"

> And lose ourselves in Thee!
> Years on years!
> And nought appears
> Save God to be.
> God! God! God!
> ....
> CHERUBIM. As sun and star,
> How high or far,
> Show but a boundless sky;
> So creature mind
> Is all confined
> To show Thee, God, most High.

Cain opens with the mortal characters of Adam and Eve in a slightly different setting, but the tone and content of their own song of praise is undeniably similar.

> ADAM. God, the Eternal! Infinite! All-wise!—
> Who out of darkness on the deep didst make
> Light on the waters without a word—All Hail!
> Jehovah! With returning light—All Hail!
>
> EVE. God! Who didst name the day, and separate
> Morning from night, till then divided never—
> Who didst divide the wave from wave, and call
> Part of thy work the firmament—All Hail![29]

Cain is also responsible for Bailey's choice of Lucifer, rather than Mephistopheles, as his hero's guide, and the journey for knowledge undertaken by Festus and his Lucifer literally covers much of the same territory as Cain and Byron's devil. Cain's progress through the "Abyss of Space" and "Hades" is clearly analogous to Festus's travels to "Anywhere," "Hell," and "[Earth's] Centre." Byron's Lucifer tempts Cain with a promise that he will show Cain "the history / Of past—and present and of future worlds," while Bailey's promises Festus that "All secrets thou shalt ken—all mysteries construe / At nothing marvel."[30] Both devils play upon the heroes' resentment at God's apparent neglect of their exceptional mental capacities, which has led Him to deny them the intellectual freedom and enlightenment they feel entitled to enjoy. Bailey's Lucifer offers Festus neither "lucre, lust, nor power," but merely "The freedom of thyself," while Byron's encourages Cain to resent his "tamed down" father Adam and to consider that "Nothing can / Quench the mind, if the mind will be itself / And centre of surrounding things."[31] Apparently, Bailey found Goethe's treatment of his protagonist too relaxed; *Festus* therefore reclaimed the Byronic view of the self, with all its attendant masochism and self-conscious profundity.

Bailey resurrected a Romantic theme and a Byronic approach, but not in an attempt to placate those suffering from poetic nostalgia. Rather, he deliberately infused *Festus* with the unmistakable flavor of his own era. The degree of his success is reflected in his contemporaries' belief that in Bailey they had found the fabled poet of the Age, as well as a guide to the particular concerns of the time. *Festus* was released at a time when its tone, more frankly pedantic than Goethe's and certainly more so than Byron's, was especially welcome. *Festus*'s brand of Romanticism proved both exciting and less threatening to early Victorian readers than Shelley's or Byron's, with their respective implications of social rebellion and aristocratic amorality. *Festus* was, in fact, explicitly dogmatic in a religious sense, introducing as it did a new theological twist in poetry, that of Universalism,[32] which provoked speculation pious enough in character to assuage the average Protestant. Readers were particularly susceptible to paternal voices like Gilfillan's, whose pandering Evangelism appealed to "thousands of readers" precisely because of its sermon-like, "wildly emotional ... strange billowing style." Gross goes so far as to attribute the success of "grandiose spiritual epics of the type best exemplified by P.J. Bailey's" directly to Gilfillan's influence.[33] Tellingly, Dobell was also an ardent admirer[34] of Bailey.

That *Festus* was particularly a product of its time is supported by two anecdotes. Gosse observed that many invalids kept *Festus* beside their sickbeds, along with the Bible; "it has helped and comforted me," he imagines a typical admirer asserting, "and it helps me still."[35] Weygandt, examining an 1889 edition of *Festus*, notes that the volume's previous owner seems to have read the poem by "skipping" through the various labyrinthine sections, marking with "X" those passages he apparently "wish[ed] to remember." Yet, after page 276, "the pages are cut but they bear no signs of being read or even of a rehandling."[36] Obviously, the 1889 reader had attempted to study *Festus* with the self-informing intentions of its original audience, but eventually found, just as Weygandt does forty years later, that he had overestimated its instructional potential and could not go on. By 1901, *Chambers'* could safely assert that "*Festus* joined the limbo of books that are revered unread"[37]; time, taste, and attitudes toward poetry and religion alike were on the march, leaving Bailey forlorn and forgotten.

Festus's supposed combination of instruction with liberating sentiment brings up another necessary contrast between *Festus* and a work

3. "Barbaric Jewelry"

which enjoyed simultaneous popularity. The moralizing volumes of Martin Farquhar Tupper, as we have seen, were often deemed insipid and unworthy of close critical attention. Still, in light of Bailey's supposed spiritual dimension, of which so much was made at the time, a further comparison between his poem and the productions of Tupper seems warranted. Significantly, in retrospective essays and in historical surveys Bailey and Tupper are often discussed together, usually in terms of their perplexing success. For example, Walker expresses his distaste for some of Bailey's more fanciful images like the paradoxical "soul-bones" and "marmoreal floods" of snow (which is difficult to reconcile with marble) with amazement that "this passes for poetry.... The aberration of taste is not quite as great as that which raised Martin Farquhar Tupper and his *Proverbial Philosophy* to the highest popularity, but it is similar in kind."[38]

Some literary histories, such as the *Cambridge History*, have lumped Tupper in with the Spasmodics because of *Proverbial Philosophy*'s popularity with undiscerning readers as well as its legendary purple patches and grating banalities. It is true that Tupper's method of composition recalls Smith's layering of disconnected and perhaps tasteless images (as well as *Balder*'s apparent infanticide) in passages like

> MEMORY is not wisdom; idiots can rote volumes:
> Yet, what is wisdom without memory? a babe that is strangled in its birth,
> The path of the swallow in the air, the path of the dolphin in the waters,
> A cask running out, a bottomless chasm: such is wisdom without memory.[39]

Yet Tupper's near-doggerel verse is arid and sentimental rather than imagistic and expansive, and as such cannot be considered truly Spasmodic. His book did, however, help generate the early Victorian public's receptiveness to *Festus* and the other Spasmodic works, and was probably partially responsible for the eventual critical disdain accorded these later works.

As might be expected, many of the topical headings in Tupper suggest subjects which *Festus*, and later *A Life-Drama* and *Gerald*, would tackle in ostensibly philosophical passages: Love, Reading and Writing, Ambition, Fame, and Self-Acquaintance. Like Bailey, Tupper attempted to explain, albeit in a less fanciful manner, the relationship of God's heavenly kingdom to the mundane Victorian sphere. A passage from "Of Subjection" strongly resembles many of the speeches exchanged between various characters during *Festus*'s frequent theological debates:

The Spasmodic Poets

> So then, start ye from the fountain, and follow the river of existence,
> For its current is bounded throughout by the banks of just subordination:
> Thrones, and dominions, and powers, Archangels, Cherubim, and Seraphim,
> Angels, and flaming ministers, and breathing chariots and harps.
> For there are degrees in heaven, and varied capabilities of bliss,
> And steps in the ladder of Intelligence, and ranks in approaches to Perfection:
> ....
> Where is there an atom out of place? Or a particle that yieldeth not obedience?[40]

Here, Tupper provides a comfortable variation on the concept of a Great Chain of Being in a tone meant to convey mature, benevolent (and patriarchal) authority. This particular explanation appealed to his trusting middle-class audience (a vast readership he shared with Bailey) for two reasons. First, it rendered the spiritual kingdom concrete and easily visualized by borrowing vivid Miltonic imagery but removing the difficult intellectual content; and second, it reaffirmed the complacent political vision which had long contrived theological excuses for the persistence of poverty in a prosperous industrialized world and had proven effective in keeping the poor from revolting. Tupper's instructional message, therefore, was calculated not exactly to forestall progress, but to limit its fearsome transfiguring effects.

Despite his ostensibly Romantic agenda, Bailey included the voice of religious conservativism in his epic. Clara, whom Festus eventually chooses over his many other loves, represents exactly the sort of reader who might have memorized Tupper. As Festus begins his investigation into personal sin, Clara encourages him to practice an obeisant worship closer to her own. "For spiritual life is great and clear," she informs him, "And self-continuous as the changeless sea." She then suggests that, contrary to his defiant, flamboyant approach to God, "The bended knee, the eye uplift is all / Which man need render; all which God can bear."[41] Tupper and Bailey share a uniquely Victorian approach to modern problems, involving the promotion of Colonialism, self-discipline for the poor, limited extension of democratic processes, and pious cultivation of industrial boons.[42] The view of a beneficent God who loves Englishmen and English politics unequivocally informs both texts.

Bailey does differ from Tupper in one important respect. Tupper's "Of Experience" admitted that periods of youthful excess and even agnosticism were to some degree inevitable for men of Festus's exuberant temperament, but were fortunately only temporary. In Bailey's neo–Romantic theology, such phases are not to be regretted. The humble and complaisant faith advocated by *Proverbial Philosophy* mollifies the hero

3. "Barbaric Jewelry"

only after the opposite extreme has been tested and found less satisfying. Festus, in some ways the early Victorian Everyman, undertakes precisely this investigation into the limits of personal faith, with far more edifying results, and it is not difficult to see why *Festus*, appearing one year after *Proverbial Philosophy*, was considered an equally useful, and perhaps even more congenial, tool for spiritual enlightenment in an age of declining faith.

As the Proem of *Festus* demonstrates, P.J. Bailey saw himself as a second Milton, setting to work on an epic poem that would explain God's plan to humankind (*Festus* was, in fact, to become more and more Miltonic as it went through its successive editions[43]). Bailey also imitated Milton in withdrawing to his father's care at twenty so that he could set to work with complete concentration. This youthful zeal and narcissism, common to both the Spasmodic poet and his protagonist, would eventually cause Hugh Walker to observe with amusement that "At thirty-four ... Milton was still meditating his great work; while at twenty-three Bailey was confident that he had adequately executed one of the most ambitious poetical schemes ever conceived."[44] Bailey's ability to work at his desk undisturbed by economic concerns does bring to mind another major difference between him and the later Spasmodics, who were also young and idealistic but barred by their social class from formal education and always on the brink of poverty.

Bailey's monastic seclusion (similar to what Dobell would experience in his grandfather's isolationist sect), McKillop believes, may account for *Festus*'s curious estrangement from the mundane world and the attention spans of its readers.[45] "How I wish I could love men!" Festus cried in a moment of alienation; in a letter of 1834, his creator expressed a misanthropist sentiment worthy of Balder himself: "To labour apart from others is in my opinion the way to get on."[46] By "others," Bailey also meant other poets, for like Gilfillan he believed that God had "made His prophets poets," and that he, as one such prophet, should be entitled to create spontaneously, without regard to established form or convention. His poetic utterances were nothing less than revelatory:

> He spake inspired
> Night and day, thought came unhelped, undesired,
> Like blood to his heart.[47]

Revision was unnecessary and perhaps even heretical; predictably, Bailey viewed adverse criticism of his poem as theological, rather than aesthetic, in intent. "If the Metaphysics of the Poem be just and in accordance with scripture and reason," he insisted, "I will not for the sake of any, consent to qualify a single syllable or soften a single breathing." The fact that his poem had no need of conventional attributes like plot and action remained a source of pride to him, and in fact Bailey's most original touch is his complete renunciation of the demands of form and dramatic unity.

Festus is not exactly a patchwork of ideas from other sources, since it does reflect its author's idiosyncratic religious doctrine throughout, but its form is unarguably jerky, confused, and often anticlimactic. Walker recounts the experience of one reader who actually hurled his copy of *Festus* across a room in frustration with its tedious bombast, and concurs that "Perhaps about a tenth part of *Festus* is good, and a tenth of that tenth is really admirable; but what is good is so lost and buried [in] the mediocre and worthless" that such a disgruntled reaction is more than understandable.[48] A good deal of the excess found in *Festus* is the direct result of Bailey's incorporating his later unsuccessful poems into the original text, but much of it is also owing to his didactic and declamatory intention. Often, Festus becomes an orator, declaring his own spiritual tenets. With a nod to Shelley's "Ozymandias," Bailey also manages to explain the place of pagan gods from several mythological systems in his Universalist scheme:

> I am an omnist, and believe in all
> Religions,—fragments of one golden world
> Yet to be relit in its place in Heaven—
> For all are relatively true and false,
> As evidence and earnest of the heart
> To those who practice, or have faith in them.
> The absolutely true religion is
> In Heaven only, yea in Deity.[49]

In addition, no doubt to ensure that his audience would understand every detail of his Universalist vision of the Apocalypse, Bailey composed nearly interminable sections in which Festus and Lucifer discuss a variety of topics in Tupperesque succession. These topics include the existence of evil, salvation, and even romantic courtship and foreign politics. In one scene, Lucifer and Festus fly over Earth and comment on different countries, in particular "America! half-brother of the world!" with its "dark cloud of slaves / Which yet may rise" in domestic rebellion[50]; in another instructional dialogue, Lucifer actually defends God's rationale in creating the imperfect human race and in permitting

3. "Barbaric Jewelry"

the existence of evil. Byron's Cain had asked his Lucifer this same question, having received an unsatisfactory answer from Adam: "why is Evil—[God] being Good?"[51] But whereas Byron's Lucifer remains merely Socratic in his responses, countering question with leading question, Bailey's devil happily provides a detailed explanation.

> LUCIFER. The idea of good
> Is owned in imperfection's lowest form.
> God would not, could not, make aught wholly ill,
> Nor aught not like to err. Man never was
> Perfect nor pure, or he would be so now.
> Thy nature hath some excellences,—these
> Oft thwarted by low lusts and wicked wills.
> What then? They are necessitate in kind,
> As change in nature, or as shade to light.
> No darkness hath the sun—no weakness God:
> These be only the faulty qualities
> Of secondary natures—planets, men.
> ....
> FESTUS. Is God the cause of evil?
> LUCIFER. So far as evil comes from imperfection,
> And imperfection from the things He hath made,
> And what He hath made from His will to make.[52]

This excerpt, even in abbreviated form, affords a taste of *Festus'* overall tone, and helps explain both the violent reaction described by Walker and the adulation of readers with a taste for the pedantic. Were Lucifer's pronouncements extracted from their context, they might easily be passed off as selections from Tupper's book. In fact, Tupper does include a section entitled "Of Good in Things Evil," which expresses his belief that

> The characters of God were idle, if all things around him were perfection,
> And virtues might slumber on like death, if they lacked the opportunities of evil.
> There is one all-perfect, and but one; man dare not reason of His Essence.
> But there must be deficiencies in heaven, to leave room for progression in bliss:
> A realm of unqualified BEST were a stagnant pool of being.[53]

Though the particulars of the two men's theologies differed, both attempt to answer standard Victorian questions regarding the individual's place in a heavenly scheme whose existence had to be taken for granted lest an even greater despair prevail. Festus takes advantage of Lucifer's presence to inquire about several Victorian theological topics like redemption, just punishment for sins, and even whether it is true that "God hates man's nature."[54] It is not fair to say that Bailey abjured

The Spasmodic Poets

plot in favor of discourse; the rhetorical content of *Festus* is, in fact, its plot.

Given these aims, Bailey's dismissal of critical charges of diffuseness and lack of real conflict in the drama seems easier to understand, if only slightly less wearisome. Long after the publication of *Festus*, Bailey claimed that not only had he been captivated by Goethe's *Faust* in his youth, but he had been determined to improve on it from the first.[55] One aspect of his "improvement," of course, was intensifying the hero's Byronic attributes, but another involved deflecting the poem's emphasis from the question of individual salvation.

Bailey's God is a Universalist conception of the beneficent creator promised to Festus earlier on his journey; with the Apocalypse, evil itself is obliterated and, from the second edition of the poem on, even Lucifer, who has found love with a mortal and moral woman, is saved during God's Final Judgment. Sin in Bailey's epic represents the path to understanding rather than ruin, for once Festus realizes that earthly pleasures cannot satisfy his lust for beauty he returns to God almost effortlessly, and is in fact rewarded by being reunited with the spirits of his former lovers. Bailey has often been accused of failing to develop the main source of conflict in *Festus*, for in his Faustian legend, the hero's soul is never really in peril. Unlike the protagonist of Marlowe's or Goethe's dramas, Festus needs never realize that by renouncing God he has also renounced the true source of knowledge, for aside from the fact that Lucifer patiently responds to his every inquiry, Festus never rejects God completely. The pact between the hero and Lucifer is closer to that in *Cain* than in Goethe or Marlowe: "If thou dost long for knowledge," Byron's Lucifer tells Cain, "I can satiate / That thirst; nor ask thee to partake of fruits / Which shall deprive thee of a single good / The Conqueror has left thee."[56] Though Bailey's God grants his Lucifer the "youth" to "tempt," it is with the condition that "Upon his soul / Thou hast no power" and asserts that "though he plunge his soul in sin like a sword / In water, it shall nowise cling to him. / He is of Heaven." Festus' personal Guardian Angel is even on hand to affirm his own devotion to this "soul elect" even though Festus occasionally demonstrates understandable human doubts and failings.[57]

Festus is also unique, and undoubtedly aesthetically unsatisfying, in that Lucifer's character seems neither particularly demonic nor creative in the temptations he offers his pupil. Besides engaging in long-winded discourses on theological problems and flights through the atmosphere, Festus and Lucifer do nothing more dangerous than visit

3. "Barbaric Jewelry"

country gatherings and literary parties (one of which would become the model for a similar scene in *A Life-Drama* and even includes an attendee named Walter), and flirt with a variety of attractive young women. While all of these women eventually become Festus' mistresses, one of them also falls in love with Lucifer. In this section, perhaps the most potentially dramatic in the poem, Bailey's poetic limitations become clear. His characters seem to communicate via lofty oration that precludes the illusion of intimacy, and Lucifer's speech to Elissa might be any human lover's to any of the cipher-like women in the poem.

> I love thee, and am full of happiness.
> My bosom bounds beneath thy smile as doth
> The sea's unto the moon, his mighty mistress;
> Lying and looking up to her, and saying—
> Lovely! lovely! lovely! lady of the heavens!
> Oh! when the thoughts of other joyous days—
> Perchance, if such may be, of happier times—
> Are falling gently on the memory
> Like autumn leaves distained with dusky gold,
> Yet softly as a snowflake; and the smile
> Of kindliness, like thine, is beaming on me—
> Oh! pardon, if I lose myself, nor know
> Whether I be with Heaven or thee.[58]

The last line is particularly curious, spoken as it is by a devil, and the whole passage is not strikingly different from Festus' own speech to Elissa once he has all too easily won her for himself.[59] The surplus of disconnected images, such as moons, leaves, and snowflakes, is substituted for real analysis by both speaker and poet and thus rob the situation of irony or genuine emotion.

These simplistic lyrical passages, however, captivated Bailey's Spasmodic imitators. All the later Spasmodic heroes were ardent lovers, and Alexander Smith wrote similar love-scenes for his own hero, Walter. Walter and Festus would share more than diction with regard to love-making in both its Victorian and modern sense: since both protagonists spring from a common Byronic source, they are equally concerned with self-gratification and the pre-eminence of sexual love. Festus and Walter share with Cain and Manfred an extroverted virility which Aytoun, the Spasmodic parodist, came to regard as nothing more than offensive prurience; his Firmilian's plan of research for his epic on sexual passion, which requires his participation in an orgy with his three mistresses, was clearly modeled on Festus' exploits.

Festus' insistence that physical love is of at least as much value as

The Spasmodic Poets

Christian *agape* is central to his spiritual quest, since he is both possessed and defined by an overpowering Romantic sensuality. When Lucifer tries to win his trust by promising him "worldly things," Festus demands to know "What can be counted pleasure after love?" and is finally won over when Lucifer suggests that "Hell become[s] a tolerable torment" when lovers see each other there.[60] In fact, Festus reaches his emotional nadir when he suddenly finds that the stress of his adventures has robbed him of the ability to "love as I have loved" and declares that "It is the one great woe of life / To feel all feeling die." On the other hand, his happiest moment during the Apocalypse occurs when he realizes that his harem awaits him in Heaven.[61]

Curiously, Smith would suffer more public disapproval in this respect than Bailey, even though Festus takes twice as many mistresses as Walter, and even declares at one point, "Oh! why was woman made so fair? ... It is impossible to love but one."[62] Perhaps readers were inclined to look the other way in Festus' case because of the story's obvious moral intent. After all, Lucifer was expected to make a show of tempting Festus, and Bailey's portrayal of such love affairs never exceeds lengthy sentimental professions and courtly kisses. Readers may also have expected parallels with *Faust*'s Gretchen and Helen seduction plotlines, though Elissa, Clara, Angela, Marian, and Bailey's English Helen are far less developed and instead become prototypes of the typical Spasmodic heroine, "singing" to the hero when he becomes weary and praising his intellectual prowess.[63] Perhaps the most obvious reason that Festus' promiscuity was excused, however, is that it is justified in its context as an expected and even commendable byproduct of the poet's dedication to the worship of beauty in all its natural forms. As in Shelley's "Hymn to Intellectual Beauty," Festus has a moment of revelation which singles him out as a kind of emissary to the world of the sublime.

> Oh! I was glad when something in me said
> Come, let us worship beauty! and I bowed;
> And went about to find a shrine; but found
> None that my soul, when seeing, said enough, to.[64]

The importance ascribed to the Spasmodic hero's status as a poet would, needless to say, become the School's predominant characteristic, and in this respect *Festus* was, despite Bailey's later claims, especially seminal. Festus had no time for subtlety when he declared his frustration as a poetic soul trapped in an essentially powerless mortal husk; his lament must have expressed, in raw form, what many accepted as

3. "Barbaric Jewelry"

an appropriate concern for the would-be seer. Bailey can have Festus declare, apparently without any sense of his pompous absurdity, that

> I am an universall [sic] favorite.
> Old men admire me deeply for my beauty,
> Young women for my genius and strict virtue,
> And young men for my modesty and wisdom.
> All turn to me, whenever I speak, full-faced,
> As planets to the sun, or owls to a rushlight.[65]

Nor was Festus afraid to challenge even God's wisdom in assigning him a subordinate role in the Universe:

> Why mad'st thou not one spirit, like the sun,
> To king the world? And oh! might I have been
> That sun-mind, how I would have warmed the world
> To love and worship bright life!

since he accepts, as Dobell's critical theory would later reaffirm, the necessity for poet-kings:

> The world must have great minds, even as great spheres
> Or suns, to govern lesser restless minds,
> While they stand still and burn with life; to keep
> Them in their places, and to light and heat them.[66]

Festus also believes, as will Balder, that he is deserving of divinity. As he declares to Clara,

> I but feel,
> That were I—as I ought to be—a god,
> I would just sacrifice the sun to thee,
> In bright and burning honour of thy love.[67]

All the major Spasmodic poems would assume that the artist occupies a special place in a theological hierarchy; for example, Dobell's famous article on "Currer Bell [Charlotte Brontë]" explains how, since the artist exists "a little lower than the angels, and a little higher than men, the hand of the one [the poet] links his glorious group to the superior, that of the other [the novelist] to the subordinate intelligence."[68] Festus, though, is given an opportunity that no other Spasmodic poet dared bestow on his hero: literal monarchy of the entire world for the last day before the Apocalypse. Festus presides over a coronation scene arranged by heavenly agents and attended by both kings and laymen. Such a show of power would have been welcome to either Marlowe's or Goethe's Faust, since the desire for sovereignty was the basis for their Satanic pacts, but Festus' case is different. As in *Cain*, his is less a pact

The Spasmodic Poets

with Lucifer than a loose arrangement for a series of gratuitous tutorials, and, more importantly, his desire for omnipotence is not a tragic flaw but a forgivable byproduct of the divinely-sanctioned poetic imagination. Despite his attempt to immerse himself in the forbidden, he has ultimately "sinned sublimely"[69] in a valiant effort to unravel the mysteries of the Universe and the nature of fleshly temptation. This high-spirited excess surely must account for the fact that Bailey's poem became a rallying-point for those who shared his desire for passion and metaphysics in literature and this attitude became not only a staple of subsequent Spasmodic poetry, but of Gilfillan's criticism as well.

Festus's identity as the philosophical parent of the later Spasmodic productions, therefore, is not particularly difficult to establish. All that remains is to explicate its stylistic similarities, and this is not a particularly challenging task. As would be the case with subsequent Spasmodic poems, *Festus* is long and thematically diffuse to the point of rambling, and its tone is irregular. The bulk of the poem consists, as do the other Spasmodic works, of the stockpiling of periphrasis both appropriate and convoluted. In *Festus*, the idea is to explain the metaphysics of Creation by translating every sensation into metaphor and then attempting to fit these metaphors into a universal system. Most have an epistemological dimension and strive to reconcile the concrete and spiritual, as when Lucifer declares that

> Souls see each other clear
> At one glance, as two drops of rain in air
> Might look into each other, had they life.[70]

For Bailey, the successful fitting of metaphor to the object or situation described depended upon chance rather than sustained vision, since such excess might be expected to yield an interesting image periodically. Bailey also alternates high and low styles even more frequently than did Goethe in *Faust*. Sometimes, these attempts at humor are meant to brighten single scenes, as when a villager responds to Lucifer's pronouncement of his Satanic identity, "I am the Devil," with "I think you are. / You look as if you lived on buttered thunder," and again when Lucifer declares that "I should like to macadamize the world; / The road to Hell wants mending."[71] At other times the interruption is distracting and prevents one from taking the sentiments expressed with the seriousness Bailey obviously intended. One such passage probably provided the inspiration for the scene in *Firmilian* in which the Spasmodic hero causes a church to explode: after a pseudo-philosophical

3. "Barbaric Jewelry"

discussion with Lucifer and an alchemist on the larger scheme of the elements, Festus wonders whether the alchemist will perform an experiment mischievously suggested by Lucifer and find that

> Perhaps the nostrum will explode and blow him
> Body and soul to atoms and to—
> LUCIFER. Nonsense![72]

After this moment of low comedy, the two move on to a somber discussion of martyrdom, war, and politics.

Another form of digression in *Festus* involves the insertion of shorter poems spoken by one of a given dialogue's interlocutors. This was to become common practice in *Balder* and *A Life-Drama*, in many cases giving the impression that extending the poem's length was the sole justification for the digressive inclusion. Although *Festus* seems never to have suffered from brevity, even in its earliest editions, these shorter poems are to some extent suited to their context and are less distracting than merely unimpressive. One such inserted "song," performed for Festus and Lucifer by a travelling bard, seems irrelevant in terms of its specific content, which describes a doomed affair between the bard and a Gypsy Maid, but actually does reflect themes in the larger poem. While the lover in the ballad is a Christian, the Gypsy maid is not, and eventually she convinces him to choose her over his faith. This recalls Festus's spiritual struggle to choose between lust and submission, and provides a point of contrast in that his own lovers are invariably more obediently Christian than he. Though Bailey is unable to exploit this device as a more skillful poet might have, he is at least justified in making the attempt to enlarge on the sphere of the action.

Other insertions are more difficult to explain, such as the curious and nearly incomprehensible Burnsian dialect poem which directly follows the Gypsy ballad ("Oh! the wee green neuk, the sly green neuk, / The wee sly neuk for me!"), a rather hollow Blakean lyric recited by Lucifer, and an unmistakably Spasmodic tribute to a tree which arouses fervid emotion in Festus.[73] Bailey also apparently developed an additional technique which would become commonplace in Spasmodic poems, particularly *A Life-Drama*, as the hero sketches the biographical portrait of a poet friend, usually deceased, who either inspired the hero or struggled with the same emotional burdens currently besetting him. In Smith's poem, as will be shown, the poet described resembles Keats; in Bailey's, the model is obviously Byron.[74] In both cases, however, the "friend" is eventually revealed to be the poet-hero himself, and the

The Spasmodic Poets

anecdotal form of the story intended as an expression of modesty which in most cases impresses the reader as exactly the opposite.

The *Cambridge History* referred to Bailey's poetic style as his "barbaric jewelry,"[75] which alternately attracted and repelled readers. In a sense, the strained voice one often encounters in *Festus* is appropriate to its hero's lofty mission and ambition. Though Bailey was in part inspired by a minor craze for Apocalyptic and openly metaphysical novels which attained some popularity between the years 1819 and 1828,[76] his was a poetic forage into the same fantastic territory, and his argument for the superiority of the poet as a leader of men therefore received more serious critical attention than any work of prose fiction.

It might be said that Festus is not quite as obsessed with his poetic calling as Balder or Walter, and never regards it as his actual profession. Still, he does expound freely upon the necessary seriousness with which one should regard it, telling his lover of the moment, Helen, that "poesy" is what he loves most next to her, and that a poet should always "Burn to be great. / ... The bard cannot have two pursuits." Festus here obviously speaks for his creator, for even though Bailey introduced a variety of supernatural beings and situations into his poem, his attention remained focused on Festus's private intellectual development. Subsequent Spasmodic dramas go even further and eliminate the separate character of the poet's tempter. Balder and Walter require no Lucifer to coax them into indulging the lower aspects of their natures; it is enough that the possibility of sin exists in their own minds, and their own determination to test moral boundaries leads them to murder and sexual transgression. In championing his hyper-Romantic poet's right to subjective ideals, Bailey licensed other poetic heroes to do the same.

One ambitious poet who took inspiration from *Festus* was Richard Henry (later Hengist) Horne; like Bailey, the eccentric Horne would be retroactively styled a Spasmodic on the basis of his 1843 epic poem, *Orion*. As Edmund Gosse put it in 1912, both *Festus* and *Orion* were "typical products of the transitional period between Shelley and Keats on the one hand and Tennyson and Browning on the other."[77] Though his subject was the giant mythological huntsman who eventually took his place in the cosmos, Horne's real goal was "to illustrate the growth of a poet's mind by means of abstract ideas" using mythological figures as allegories.[78] Thanks to a brief fad for philosophical poetry, *Orion* proved a great commercial success and numbered among its admirers Robert and Elizabeth Barrett Browning, who became Horne's lifelong friends and thereby cemented their Spasmodic connection. Like the

3. "Barbaric Jewelry"

later Spasmodics, Horne's commercial success (as well as his decline) owed much to a gimmick that took full advantage of the burgeoning early Victorian market for books. The 1843 edition of *Orion*

> was brought out at the price of one farthing. Elizabeth Barrett sent out to the nearest bookshop for a shilling's worth, but was refused her four dozen copies. Purchasers had to produce their brass farthing for each *Orion*, and no change was given. This was done "to mark the public contempt into which epic poetry has fallen," but it was also a very good advertisement. Everybody talked about Mr. Horne's "farthing" poem, and after some editions had run out the price was cautiously raised. But when the tenth edition appeared, at a cost of seven shillings, the public perceived that its leg was being pulled, and it purchased *Orion* no more.[79]

Despite their great popularity with the public (*Orion* exhausted six editions and prompted its author to take "Orion" as his middle name), neither Bailey nor Horne inspired much critical acclaim. The reviews anticipate the accusations of formlessness and incoherence that would become a staple feature of all the later Spasmodic productions. Many of these points would be repeated again and again, in only slightly altered form, in the later reactionary reviews of *A Life-Drama*, *Balder*, and Dobell and Smith's two books of sonnets.

In April 1850, *Blackwood's Edinburgh Magazine*, which would eventually lead the anti–Spasmodic campaign, published William Henry Smith's review of *Festus*. Since the poem had appeared no less than eleven years earlier, the magazine's sudden interest in it suggests that its contributors were aware that they were witnessing the evolution of a trend. The flaws singled out for ridicule in *Festus* are now considered to define Spasmodic poetry: formlessness, unevenness in tone, deliberate obscurity of language masquerading as philosophy (often leading to the coinage of absurd words and the employment of twisted diction), lack of dramatic conflict, and the distasteful morality of the protagonist. Followers of Bailey should remember, the review cautions, that despite their poet's genuine artistic fervor, "in none of the arts is it necessary to alarm the whole country by a conflagration, in order that some dainty morsels may be gathered out of the ruins."[80] While originality is commendable, torturing the English language and the ear of the reader should not be accepted as an adequate substitute. Inappropriate metaphors (presumably like a flood of marble snow) pepper *Festus*, Smith declares: "We are told that one thing is like another, and have to puzzle ourselves, as in a riddle, *why* is it like … ?"[81] The essay concludes with a critical sigh which wishes both that Bailey had postponed completion of his epic until his admittedly admirable intellect and poetic powers had matured, and that critics of English poetry would apply more rigorous standards to future productions. As it happened, Smith and his colleagues at *Blackwood's* would be forced to endure four more years, and three more Spasmodic epics, before this advice would be heeded.

4

"With a Halo Crowned"

Gerald, A Life-Drama,
and the Coming of the Vates

Festus was not the only seminal Spasmodic work to gain currency in the 1840s. Even though it never achieved the popularity of Bailey's work, John Westland Marston's *Gerald: A Dramatic Poem* certainly exerted a conspicuous influence over the later Spasmodic poetic dramas and Smith's *A Life-Drama* in particular. Marston was born in 1819, three years after Bailey and ten years before Alexander Smith. Like Bailey, he had planned for a career in the law, but turned to literature after completing his education. After his death in 1890, he was remembered not as a poet, but as a dramatist as well as the father of another minor Victorian poet.

The elder Marston's *Gerald*, like so many other Spasmodic poems, is the product of youth and naïve poetic exuberance. This "poetic drama" was part of a longer volume of poems Marston wrote in his early twenties, around the same time that Thomas Carlyle, the great Sage of Chelsea, published his lectures on "Heroes and Hero Worship." Carlyle had famously expounded on the need for a great man in the tradition of Dante or Shakespeare to lead the new Victorian age, a person who would be known as both "Poet and Prophet"—or, more simply, *vates*. "Fundamentally indeed they are still the same," Carlyle assured his audience, "in this most important respect especially, [t]hat they have penetrated both of them into the sacred mystery of the Universe ... is a man sent hither to make it more impressively known to us. That always is his message; he is to reveal that to us,—that sacred mystery which he more than others lives ever present with."[1] Marston, like so many other Spasmodic poets, and certainly like Gilfillan himself, seemed to have Carlyle's booming edicts ringing in his ears when he sat down to write.

Gerald follows what would eventually become a recognizable pattern. The hero, Gerald, is a tormented country poet who moves to London to seek success and convey his urgent message to the world. Instead, he is brought to the brink of suicide by the Philistinism and corruption he finds there. Gerald remains a tormented soul until he realizes that his happiness depends not upon fame or material prosperity, but upon spiritual surrender to the Christian principles of humility and love. Unlike Festus, who remains magnificently self-centered even in his afterlife, Gerald relinquishes his own egotism on his deathbed and embraces instead the humanitarian ideals of the fiancée he had earlier abandoned. In this respect, *Gerald* clearly prefigures *A Life-Drama* and the thwarted quest of Smith's fame-seeking hero, Walter, who fortunately finds a happier end.

Gerald was written in 1841 and appeared in print in 1842, making it nearly contemporary with the first edition of *Festus*. Although the degree of Marston's familiarity with *Festus* is unclear, there are good reasons for accepting Buckley's classification of *Gerald* in *The Victorian Temper* as a full-blown Spasmodic drama. Buckley sees *Gerald* as an example of tragic Romanticism which has been afforded the full Spasmodic treatment. He finds in *Gerald* all the familiar characteristics: the diffuse and jerky form, the contemporary setting with its pseudo-political message, and the personality of the poet-hero who attempts to find inspiration in a hostile world.[2] However, since *Gerald* predates by more than ten years the works that established these characteristics as "Spasmodic," it would be less than accurate to suggest that Marston adopted them. *Gerald* was, in fact, crucial to their development, and was in some ways more directly responsible for the form they would take in Smith's and Dobell's works than was *Festus*.

There can be little question that J.W. Marston identified with the somewhat anachronistic Romanticism of Bailey and the later Spasmodics. A strain of nostalgic Romanticism apparently ran through his family, for his son, Philip Bourke Marston, is remembered as the blind poet who was for a time associated with a young group of Pre-Raphaelites.[3] The elder Marston may also be responsible for the similarity of the Spasmodic dramas to contemporary melodramatic plays. Around the time that *Festus* was originally released, J.W. Marston was busy composing sentimental dramas with a derivative Romantic flavor. These plays would, he hoped, demonstrate that the events of ordinary life could be raised to the level of the sublime and thus become appropriate subjects for poetry.[4] This aim was quite different from that of *Festus*, which featured cosmic and otherworldly atmospheres, but it

4. "With a Halo Crowned"

undeniably engendered the contemporary and even mundane settings of *A Life-Drama* and *Balder*. The plays were popular enough in Marston's own time and counted among their admirers Dickens, who wrote a prologue for his biggest success, *The Patrician's Daughter*. Unfortunately, they were eventually forgotten, consigned to the voluminous dust heap of Victorian ephemera.

R.H. Horne's *A New Spirit of the Age* (1844), which embraced *Festus* as the harbinger of a more vital poetry for the age, included a discussion of J.W. Marston's work and compared his efforts to the early poetic dramas of Robert Browning. Interestingly, it was a misreading of one section of this chapter which led to Robert Browning's subsequently being labeled a Spasmodic. While discussing Browning's *Strafford* and Marston's *The Patrician's Daughter*, Horne remarked that both were "examples of men of genius going astray, the one turning tragedy into a spasmodic skeleton, the other carrying the appointments of what is technically and degradingly termed a 'coat-and-breeches comedy' into the tragic arena."[5] Horne's syntax is convoluted, but the context of this passage suggests that the "coat-and-breeches comedy" is the historical *Strafford*, and therefore the term "spasmodic skeleton" must refer to Marston's play, not Browning's.[6] Nonetheless, the label stuck to both poets for decades.

Although Horne was an enthusiastic "Festonian," and admired Browning's artistic eccentricities, he had more serious misgivings about Marston's dramatic practices. Marston, according to Horne, favored a "realistic" style, which in his opinion should not replace the "ideal and imaginative" qualities innate to the "spirit of Fine Arts."[7] Since Marston's sentimental melodrama is hardly "realistic" in the common sense of the term, Horne was obviously taking issue with Marston's decision to make his plays contemporary (another common practice of all the Spasmodics, arguably to their eventual detriment). Horne did, however, recognize that Marston's "language ha[s] a strong smack of the olden time," namely an "Elizabethan" quality.[8] This remark is significant, for Horne was the first of many critics to note the Spasmodic tendency to imitate the Elizabethan drama; in 1959 William Wimsatt was still identifying the Spasmodic School by its characteristic "pseudo-Elizabethan dramatizing."[9] Horne also criticized a few more of Marston's devices which would become Spasmodic staples, such as spontaneous bombast, excessive morbidity, and religious dogmatism.[10] One can only suppose that he excused these same shortcomings in *Festus* because Bailey had not attempted to circumscribe his protagonist's sphere as did Marston;

the Miltonic (or even fantastical) interdimensional setting made its extravagance more palatable, or at least allowed a greater suspension of disbelief.

Horne found one aspect of *Gerald* worthy of particular attention. This was Marston's insistence on portraying a hero who was not merely idiosyncratic and sensitive, as Festus might be said to have been, but who could be singled out from other men by virtue of the "genius" (specifically of a literary nature) he possessed. Interestingly, Horne considers that Marston failed in this respect not because the idea of such a protagonist is in itself flawed, but simply because, in his opinion, Marston had not sufficiently proved that either Gerald or the hero of *The Patrician's Daughter* "*is* a man of genius."[11] In other words, had Marston been more successful in convincing his audience that Gerald was actually endowed with superior intellectual prowess, both the author's and the character's actions would be commendable rather than perplexing and mildly exasperating. It is hardly worth noting that *Balder* and *A Life-Drama* would go to even more extreme lengths to prove their own protagonists' genius; perhaps Dobell and Smith kept Horne's complaint in mind when composing their heroes' elaborate self-promotions and the supporting characters' often-bizarre tributes.

That Horne felt Marston had failed in this respect probably proved especially galling to the aspiring dramatist, for Marston's conscious manipulation of form and technique is apparent throughout the text of *Gerald*. He even explicitly stated his design for Gerald's character in an elaborate Preface which undoubtedly helped inspire that presented by "T. Percy Jones" in *Firmilian*. Here, Marston declares that his "intention" was "to choose the struggles and experiences of *Genius* as a subject."[12] After all, he asks, "what is the heroic in Man, but *his Genius*?" The scope of his drama, which he hopes might even have "Tragic" interest, will indeed be strictly subjective and clearly defined: "The Reader will bear in mind that all I have contemplated is the illumination of *certain points* in Gerald's mental history," namely "the delineation of a great mind, subject to infirmities and swayed by passions."

Since *Gerald* would be so unique in intent, it would also of necessity remain a closet-drama, as was *Festus* and all subsequent Spasmodic creations. "I have not thought it necessary," Marston noted, "to adhere to the canons of the Drama, so strictly, as if the Poem had been intended for Theatrical representation." Likewise, in a note appended to the very first scene, he emphasized the difference between

4. "With a Halo Crowned"

"soliloquy and reverie" as indulged in by his hero; "reverie" represented the spontaneous and therefore true reflections of his protagonist, especially "thoughts by which the mind is borne along without any conscious effort of its own."[13] This cannot help but recall Bailey's reliance on unedited effusions born of inspiration alone, and prefigures Smith's and Dobell's distrust of rewriting and structural editing.

Many of the themes in *Gerald*, and the particular obstacles faced by the downtrodden poet-hero, elaborate on those touched upon, but not fully exploited, in *Festus* and prefigure many of those found in *A Life-Drama*. As would be the case with Walter, Smith's protagonist, Gerald repeatedly argues with ignorant and even villainous characters who promote empiricism and Mammonism over the subjective ideals the poet must obviously cherish. A captain of Industry, for example, retorts, "Think you 'twas the Ideal lined my floor / With this soft carpet?" and antagonists named Clayton and Ashton bait Gerald with observations like "The world has outgrown Poetry" and

> You Phantom-chasers ever thus contemn
> The real and useful.
> ....
> Give me the senses for my guides in life;
> I'll trust none other.[14]

Gerald, like Walter, adheres steadfastly to his belief in the poet's divinity and mission. "Poets," Gerald exclaims at one point, are like "Sages," and not coincidentally like Christ, in that

> their speech sublime,
> Inspires the general heart; their beauty steals
> Brightening, and purifying, through the air
> Of common life; the Patriot wakes the soul
> Of apathetic nations, with their breath
> To Freedom's energies; their language gives
> Voice to Love's mysteries; the evening hearth
> Grows shrine-like, when is hymned their holy chaunt
> Of social concord; and their pathos speaks
> With a Fiend's accent to the desolate!
> The thought that *they* were men, makes other men
> Exult in manhood; and Eternity
> Preaching HEREAFTER to the world, attests
> Her Gospel by their deeds! And thus the Sons
> Of Genius have prerogative to stand
> Exempt from Time's decree; immutable
> In change!

The Spasmodic Poets

"Bards," Gerald believes, "write / The life of soul—the *only* life."[15] Though Gerald learns many hard lessons as he seeks worldly recognition as a poet (the same lessons, ironically, that would bring the real-life Spasmodics to their poetic knees), in this belief he is eventually vindicated. On his deathbed, he expresses his certainty that he is about to depart to a kind of Poets' Corner in Heaven, where "Sages, Poets, Potentates are throned!" and be "crowned" with a garland resembling both Christ's thorns and the traditional laurel, though in this case "woven from the Tree of Life!"[16]

The kind of poetry favored by Gerald, and supposedly written by him, is also recognizably Spasmodic. Gerald most resembles Walter in his sensuous personality, and this is reflected in his diction. For example, in a particularly Smithean passage, Gerald notes,

> On the brow
> Of the bleak Crag, oft have I marked a flower,
> So exquisite in form, in tint so pure,
> It seemed the child of dew-drops, and the Sun,
> There resting, like a memory of Heaven
> In stern, and guilty bosoms.
>
> ....
>
> My peerless one! Whose features are impressed
> On all Creation's beauty—I *must* speak,
> My heart o'erflows![17]

Gerald most resembles the belligerent Balder, however, in his misanthropy, which represents the main spiritual limitation he must overcome in the course of the poem. At one point, Gerald's "peerless one," Edith, rebukes him: "Ah, love! I would not have these moods recur / In which thou spurnest so the humbler minds." Even though "the coarse, unlettered hind" may not be able to understand Gerald's lofty words, he is subject to the same "Feelings" and is therefore worthy of respect. Unlike Balder, however, Gerald eventually renounces his supercilious attitude and embraces his cottager neighbors as "good Friends," apologizing for the fact that "I scorned ye once!"[18]

This temporary short-sightedness can be seen as the result of Gerald's enhanced intellectual capabilities, still worthy of praise in Marston's view. It also reflects, though, his masculinity as a prophetic bard, perhaps intensified directly in reaction to critics' repeated charges of Romantic effeminacy. Naturally, Edith's feminine receptiveness to the decency of even the lower classes re-educates Gerald; she is also a typical Spasmodic heroine in that this receptiveness allows her to become

4. "With a Halo Crowned"

her poet-lover's ideal reader. For this purpose, Festus was given an entire harem, and Smith created Walter's Violet and Flora; so ingrained did this motif become to Spasmodic poetry that Dobell would eventually attempt to invert (and perhaps even satirize) this process by having Balder's devotion to his art drive Amy mad. Through Edith, we are for the first time explicitly instructed how to receive, and learn from, the oracular Spasmodic poet, of whose teachings so much had been and would be made:

> Her eyes are bent upon the Poet's lay,
> And as she reads with holy light they shine;
> Partaker of his Being is she made!
> ....
> Yet, as she reads, her mind is upward borne
> By the Companion Spirit; and she owns
> A loftier pride than earthly state imparts;
> Which dwarfs the wide inheritance of thrones,
> To that which genius founds in human hearts.
> From all that only *seems* her soul is free,
> And learns a season, what it is—*to be*![19]

Whatever Marston may have hoped for *Gerald*, it must eventually have become obvious to him that his own goals, like Gerald's, were too idealistic for the temporal confines of 1842. He soon turned to writing plays, and his later works bore little resemblance to *Gerald*, though no doubt some of the familiar Spasmodic bombast found a more natural home on the Victorian stage. He was therefore spared the critical wrath endured by the younger Spasmodics. Still, had he not apparently outgrown his vatic phase, he might have felt joyously vindicated by a hopeful Glasgow mechanic's optimistic reinterpretation of his prototype ten years after his hero, and his ambitious poetic drama, had sunk into the bitter abyss of bourgeois indifference.

Alexander Smith (1829–1867), should not be confused with an earlier literary critic who shares his name. Alexander Smith of Banff, who died in 1851, published "The Philosophy of Poetry" in the December 1835 issue of *Blackwood's*, when the Spasmodic Smith was a small child. The elder Smith, however, made one point in his article with which the younger Smith would have heartily concurred: poetry, the article states, "is *essentially the expression of emotion*" accomplished by using "figurative phraseology." Poetic failures, Smith argued, are the result of the poetry's attempt in "conveying some mere *information*, not subsidiary to the prevailing emotion, and breaking the continuity of that

The Spasmodic Poets

emotion."[20] Alexander Smith the Spasmodic not only put a similar conviction into practice through his works, but enjoyed a career that was itself based on an emotional response not entirely of his creation.

As had been the case with some of the earlier working-class poets, Smith's obscure language and flattened political awareness did his popularity no initial harm. Yet, like many other working-class poets, Smith is now remembered more as a cultural phenomenon, an index to mid-nineteenth century taste than a serious thinker or artist. Even more than Sydney Dobell with his sickly disposition and frail wife, Alexander Smith displayed many of the characteristics required of a sentimental figure. In fact, in a perverse way Smith was fortunate to be born into poverty. Working class writing, providing the politics expressed were not radical enough to embarrass the sponsors, was an outgrowth of the Romantic appreciation for the common man's song; Burns was one such example. Much to Byron's disgust, even Robert Southey got into the act in 1831 with an "Introductory Essay on the Lives and Works of our Undereducated Poets," which was published as the Preface to the collected works of John Jones, "a Servant." Though the craze for working class poetry had peaked in 1833 with a volume called *Sketches of Obscure Poets*,[21] Smith's brief celebrity proved that the concept had not lost its pull on the public imagination. He and his mentor, Gilfillan, unabashedly petitioned for his literary recognition on that very basis. In *A Life-Drama*, Smith described a poet, much like himself, who longs for understanding, and, even more importantly, acclaim:

> Dungeoned in poverty, he saw afar
> The shining peaks of fame that wore the sun;
> Most heavenly bright, they mocked him through the bars.

Even more explicitly, one of the Sonnets appended to *A Life-Drama* describes how "I think on Poets nurtured 'mong the throes, / And by the lowly hearths of common men," and then candidly discloses that "my heart is burning to be one of those."[22]

Ambition was nothing new to Smith, but his aspirations had not always been literary. In his youth, Smith had entertained hopes of joining the ministry, but his family's financial distress forced him to give up his schooling at ten and settle for employment tracing patterns in a Glasgow muslin factory, where he was able to snatch the occasional moment to read and write. Since he preferred the Romantics, Smith came to believe, as they did, that poetry must be a product of inspiration, not training, and thus, like his predecessors Bailey and Marston,

4. "With a Halo Crowned"

he neglected the technical aspects of composition in favor of learning to create striking images and isolated metaphoric triumphs.

After a few years of poetic dabbling, Smith hopefully submitted a small collection of his poems to George Gilfillan, who had by 1850 established himself as an authority on literary excellence in Scotland. Though Gilfillan originally neglected the manuscript long enough to prompt Smith to ask for its return, he eventually became so enamored with Smith's youthful efforts that he decided to become Smith's mentor and create an audience for his work. Ultimately, Gilfillan's attentions were to prove a double-edged sword for Smith. Even today, scholars are divided about both his sincerity and his wisdom in championing Smith as the Carlylian *vates* he was desperate to find. Cronin is perhaps the most cynical: Gilfillan, he states, was disappointed by Bailey's decline in popularity. He therefore embarked on a "single-minded quest to find the poet of the age," and considered the manuscripts sent to him as "applications for the post."[23] The implication is that Gilfillan sought to enhance his own reputation as much as his preferred poet's. An opposing view may be found in Boos, who depicts Gilfillan as a gentle, supportive mentor[24] who acted out of altruism, a genuine love of literature, and a belief in its ability to reform an unjust society. There can be little doubt about how Smith and Gilfillan's contemporaries viewed their relationship in the aftermath of *Firmilian*, however. One letter-writer ("J.W.") in the 10 January 1857 issue of *The Athenaeum* defended Smith by admitting the derivativeness of his poetry but with an important qualification: "It has been Mr. Smith's misfortune to have known the truth of the old proverb, 'Save me from my friends.' Better had it been for him to have received poor Keats's treatment from Gifford than his own from Mr. Gilfillan. A worse critic than this last gentleman I cannot conceive."

Still, in the beginning, Smith's disadvantaged status actually worked in his favor. The manner in which Gilfillan introduced his new protégé to the public was calculated to play upon its hunger for the poet-prophet, or *vates*, for the age, as well as upon its taste for proto–Samuel Smiles stories of personal betterment. When he introduced Smith's unpublished manuscript in the October 1851 *Eclectic Review*, Gilfillan made it a point to praise Smith for educating himself and for using poetry not only as a method of self-expression but as a way to work his way up from the factory to "a situation more congenial to his mind, more worthy of his powers and allowing him more time for his favourite pursuits," which were of a "praiseworthy" educational and spiritual nature. Gilfillan was not hesitant to imply his own virtue in "aiding" Smith to reach these goals, and thereby suggested that his readers show equal moral rectitude in joining him on Smith's behalf.[25] Nor was he above an attempt to shame these same readers into accepting his new discovery. Alluding to an earlier working-class poet who had unjustly been consigned to an early grave through critical snobbery, Gilfillan begged them not to let Smith "pine away amid much drudgery" and become no more than a "dried-up spirit, crushed heart, and daisy-covered sod" like his great predecessor, John Keats.[26] Here, Gilfillan must surely have been thinking of "Ode to a Nightingale," with its climactic line, "to thy high requiem become a sod."

Smith himself seems to have been only too happy to follow Gilfillan's lead. In *A Life-Drama*, Walter frequently refers to an unnamed poet who served as his inspiration, perished unknown, but found posthumous recognition. As was the case with Keats, "the fame that scorned him while he lived / Waits on him like a menial." Keats' legendary withering in the face of critical scorn is again alluded to when Walter laments,

> No sooner was he hence than critic-worms
> Were swarming on the body of his fame,
> And thus they judged the dead: "This Poet was
> An April tree whose vermeil-loaded boughs
> Promised to Autumn apples juiced and red,
> But never came to fruit."[27]

The similarity between the fictional critics' carping and early reviews of Keats cannot be accidental, nor can the reference to "Autumn" fail to put us in mind of Keats' "To Autumn," lines 4–6, with its juicy apples bending the "moss'd cottage-trees." Finally, in one of the appended sonnets near the end of his volume, Smith attempts to shame his own potential critics into recalling their previous obtuseness (and presumably be gentler with him): "Critic, let that soul moan / In its own hell without a kick from thee" (182).

Gilfillan's promotion of Smith as new poet was for a time extraordinarily successful. After all, not only the language but the context of Gilfillan's review had been aggrandizing: his accolades had appeared in both *The Eclectic Review* and *The Critic* before Smith had actually published a line. This tactic increased the mystique surrounding this new poet (and, not incidentally, ensured Gilfillan an even surer monopoly than he held on the well-known Dobell), and Smith was increasingly, and quite prematurely, regarded as a genuine and important new artist. By the time *Poems* was rushed into print, Smith was already a

4. "With a Halo Crowned"

well-known figure, and the finished volume received unprecedented attention. Clough's *North American Review* article of July 1853, for example, admits that Smith's collected *Poems* had already enjoyed "a good deal more notice" than was usual for "first volumes of verse,"[28] and other established literary figures, including Tennyson, Rossetti, and Elizabeth Barrett Browning, offered their own admiration and support. Such enthusiasm stemmed directly from Gilfillan's propaganda.

Gilfillan's efforts also determined, to a large extent, the shape Smith's embryonic "A Life Fragment" took by the time it reached print. Aware that he was already regarded as a published poet in his early twenties, Smith earnestly but misguidedly began expanding his piece in a manner reminiscent of Bailey's continual augmenting of *Festus*, interpolating independent pieces of poetry and blowing existing passages to larger proportions. This was also owing to Gilfillan's intervention, for he had encouraged Smith to study *Festus*,[29] and in his *Eclectic* review he had defended "A Life Fragment's" lax structure as laudably in keeping with Bailey's poetic theories: "It has no plot," he admitted, but then again, "'Life,' says Bailey, 'has none.'"[30]

The late 1853 edition of *Poems* consisted of "A Life Fragment," which had now been expanded into *A Life-Drama*, and a few shorter pieces which followed it. The influence of Gilfillan, and by extension Bailey, had taken full hold of the volume. *A Life-Drama* now resembled both *Festus* in its profusion of images with would-be cosmic dimensions, and *The Roman* with respect to its loose structure and reliance on bombast in place of dialogue. Smith's padding of the original "Fragment" is evident as well in the poem's numbing repetitiveness both in imagery and episode, flat characterizations, and thin storyline which forces the poet to turn again and again to overwrought description or digressions in an often feeble attempt to advance the action. Most lamentably, Smith stuffed the poem with scenes many Victorians found in questionable taste[31]—scenes of possible rape or at least seduction, prostitution, Orientalist debauchery, and even suggestions of homosexual attachment.

Ironically, as with other Spasmodic efforts like *Balder*, the excessive imagery was both the most highly praised and the most derided aspect of Smith's poetry. This makes peculiar sense: by loading every page with metaphors, Smith was bound to hit occasionally upon something successful. Still, those successes are qualified at best, for his repertoire is strangely limited to certain comparisons which recur constantly and thus deaden any impression of originality. In 1855, after the

The Spasmodic Poets

anti–Spasmodic reaction had begun, *The National Magazine* attempted to count the most common of these, and managed to tally 62 similes in *A Life-Drama* involving the sun, 58 involving the moon, 67 the sea or ocean, and no less than 72 referring to the stars.[32] In addition, though Smith was recognized as an important voice for the working class, his hero Walter is a Byronic aristocrat with access to material comforts that make his angst more cloying than moving. His introspection quickly begins to resemble narcissism rather than artistic talent.

Despite these painful shortcomings, which are understandable given Smith's youth and lack of formal education, the 24-year-old still managed to become a kind of symbolic and even allegorical figure the lingering Romantic inside each Victorian reader and poet could seize upon as a hope for both literary and social progress. Clough, especially, is remembered as Smith's champion because of his *North American Review* article in which he compared Smith and Arnold. While allowing that the Oxonian Arnold possessed greater technical virtuosity as a poet, Clough made his own socialist agenda clear to an extent that Gilfillan did not dare. In comparison to Arnold's "pseudo-Greek inflation"[33] and concentration on noble figures like Tristan and Iseult, Clough finds Smith's images evocative of the workaday world particularly inhabited by the socially downtrodden: he finds "charm" in the "continual images drawn from the busy seats of industry" and, importantly, this "seems to satisfy a want that we have long been conscious of, when we see the black streams that welter out of factories, the dreary lengths of urban and suburban dustiness." Clough argues that poetry's true function, given such a reality, should be to provide not Arnoldian grace, but "significance" and "dignity" to even the most "dingy" labor.[34] Clough further suggests that what Smith has to offer the public is the touching example of a "passionate, youthful spirit, struggling for something like right and purity amidst the unnumbered difficulties, contradictions, and corruptions of the heated and crowded, busy, vicious, and inhuman town."[35] Clough probably sensed that his American readers would find this aspect of *A Life-Drama* especially congenial in the early days of industrialized capitalism (Melville's "Bartleby the Scrivener," a figure to whom the same description might apply, would appear in *Putnam's Magazine* in November of 1853).

Clough does admit that in certain respects *A Life-Drama* is less than satisfying, being imitative and in places strained. On the whole, however, he declares that this is less a fault than the "overeducated weakness" of minds like Arnold's. For him, Smith's derivative methods

4. "With a Halo Crowned"

are both understandable and forgivable, since his learning and social contacts have been much more limited by his class and occupation. Arnold, on the other hand, exhibits in his poetry his obvious breeding and familiarity with the "refined education" and "refined society" closed to "a Glasgow mechanic." Clough denigrates the courtly abilities he attributes to Arnold as inadequate to the poetic task he has already proposed: these "highly educated sensibilities" are undoubtedly "too delicate ... for common service."[36] In Smith we see rather the raw power of the human (and perhaps specifically the masculine) soul, oppressed but still seeking beauty in a harsh external world. That Clough was speaking politically and not literally is all too obvious when one attempts to apply his description to the actual poem. Although his statements do apply somewhat to Smith's biographical situation, the poem's hero, Walter, is heir to a pleasant country estate and is plagued by artistic, rather than financial, angst. This state of affairs could hardly have diverged more sharply from the tale of a factory hand snatching a few moments to jot down verses during a grueling ten-hour workday.

If Clough's misguided ardor for *A Life-Drama* seems extreme, one should note that some reviewers besides Gilfillan went to even more astonishing extremes. Hailing Smith as a prophet in self-consciously Carlylian terms, a *Tait's* critic who has since been identified as Peter Bayne went so far as to claim Smith as a kind of second Christ, humble in origin but prophetic in essence:

> Alexander Smith! Do they call thee Alick or Sandy[37] when thou art at home? ... Who ever heard that a prophet was born in Nazareth? who ever heard of a poet among the Smith family? ... Verily, Alexander Smith, thou hast limned the poet's outline greatly to our mind: a many-sided man is he, with thoughts that wander abroad all over the universe of God, and large-souled sympathies with all the brotherhood of men.... So they judged rightly of old time, when the *Vates* was deemed a true prophet, and not merely a verse-maker, given to chiming syllables in a school-girl's album.[38]

Seldom, save in the cases of Bailey and Dobell, had such exorbitant expectations been placed on so young and untested a poet. Given these plaudits, it is rather sobering to turn to the actual text of *A Life-Drama* and to be reminded of the harsh discrepancy between its supposed and its actual contents.

A Life-Drama revolves around a young man, Walter, who is by temperament a poet but who has yet to make his mark on the world of letters. Walter is a Romantic hero, self-absorbed and distracted from the workaday world by his imaginative landscape. He is less Byronic than

The Spasmodic Poets

Keatsian, for although, like Manfred, he is conscious that his heightened poetic sensibilities place him apart from the majority, like Keats (and Gerald) he is bound to the mundane world by his craving for its approbation. The poem, like its Romantic prototypes, portrays the hero's journey from a state of relative innocence through a moral nadir to a plateau of spiritual peace. Dobell would later employ the same format in *Balder*, but would make the mistake of stalling the hero in the second phase, to his readers' collective outrage; Smith's work was, perhaps, better received because he made it a point to restore ethical order in his last pages in spite of some perceived prurience in a few scenes. The thin plot follows Walter through two unsuccessful romances to the publication of a great poem and his eventual realization that human love is superior, though still essential to literary success.

Walter is, unfortunately for the poem as a whole, a self-centered and ultimately unengaging figure. Smith replaces conventional character development with interminable, melodramatic speeches and has Walter's most important intellectual revelations occur between scenes. For example, the publication and success of Walter's poetic masterpiece is described by two friends long after the event; Walter's increasing religious doubt and psychic pain are portrayed at one remove in much the same fashion. To fill pages, Smith relied on long metaphorical passages and repetition, both of images and of the same stories told over and over by various characters.

As might be expected, given Smith's conscious effort to be considered another Keats, much of the imagery of *A Life-Drama* is concerned with producing intense sensory stimulation. Walter seems to struggle, in his every speech, to translate every thought and observation into the language of hedonism, rather ineptly resembling the Pre-Raphaelites and prefiguring Oscar Wilde. The poem's opening lines set the tone for everything that follows:

> As a wild maiden, with love-drinking eyes,
> Sees in sweet dreams a beaming Youth of Glory,
> And wakes to weep, and ever after sighs
> For that bright vision till her hair is hoary;
> Even so, alas! is my life's passion story....

More often than not such epic similes impede the minimal action rather than add layers of meaning. Some are even embarrassing, like the unintentionally phallic "My drooping sails / Flap idly 'gainst the mast of my intent. / I rot upon the waters when my prow / Should grate the golden isles."[39] Much of Smith's dialogue takes a similar rambling

4. "With a Halo Crowned"

tone and is often inane, particularly the love scenes between Violet and Walter in which the two seem to recite verse to each other rather than actually communicate. Smith's occasional attempts to sound like the Romantic poets he idolized make his shortcomings even more obvious. For example, Walter's first love, a noblewoman, is moved to a Wordsworthian reverie while weaving a wreath from flowers. She exclaims,

> I look, sweet Flora, in thine innocent eyes,
> And see in them a meaning and a glee
> Fitting this universal summer joy.
> ....
> Better for man,
> Were he and Nature more familiar friends!
> His part is worst that touches this base world.
> Although the ocean's inmost heart be pure,
> Yet the salt fringe that daily licks the shore
> Is gross with sand.[40]

Not only is yet another "sea" image cloying, it is unclear why Smith believes it has a "heart," and why the sand, also a natural element, would defile the waves. Other passages comparing rustic and urban life are likewise confused and unremarkable.

Internal evidence suggests that Smith himself was aware that his predilection for the voluptuous rendered him ripe for parody, as W.E. Aytoun was soon to realize. Perhaps for this reason, Smith had the foresight to include a burlesque of his own style, placing it in the mouth of Arthur, a frivolous guest at a literary gathering. Arthur "sings" of a Keatsian "draught from your crystalline mountains" which is

> yellowed with peat-reek, and mellowed with age.
> O, richest joy-giver!
> Rare warmer of liver!
> Diviner than kisses, thou droll and thou sage!

Arthur's song goes on, increasing in Keats-like sensuality and also in deliberate ridiculousness, for almost two pages.[41] Another character, Edward, resembles the pragmatic friend Matthew in Wordsworth's "Expostulation and Reply," who disdains Romantic sensibility in favor of a more Augustan approach to life. Edward frequently ridicules Walter by expressing not only an anti–Romantic, but an anti–Spasmodic viewpoint: "We must go down / And work our souls like mines, make books our lamps, / Not shrines to worship at," he sneers at one point.[42] Though he is intended as a foil to show the reader Walter's fuller spiritual life, Edward ultimately comes off as the most reasonable voice in the text.

The Spasmodic Poets

At the close of *A Life-Drama*, Walter decides that, to achieve lasting greatness, he must take patient and subtle steps from minute to universal action:

> I will go forth 'mong men, not mailed in scorn,
> But in the armor of a pure intent.
> And whether crowned or crownless when I fall,
> It matters not, so as God's work is done.
> I've learned to praise the quiet lightning-deed,
> Not the applauding thunder at its heels
> Which men call Fame.[43]

Nevertheless, as Walter progresses along the course paved by Gerald, Smith emphasizes the need for the poetic prophet Gilfillan and Bayne were attempting to make of Smith himself. Walter quotes, for example, a Keatsian mentor who once predicted to Walter the advent of such a figure.[44]

> My Friend! a Poet must ere long arise,
> And with a regal song sun-crown this age,
> As a saint's head is with a halo crowned;-
> One, who shall hallow Poetry to God
> And to its own high use....
>
> ....
>
> A mighty Poet whom this age shall choose
> To be its spokesman to all coming times.
> In the ripe full-blown season of his soul,
> He shall go forward in his spirit's strength,
> And grapple with the questions of all time,
> And wring from them their meanings.

Ultimately, this poet "shall ... reflect our great humanity; / ... Through every theme he touch, making all Beauty / And Poetry forever like the stars." Having supposedly achieved artistic maturity at the poem's close, Walter is finally ready to create the great song, alluded to throughout the drama, which will explain the human experience from Creation to the crises of Modernity (needless to say, *A Life-Drama*'s readers never get to see it).

The impudence attributed to Smith by the Aytoun camp (and parodied in *Firmilian* by casting Smith as an ignorant costermonger lionized by the Gilfillan character) resulted from the author's obvious identification with Walter. Given Walter's autobiographical implications, at least in terms of psychology if not social advantage, *A Life-Drama*'s implication that he is the poet of the age suggests that Smith is as well. Perhaps sensing that he might be accused of arrogance, Smith begins the

4. "With a Halo Crowned"

first sonnet appended to *A Life-Drama* in *Poems* with a curious authorial disclaimer:

> I cannot deem why men toil so for Fame.
> A porter is a porter though his load
> Be the oceaned world, and although his road
> Be down the ages. What is in a name?
> ....
> We ever hunger for diviner stores.
> I cannot say I have a thirsting deep
> For human fame....[45]

Since there is no textual evidence to suggest that the voice is not the poet's own, this statement was no doubt intended to counteract just this implication that Walter and Smith were essentially the same figure (Dobell would later be forced to add a Preface to *Balder* to correct the same damaging impression). Still, given all that has come before, especially the "burning" desire for recognition expressed in another short poem, Smith's protest cannot help but sound more disingenuous than sincere. Even Bayne, in his flattering review, felt it necessary to remind Smith to "Be in no hurry to be famous; you must first of all be great."[46] The sonnet also contradicts Walter's opening speech, where he declares that "one passion eats the rest," and that he can conceive of no greater frustration than fruitlessly wishing "in immortalness / To stand on time as on a pedestal."[47] In a line that may have stuck in Sydney Dobell's mind when he penned Balder's infamous thirteen repetitions of "ah!," Walter bursts out: "Might I so broaden on the skies of fame! / O Fame! Fame! Fame! next grandest word to God!"[48]

Walter's desire for fame is more than mere egotistical rant, though Smith's hero can certainly not be said to suffer from excessive modesty. That the poet and his works become well-known is obviously necessary if he is to assume the prophetic role dictated by Gilfillan's evangelical scheme. The "Young Apollo," albeit Christianized, of Gilfillan's review essays appears again in *A Life-Drama*[49]; clearly, if the poet's message is hidden from the multitude, he can neither stand for his age historically nor influence it morally and spiritually. Part of the Poet's duty as "Sir Bookworm" is to set an example for readers, since in Walter's view "few read books aright" among his contemporaries.[50] Eventually, Walter, like Gerald before him, finds his ideal reader. Violet, a young woman he meets at a literary gathering, reads some of Walter's transcendent work and is stunned into contemplative awe. "I shed no tear," she tells him after spending an entire day reading the poem, but instead "I laid it

The Spasmodic Poets

down in silence, and went forth / Burdened with its sad thoughts." Convinced of her lover's talent, she hopes he will now "Put off the robes of sorrow, and put on / The singing crown of Fame."[51] Obviously, Smith believed that such attuned reading would have to be inspired on a much larger scale.

For Victorian readers, the hero's (and presumably the author's) quest for poetic status was less distasteful than his extreme emotionalism and unbridled sexuality. Walter's renunciation of fame for love, a metaphor for transcending erotic love in favor of *agape*, was perhaps intended, in true Christian spirit, as a partial corrective to *Festus'* excess in this area, but Walter's unrestrained effusions soon earned Smith a reputation for licentiousness. Walter's preoccupation with the sensual is evident in both his own dialogue and in that of the characters of his own fictions: for example, he entertains his first love, a noblewoman, with an autobiographical tale of a page-boy smitten by his own Lady. The language of the tale is unabashedly erotic, as are the similes of the banging cymbals and the opening bud, as well as the suggestion of mutually ingested bodily fluids:

> I know a song, born in the heart of love,
> ....
> 'Tis of two lovers, matched like cymbals fine,
> Who, in a moment of luxurious blood,
> Their pale lips trembling in the kiss of gods,
> Made their lives wine-cups, and then drank them off,
> And died with beings full-blown like a rose....[52]

Walter's own dealings both with this Lady and later with Violet are also unmistakably sexual. His declaration of passion to Violet hardly differs at all in tone, and the sense in which he uses "love" is all too apparent.

> Gods! I could out-Antony
> Antony! This moment I could scatter
> Kingdoms like halfpence! I am drunk with joy.
> This is a royal hour—the top of life.
> Henceforth my path slopes downward to the grave—
> All's dross but love.[53]

Two scenes in *A Life-Drama* were considered especially startling by Smith's contemporaries: Walter's seduction (which some called rape) of Violet and his request that a prostitute (referred to as "an Outcast" and a "girl" by the stage directions but as "Sister" by the now-debauched Walter) pray for him on a city bridge at midnight. Here, Walter's sensual

4. "With a Halo Crowned"

language oscillates to an opposite and distasteful extreme suggesting the physical corruption of venereal disease: "My soul breeds sins as a dead body worms! / They swarm and feed upon me," he tells the Outcast, and, after he slept beside Violet, "It was a putrid corse that clung to me, / ... that rots into my being."[54] Walter's description of the consummation was actually expurgated from some later editions, among them that of Boston's Ticknor and Fields. Missing from this 1855 reprint are the fervid lines

> I ceased to sing and on the queenly lady lay
> One white hand in a golden shoal
> Of ringlets, reeling down upon her couch
> And heaving on the heaving of her breast.

This frankness, amounting to what the Victorians considered prurience, represents the inevitable byproduct of Smith's overwrought style. As his drama reeled from one false climax to another, Smith was forced to reach further in attempting to heighten dramatic tension; soon sexual indecorousness also came to be considered an aspect of Spasmody; even Clough, for all his championing of Smith, may have been sufficiently embarrassed upon recollecting the poem's sexual content that he recanted his enthusiastic recommendation to his fiancée, Blanche Smith.

Owing largely to Jerome Buckley,[55] Dobell has long been considered the primary "aesthetician" of the Spasmodic School, but Smith, too, had a theoretical basis for his ostensibly random methods. His ideas are largely afterthoughts, it is true, published long after the composition of *A Life-Drama* and the Spasmodic debacle spearheaded by *Firmilian*. Needless to say, Smith was not of the opinion shared by Kingsley, Arnold, and others, that poetry ought to promote somber educational and moral discourse, especially with respect to the middle class.[56] Though he acknowledged that literary productions required some intellectual content, he was firm in asserting that "in every work of art the style is of even more importance than the thought."[57] Since ideas themselves cannot be other than repetitive, the only true measure of artistic merit must be how the artist rearranges the old concepts into new and more striking forms. Biographical interest, for Smith, outweighs any objective observation a text might prompt: "in every work the writer's biography may more or less clearly be read," he states, while the characters an author has created are analogous to his children or a king's ambassadors in a foreign land. Meantime "we are striving to catch a

The Spasmodic Poets

glimpse of the author between the lines ... as the sunbeam constantly takes us back to the sun." The reader's pleasure depends upon how much of the artist's personality he can divine from his expression.

Smith's theories extolling the importance of the author are further delineated in his essay on Sydney Dobell, written after *Balder* had for all intents and purposes ruined his friend's career. The biographical approach was to become commonplace for anyone attempting to defend Dobell, but Smith's essay is particularly useful in that it provides a definition of the Spasmodic poet which is surprisingly and unapologetically close to Aytoun's parodic portrait. Since the poet is "the most perfect human being," a teacher with Divine dispensation, Smith insists that he should be exempt from the moral constraints binding lesser men. He goes further than Shelley in demanding that the artist actually be acknowledged as "the true legislator and ruler" of society. To judge from Smith's description, Dobell had accepted the burden of the modern prophet as did Walter, Balder, and to a lesser extent Festus:

> His mental constitution is high, solitary, disdainful. His genius is of an ascetic and *fakir* kind. He stands apart from his fellows, and wraps himself up in the mantle of his own thoughts.... He has neither written for the mere enjoyment of writing, nor for money, nor for fame, but mainly because he has a doctrine to preach, a cause to plead; and this doctrine he has preached in ears too long accustomed to sounding brasses and tinkling cymbals to give heed to high discourse. Mr. Carlyle preaches hero-worship, Mr. Dobell preaches genius-worship.... [One is] practical, the other ... ideal.[58]

Despite his good intentions, Smith probably did little to appease those convinced that Balder's amorality was also his creator's by praising Dobell because he "would have the world sit at the feet of the poets [who should] shape everything, not only private conduct, but Parliaments" and reminding the readers that such an "apostle of the Highest" should strive "to live poems." This is, of course, the same philosophy that allegedly prompted Balder to murder his infant daughter so he could perfect his poem on death. Though Smith acknowledges that *Balder* is an unsuccessful poem, he believes, as did Horne in the case of *Gerald*, that its flaw lies not in its message but in its technique. Since Balder himself was so unceasingly garrulous, Dobell was too obviously propagandizing his "cause." Had he remained more subliminal, Smith suggests, the public might have idolized him as he deserved. Since *A Life-Drama* had been pilloried along with *Balder*, at least some of Smith's apologia was surely intended to explain his own failure to maintain its interest. Many passages in *A Life-Drama* prefigure *Balder*,[59] and

4. "With a Halo Crowned"

it therefore seems likely that the storm of reaction against Dobell was partially critics' overcompensation for their earlier, now regretted plaudits for Smith.

Smith's reputation suffered its most serious blow when his inventiveness was challenged by *The Athenaeum*, which had once warmly praised Dobell's *The Roman*. Not only was Smith dull, claimed the critic "Z," but a thief as well. "Z" then aligned column after column of Smith's poetry with comparable snippets from established authors to prove him a plagiarist. Significantly, the poets Smith is most often accused of pilfering from are Shelley, Keats, and P.J. Bailey. "Z" was not even willing to allow that *A Life-Drama*'s echoes were unconscious: "Every reader of sense—and more especially every writer of sense—knows the trick of such transformations," he noted with more than a touch of malevolence. "Mr. Smith is an adept in the art."[60]

Certainly many of "Z's" parallels raise doubts about *A Life-Drama*'s integrity, and are sufficient to disqualify it from being thought of as ground-breaking in the way Gilfillan had suggested. "Z" was unable to convince all of his readers, many of whom (among them Sydney Dobell) wrote in to offer a back-handed defense of Smith as merely naïve or intellectually limited rather than dishonest. In this case, however, reasonable doubt proved sufficient to convict the Spasmodics. *City Poems*, generally acknowledged by modern commentators as a far superior collection than the first, had just been published—indeed "Z" admits that its appearance prompted him to step forward with his charges—but was summarily dismissed by both critics and readers. It, too, was accused of being a plagiarized patchwork of other, better sources.

Modern critics have sought to explain Smith's derivativeness by focusing on his place within the traditions of working-class and Scottish poetry. According to Richard Cronin, *A Life-Drama*'s style has its origin in "displaced political enthusiasms," and the poem is "written in a language pillaged from books" because it is the "production of a poet disconnected from the language of his poetry.... Poetic language is the property of a nation and of a class from which Smith is excluded."[61] As a Scot, Smith has already been politically deprived of his true voice, and thus must splice together the utterances of British poets to ease his alienation. P.G. Scott likewise postulates that since the Scottish tongue had by Smith's time ceased to be used for serious literature, he probably felt it "inappropriate to his higher calling, and so employed English from the beginning."[62] It was, of course, a curious English, constructed by the isolated factory drudge almost entirely from the poets

The Spasmodic Poets

"Z" mentions. Since the tradition of working-class poetry forbade (or at least strongly discouraged) the explicit treatment of politics in works subsidized by middle and upper-class patrons,[63] *A Life-Drama* was further robbed of the chance for expression. This is supposed to account for Walter's financial security,[64] so far removed from the borderline poverty of his creator.

Smith's poetic career was not to recover after the failure of *Balder* and the onset of the anti–Spasmodic backlash. A telling anecdote appears in one of Sydney Dobell's letters of 1854, when Dobell was "one of the canvassers" for Smith's appointment as Secretary to the University of Edinburgh, where Aytoun was a professor. Though *Firmilian* had not yet been published, gossip about *A Life-Drama*'s less restrained episodes had clearly spread. Dobell reports that "several influential people had got notions of Alexander's 'immorality.' I took the book [presumably *A Life-Drama*] with me and gave extempore lectures on the pure passages to counteract the effect of the others!"[65] Thankfully, Smith was elected to the post and secured financial stability enabling him to escape factory life, but his literary celebrity was already in steep decline. Although Smith had often reiterated his belief in the superiority of the poet over the novelist, and had complained in "Literary Work" that "novels have too much plot; interesting like a puzzle, only in the unravelling," and are composed in haste without style,[66] he was forced to turn to prose in order to support himself and his family, writing two unremarkable novels[67] (and leaving a third unfinished when he died of typhoid at age 37) in addition to many periodical pieces. Several of these pieces were published by *Blackwood's*, still under W.E. Aytoun's editorship; ironically, the man who had named and destroyed the Spasmodic School became a financial boon to Smith when all the other critics, most notably Gilfillan, had turned away.[68] Having outlasted their poetic welcome, Dobell and Smith could do little but ineffectually protest their humiliation and attempt, in vain, to restore their reputations through their collaborative effort, *Sonnets on the War*. The volume failed to attract anything but negative attention and even a few cruel jibes (notably by Aytoun,[69] whose humor at Smith and Dobell's expense had gone cold and vindictive).

Though *City Poems* is still occasionally praised, and selections from that volume can be found in anthologies of Scottish literature, *A Life-Drama* (along with Smith's prose) is now forgotten except in relation to the Spasmodic debate, Clough and Arnold's epistolary quarrel over its merits, and Aytoun's jabs in *Firmilian*. Ironically (or perhaps

4. "With a Halo Crowned"

fittingly), it was only when Smith left behind his neo-Romantic fantasy of Walter and Violet—what Trilling called a "trivial world of his own contriving"[70] and his ambitious but sterile historical poem "Edwin of Deira" that he found his true voice. As an urban poet documenting the grime and human cost of industrial Glasgow and Edinburgh, the "Iron World" from which he had come, Smith has caught the notice of modern cultural scholars equipped to appreciate his "particularly Scottish"[71] voice.

One passage in *A Life-Drama*, though typically over-written, could serve as an epitaph for Smith and the Spasmodic School after the 1854 *Firmilian* imbroglio.

> O! There are men who linger on the stage
> To gather crumbs and fragments of applause
> When they should sleep in earth—who, like the moon,
> Have brightened up some little night of time,
> And 'stead of setting when their light is worn,
> Still linger, like its blank and beamless orb,
> When daylight fills the sky.
> ....
> Strive for the Poet's crown, but ne'er forget
> How poor are fancy's blooms to thoughtful fruits[.][72]

5

"The Unstable Bubble of Inflated Thought"

Dobell, Bigg, and the Flowering of High Spasmody

Sydney Dobell (1824–1875) may be called the archetypal Spasmodic poet, with the possible exceptions of the fictional Firmilian and his equally fictional creator, "T. Percy Jones," who is in some ways even more fully developed as a character in Aytoun's parody. In his poetry, prose, and even an extraordinary 1857 lecture that may have taken hours to deliver,[1] Dobell disseminated Spasmodic ideals for poetry and life with quasi-religious fervor. During the anti–Spasmodic backlash, spurred by the 1854 publication of *Balder*, he was the most viciously lambasted and the most profoundly embarrassed. Smith, Bigg, Marston, and Bailey all forfeited their laurels in the wake of Aytoun's attacks, but Dobell, who displayed genuine poetic and even critical promise, may have been the most grievous loss to Victorian letters.

Though it is not difficult to ridicule Dobell's (and his hero, Balder's) excessive seriousness and apparent self-regard, he is in many ways a poignant figure. Taking their cue from Alexander Smith's *Last Leaves* and John Nichol's biographical notices of his late friend, defenders have emphasized Dobell's good humor and personal generosity and lamented the invalidism which led to his doctors' forbidding him to write or undertake other stressful "brain-work."[2] Robert Buchanan, best known today for his attacks on D.G. Rossetti, went so far as to portray Dobell as a martyr who, as the Philistines closed in around him, "went to the stake of criticism with a smile on his face, almost disarming his torturers and executioners."[3] The tradition is alive today, as Malcolm Pittock excuses *Balder*'s domestic horror by postulating that Dobell's marriage may have been a good deal less happy than it is often portrayed and Martha Westwater pleads that Dobell be recognized as a proto-feminist

5. "The Unstable Bubble of Inflated Thought"

victimized by the malicious W.E. Aytoun.[4] Dobell also holds a special place in the voluminous scholarship on the Brontë sisters, as he was among the first to recognize not only their genius but their gender. His warm correspondence with Charlotte Brontë, who sent him a copy of the 1850 reissue of *Wuthering Heights* as thanks for his admiring review, offers not only biographical but theoretical insight into both authors. Charlotte's encouraging comments on Dobell's anti-hero, Balder, hold particular resonance for anyone familiar with a similarly controversial character called Heathcliff.

It is true that Dobell and his fellow Spasmodics were (and in a sense still are) primarily casualties of critical upheaval, specifically a reaction against extreme Romanticism. The glorification of poetic solipsism, so central to Spasmodic technique, struck some reviewers as not just aesthetically displeasing but socially irresponsible and even dangerous. The effusions of the Spasmodics' admirers remind us that poet-worship was not limited to Gilfillan's circle. As late as 1887, Buchanan could invoke, without fear of sounding unintelligible, the cultural motif of the divinely endowed poet who possessed mystical perception: "Why this divinely gifted being, whose soul seemed all goodness, and whose highest song would have been an inestimable gain to humanity, should have been struck down again and again by blows so cruel, is a question which pricks the very core of that tormenting conscience which is in us all." Of all the Spasmodics, Dobell was both the best suited and most willing to assume this prophetic role, and at least some of his admirers were (and perhaps still are) loath to admit he had failed.

Testimonials regarding Dobell's messianic qualities, of course, did not originate with Smith, Gilfillan, or other enthusiastic critics of the same Romantic stripe. On the contrary, Dobell had grown accustomed to similar plaudits throughout his youth, coming as he did from a singularly eccentric family. His grandfather, Samuel Thompson, had founded a religious sect that denied the existence of Satan and the need for atonement but affirmed, as did the Unitarians, the oneness of Christ and God as well as its own position as the one true Church. It required its adherents to shun outside social involvements, and Dobell's psychological and educational isolation was increased by his family's high expectations for him as the future head of the "Church of God."[5] He was educated rigorously, but within the home. Like P.J. Bailey, who wrote in seclusion, and Alexander Smith, who toiled unschooled in a factory, Dobell therefore lacked contact with the main currents of Victorian

The Spasmodic Poets

culture and artistic tradition. Atrophied communications skills could easily account for the syntactical and psychological idiosyncrasies of all three major Spasmodics, just as alienation would preoccupy all the Spasmodic protagonists.

Still, Dobell's private education was not deficient or exclusively evangelical. According to Emily Jolly, the family friend who became his biographer, his father set him to studying not just theological texts, but also Tennyson, Shelley, and Keats as well as Milton and Spenser. Most importantly, he was encouraged to revere Byron as did the elder Dobell, and sometime before his seventeenth birthday, he memorized the entire text of *Manfred*.[6] Sydney's bond with Byron was taken seriously by the Dobells. After the poet's death, one of his brothers recalled proudly that "those who knew Lord Byron personally, said that Sydney's face recalled his ... both had straight Greek features, curly dark brown hair, and remarkable blue eyes." Phrenology, so widely accepted at the time, hinted at even greater potential in Sydney, for "Byron's head, though of similar proportions, was small, while Sydney's was exceptionally large, some three inches larger in circumference than the ordinary full-sized man's head."[7] His brother also recalled that Sydney's eyes were "for ever trying to read and solve some unknown problem."

In adolescence Sydney decided to become a poet, composing a miniature "epic" on Napoleon and several short poems which were published in periodicals. Professional recognition and critical success came in 1850 with *The Roman*, a fragment of which first appeared in *Tait's*. Though Dobell probably composed *The Roman* in a torrent of Byronism rather than social conviction, its subject could hardly have been more propitious. English liberalism had already resulted in the passage of the Reform Bill and numerous Acts addressing sanitation and humanitarian issues, and the Italian struggle for independence from Austria became a popular cause at mid-century. The bombastic tone of *The Roman* appealed to political agitators, while its vaguely Gothic flavor, perhaps recalling the Italian settings of well-known romances like those of Ann Radcliffe, accommodated more general public tastes. One of the happiest achievements of *The Roman* was that it allowed Dobell entry into the society of other celebrated authors, where he was cordially received. As his father remarked after his son made a particularly successful visit to the city, "I can hardly expect him to have escaped internal injury, as he has been much flattered."[8] Jolly reports that aspiring young poets began to send their manuscripts to Dobell[9] even as they did Gilfillan and other popular authorities. Some, she wryly notes, asked for "more substantial

5. "The Unstable Bubble of Inflated Thought"

assistance," perhaps in the way of the ten pounds Dobell loaned Alexander Smith for the publication of his own volume of verse.

As has been noted, the majority of periodical reviews were warm with regard for *The Roman*. In addition to those already mentioned, *Chambers' Edinburgh Journal* praised Dobell in the lofty, quasi-prophetic language now commonplace with regard to the Spasmodics. Discussing a recent profusion of newsworthy events, the unidentified reviewer declared that foremost among such events "we are inclined to reckon the advent of a poet." While their age has perhaps accommodated too much "clever mediocrity," he confessed, Dobell's *Roman* is an invigorating departure. Because it is "full of unquestionable merit; full of lusty and exalted thoughts; strongly and often beautifully expressed ... with strains and strokes of passion,"[10] this reviewer believes that even the scattered selections reproduced in his review "are sufficient to prove the author's title to the honoured name of *poet*" and compare favorably to the work of such established authors as Tennyson and Thomas Babington Macaulay,[11] author of the widely read *Lays of Ancient Rome*.

The Roman is not a full-blown Spasmodic epic; at approximately three thousand lines, it does not even approach the size of *Balder*, which has nearly eight thousand. However digressive its structure, *The Roman* does deal with issues other than the omnipotence of art, and its main character, however bombastic and irritating, is not nearly as consumed by egotism as are Walter and Balder. Still, *The Roman* is certainly composed in the yet-unnamed and undeveloped "Spasmodic" style. Its scenes are stitched together loosely to form a poetic drama, but since there is little underlying unity, many could easily be dropped or rearranged. The poem's motivating force is its protagonist, significantly dubbed Vittorio Santo—suggesting a victorious saint. He is not unlike Balder or Dobell himself in his capacity as bardic hero or *vates*, and the story's events mainly provide a framework for various purple patches and expository monologues detailing his myriad virtues. Santo's character is sketchy and unappealing; in one scene he approaches some children playing and expresses his hope that a certain one of them may be the first of the group to die.[12] He is, again like Balder and Dobell, impatient with the intellectual limitations of his fellow mortals: in an unintentionally prophetic scene, Santo delivers an impassioned, ranting speech on the sanctity of Roman soil and then looks around to find that his audience has disappeared.

It was ironic that Dobell's first long poem was political in nature, for, perhaps due to his insulated childhood, he generally preferred sentimental to topical subjects. Dobell's reticence on social issues starkly contrasted with, for example, Matthew Arnold's continual grappling with science, class conflict, education, the Irish question, and other topics.[13] Dobell's two later books of war poems, for example, invoke the Crimean War primarily as a backdrop for a series of character studies in ballad form, some melodramatic or even maudlin (though D.G. Rossetti, among others, identified one of the shorter Crimean poems, "A Nuptial Eve," as Dobell's masterpiece[14]). Still, the mistaken attribution of political activism to Dobell initially worked in his favor, as did Smith's supposed concern for his fellow downtrodden members of the working class. *Chambers'* reviewer, like many others, did touch briefly upon *The Roman*'s faults, notably its rhetorical puffery and its stilted characterizations, but excused them as natural byproducts of authorial inexperience and admirable revolutionary fervor. The misunderstanding also had embarrassing consequences: Bryant relates how Dobell's Cheltenham home became "something of a shrine" for displaced Italian radicals much like those who filled the Rossetti home in Dante Gabriel's youth. As his brother Clarence recalled, the Italian rebels became "puzzled and dismayed" with Dobell, whom they had "eagerly sought out [as] the man who of all Englishmen had best expressed [their] thoughts and aspirations."[15] Dobell could offer the rebels little in the way of practical action or strategy; in some discomfort he protested that he felt he should limit his partisanship to the written word.

This fiasco, like Dobell's fall into a subterranean cavern as he mounted a rocky incline in emulation of St. Paul,[16] exemplifies his inability to apply either personal strength or sufficient intellectual dexterity to his expansive ambition. As *Chambers'* had reluctantly pointed out, in *The Roman* "The light and fire of genius are both present, but there is also something of the smoke."[17] Soon Dobell no longer relied on the indiscriminate praise of his grandfather's admiring followers, but instead made Gilfillan, with whom he struck up a correspondence, their surrogate. The young man admitted to Gilfillan in 1849 that "I have had always—you must not think me self-sufficient—an unconquerable ever-welling confidence that *some* of my thoughts were sterling." Gilfillan constantly reassured Dobell of his genius, stoking the young poet's pride or even vanity. Dobell thanked him by declaring, with unintended irony, "If in after years I should ever be called 'Poet' you will know that my success is, in some sort, your work."[18] Since Gilfillan shared his

5. "The Unstable Bubble of Inflated Thought"

evangelical ardor, Dobell became more certain than ever that he was indeed God's own "mouthpiece."

Once the success of his first work was confirmed, Dobell set to work on a new poem for which he conceived a much grander design. The saga of *Balder* was originally intended to encompass three parts. Each would be epic in scope and as a group they would detail the progress of a soul from irreverence to total Christian surrender. Balder takes his name, though not his identity, from the same hero of Norse mythology Arnold would depict in "Balder Dead." Though it is tempting to consider Arnold's title as a possible reference to Dobell's disgrace, which was sadly complete by the time Arnold published his poem in 1855, it seems more likely that the two poems were begun around the same time.[19] Thale suggests that the allusion might have appealed to Dobell because of the original Balder's status as an Apollonian figure as well as a "symbol of moral goodness."[20] In any case, Dobell's plan was to create a "Christian Balder"; moreover, the full name of the hero (though it is not stated in the text) was to be "Balder Sorgivin, [which] signifies 'Balder in the strife of Sorrow.'"[21] In a letter to Gilfillan, Dobell explained the design for his "epic" with great enthusiasm. His subject is, he admits, the "inner life" of his main character, whom he describes as "a student" (in the actual poem, Balder is described solely—and repeatedly—as a "poet"). Conveniently, this "student" is "writing an epic, of which passages and best points, introduced in various manners, come naturally into the more subjective matter of the piece."[22] With this elastic structure, Dobell felt, he had hit upon a perfect vehicle for the widest possible range of expression. "You see, therefore," he announced to the admiring Gilfillan, "that without destroying the unity of my work, I have already every outlet for every variety of thought and passion." Dobell probably also saw this free-ranging structure as an opportunity to experiment with sound and rhythm, another area of creative interest and innovation for him.[23] This would explain the variety of poetic forms and "song" used throughout the text.

It may seem puzzling that, rather than making any attempt to ameliorate the flaws so gently and so specifically identified by critics of *The Roman* (not to mention *Festus*), the burgeoning poet chose to exaggerate each of them until *Balder* was virtually unreadable, and it must be admitted that Dobell's superior attitude impeded his success to an even greater extent than his poetic inadequacies. Reviewing Dobell's second effort, a severely disappointed *Chambers'* critic thrashed the poem, but noted sadly that "unqualified praise is misleading kindness,"[24]

The Spasmodic Poets

without doubt recalling the magazine's own celebration of *The Roman* as well Gilfillan's unadulterated worship. Aytoun, elsewhere preparing his scathing indictment of both Dobell and Gilfillan in *Firmilian*, must have fervently concurred. This review, like many others, also sees *Balder* as part of an unhealthy (and uncomfortably democratic) trend in poetry: "The poets of the rising generation are going sadly astray ... [in them] we have little else save mist and moonshine. Poets are going to the dogs—or at the very least, their books are going to the pastry-cook and the butterman—not to the people and the heart of ordinary humanity" (26). Clearly, the currency of such sentiment accounted for the rapid and lasting adoption of Aytoun's "Spasmodic" epithet (and possibly inspired the character of the costermonger in *Firmilian*).

Summarizing *Balder* is both an easier and a more exasperating task than its length (nearly three hundred pages) might at first suggest. The story's somewhat gothic setting recalls that of Poe's 1842 story, "The Oval Portrait," with its isolated mad artist and long-suffering wife-victim.[25] The plot, such as it is, concerns Balder, a poet who dwells near some unnamed mountains with his wife, Amy, whose difference in status and perception is as great as her more prosaic name suggests. Apart from Amy, their baby, a physician and a single caller, Balder is as isolated as was Dobell in his own childhood. *Balder* begins, as does *A Life-Drama*, with a Faustian scene depicting the poet in his study, significantly located in a high (and undeniably phallic) tower. Here he meditates surrounded by manuscripts, statues, and other artistic props. This princely solitude, though in some ways hard to endure, has had unexpected compensations. Not only have his "keen ears / Heard each careening star that rounds the sky" and learned to identify each by sound, Balder believes he has also been entrusted with guiding

> The pen of sovereign Nature when she bent
> To send her message to the sons of men,
> Nor,—being her Scribe, and finding in her eyes
> Maternal favour—undismissed to sit
> At her dread feet, while her much-musing Voice
> Like muffled thunders of a storm unburst
> Did murmur to her heart.[26]

Like Faust (with an echo of Rasselas's acquaintance, the mad astronomer), Balder feels that he has reached the summit of mortal experience and is ready to take the next step to godhood, or at any rate supreme poethood. The next day will be Balder's twenty-ninth birthday, and he frets over finding fame and making a lasting mark on the world by

5. "The Unstable Bubble of Inflated Thought"

writing an epic which will alter the intellectual context of his age (which we may assume to be Victorian but which is nowhere specified). His ambitions are frustrated because he feels unqualified to address the subject of death, which he has never experienced firsthand. After a series of anguished monologues, though, Balder hits upon a rather diabolical plan to further his work: he will closely observe the death of his infant daughter and finally look death directly in the face as a mode of inspiration. The murder, if that is what causes the death, is not depicted in the poem, and we are left to wonder exactly when and how it was accomplished. Later references to the baby's gradual wasting away seem to imply poison, parental neglect, or even natural causes, but Dobell never makes the precise circumstances clear. Balder does, however, ruminate on what he has seen (or perhaps done) and speaks elatedly of being able to set to work at last. Unfortunately, Amy's grief upon being bereft of her child, and her egotistical husband's neglect, drive her mad. This distracts Balder from his writing and renders him increasingly bitter and disposed to further violence.

During this time Balder receives visits from a fellow artist, Gerald (perhaps intended as homage to J.W. Marston's hero) and Dr. Paul, a physician who was once a poet but who now attempts to cure Amy of her derangement. Both visits give Balder (and Dobell) an opportunity to unfurl various poetic effusions which have nothing whatever to do with the plot. In spite (or perhaps because) of these diversions, Amy's madness worsens and she begins to wander the landscape and the rooms adjoining Balder's study, wailing in a state of disarray. After much painful soliloquizing, Balder resolves to murder Amy and proceed with his epic, which is growing grander in his mind but not on paper. This second death would have the incidental benefit of relieving Amy of her great suffering. After Amy flings her husband's manuscript from the tower window in a fit of accusatory rage, Balder takes up a dagger and strips Amy's upper clothing away. As he masks her face and prepares to stab her, the poem abruptly ends.

Originally, Dobell had intended to reveal the fate of Amy in a second volume. The public's overwhelming distaste for *Balder*, however, prevented him from completing it. His ultimate intention, and Amy's prospects for survival, would remain a mystery if not for a fragment found among his notes and published after his death by his friend John Nichol. In the fragment, Balder is asked by another character how he came by his (now apparently exemplary) Christianity. Balder replies: "I was in the very dust, I had found ... the impotence of Philosophy. I

The Spasmodic Poets

had trusted to the heart and found myself in the act of Murder. I found my whole soul crying out for a revelation of Truth." At the second volume's conclusion, Balder's Pauline conversion was to be so complete as to necessitate a name change, and the fragment concludes as "the man who was once called Balder, but now—[not revealed], arose with his wife to go unto the Lord that He might heal the scar upon her breast."[27] Amy's literal resurrection, then, was intended to echo Balder's analogous spiritual experience. It is unclear what the third planned volume would depict.

Balder is not particularly complicated and would seem a bit thin to comprise an entire volume, although it might have functioned adequately as the first third of a trilogy. Had Dobell scaled down his original plan and included parts two and three (or even parts one and two) in the same volume, *Balder* might have been better understood and received. However, in his rush to meet Gilfillan's expectations, Dobell followed Smith's and Bailey's examples and merely padded his fragment until he had stretched it to book length. Early in the work, Dobell unwittingly exposed the central difficulty of the poem, and indeed of Spasmodic poetics as a whole, by having his hero look to the heavens and muse, "How far a little breath may blow / The unstable bubble of inflated thought!"[28] Having reassured Gilfillan of his epic's wonderfully elastic structure, he proceeded to drape this skeletal rack with assorted shorter poems and songs employing varying, and sometimes jarringly incompatible, meters, themes, and styles.

Balder contains digressions of two classes, both of which are equally distracting (not to mention wearisome) to the reader. First, Dobell inserts miscellaneous poems (sometimes within poems), as in the seemingly interminable scenes in which groups of people "sing." Balder reads his own poems aloud at times, or hands Dr. Paul manuscripts, which he recites in turn. At one point, a group of sailors (apparently on their way from the mountains to the sea) passes beneath the tower window for no reason other than to allow Dobell to insert a sea-ballad, which in turn moves Balder to poetic musings of his own. Amy sings to herself, her baby, and for her guests, and on at least two occasions Balder actually sits down at "a harp" and entertains, *scop*-style, changing meter four times, for seven and a half pages. In another scene Dobell divides the page into three columns and has Balder, Amy, and Gerald carry on a spontaneous harmony. Since these songs typically have nothing whatever to do, even symbolically, with the action, they slow the poem's pace and provoke the reader's annoyance.

5. "The Unstable Bubble of Inflated Thought"

Second, Dobell constructs his narrative around the continual parade of similes and metaphors, a technique which was by now regarded as the Spasmodic signature. Balder constantly interrupts his running commentary on events with the phrase "I am as one who..." or the like. These digressions, possibly attempts to echo Homeric similes that would please Classically trained critics like Clough and Arnold, occasionally become so elaborate that Dobell apparently forgets to insert a main verb and his syntax becomes unintelligible. At other times, he seems to lose track of what prompted his comparison and never returns to the point. These habits, not unjustly, earned him a reputation not for Homeric majesty but for incoherence.

One digression which particularly exemplifies the damaging effect of this diffuseness on *Balder* occurs just after Balder has (possibly) murdered his daughter. While it would seem that the guilty ruminations induced by such a heinous event would provide an opportunity for characterization, Dobell shies from exploiting the dramatic possibilities in favor of describing, in extravagant language, figurative situations only superficially similar. Although Balder's hypocrisy (or sociopathy) is exposed by his indifference, it is not dealt with in a complex or even an ironic manner. Like Balder himself, Dobell simply ignores it. Meditating on his child's funeral, Balder wonders where her soul has drifted "In this great universe" and reflects how

> We also went a little way with thee,
> As they whose best-beloved doth cross the seas
> Attend him to the shore—even to the brink
> Of the great deep, and stretch along the sands
> Wringing vain hands of sorrow; yet none saith
> "why goest thou?" nor with naked sword of love
> Denies; and none doth leap into his fate,
> Crying "I also," and with desperate clasp
> Hang on his neck till breakers far behind
> Forbid return. Spell-bound they stand and dry
> On the sea-line, and not a quivering lip
> Murmureth "To-morrow"; but his sire doth seize
> The prow that would recede, and with stern will
> Holds it, rebellious, to the task, and she
> Who bore him, with her tears and trembling hands
> Constrains and hastes him lest he lose the tide.[29]

Clearly, Balder's metaphoric equation is inadequate, to say the least. Bidding a sailor farewell at the sea-side is hardly comparable to burying one's child after having murdered her or at least contributing to her death through neglect. The sentimental posturing of the characters and the stilted language in Balder's vision gives the scene an artificial, uninvolving flavor, which in turn dissipates the dramatic potential of the framing event. As usual, Dobell proves himself reluctant (or unable) to exploit the possibilities of the situation and instead turns to melodrama for a reliable, but dissatisfying, escape. Balder soon goes on to create another bizarre image, this time of a sleep-walking woman who, caught up in a nightmare, carries her baby out into the snow and hurls the child over a precipice. Although this scenario is certainly closer to what has actually taken place, and does offer some insight into Balder's peculiarly guiltless turn of mind, it comes too late to prove effective, and its proximity to the original comparison renders it tasteless or even darkly ludicrous, better suited to an old-fashioned gothic tale like *The Monk* (or even the parody *Nightmare Abbey*).

Since it would be absurd to argue for the coherence of Dobell's long poems, one possible approach to his work might be, as the admirers of the more unwieldy *Festus* discovered, to sort through *Balder* and *The Roman*, extract a few successful passages, and then argue the poetic merit of those isolated examples. Many of Dobell's images are indeed striking and are sometimes beautifully depicted. Some attain a grace and immediacy that would not have shamed Rossetti, with whom Dobell shared a poetic interest in exploiting the visual.[30] Occasionally his verbal picture coheres arrestingly, as in

> Shall not sweet colors in the slanting sun
> Cross and recross, and floor the empty space
> with rainbows?

Unfortunately, even in the same scene he can slide abruptly into the ridiculous, as when Balder melodramatically turns from these "rainbows" to his floorboards, "in whose black oak / The straitened hamadryad lives and groans."[31] Dobell earnestly attempted to explore the metaphysical by challenging accepted extremes of language and metaphor, but he usually ended up with the merely incomprehensible or even the laughable. At one point Balder becomes so overwrought with contemplating Nature personified that when Amy walks across a field towards home, he exclaims, "That figure stealing down the linden-grove! / 'Tis Evening or she!"[32]

Needless to say, Dobell's penchant for the overwrought and ludicrous fueled Spasmodic pastiche, and *Balder*'s most preposterous lines have become virtually legendary. These include "Bring me the inflated

5. "The Unstable Bubble of Inflated Thought"

skin thou callest Life, / And I will turn the wind-bag inside out / And clothe me," the bizarre (and gothic) "I saw the grim and clanking skeleton / Of the dead dog, licked bare to the white bones, / Run as alive," and, of course, the line made famous by Jerome Buckley, in which Balder exclaims "ah!" no less than thirteen times in succession.[33] Given this tendency, it is not surprising that *Balder* occasionally reads like a Spasmodic parody itself. Not all the humor in *Balder*, though, is unintentional. Like Smith, Dobell included an element of self-satire, and although he handled the attempt inadequately, it represents a surprising touch of both wit and humility, qualities with which he is not often credited. In contrast to Amy's near-worship of her poet husband is set Dr. Paul's comic reaction to the manuscripts Balder compares to "the enchanted elements / On a magician's table" and forces upon him.[34] Looking at one of his host's nature poems, Paul snorts, "Nay, no more; one knows / This better out of doors" and finds himself growing "sleepy" at the tedium of the verse: "nay, nay, I must keep my eyes open." Upon completing a tour of Balder's study, where the manuscripts are arranged like exhibits in a museum, he sighs, "Wheugh! what a roomful; I'm not half-way round. / Courage, Paul!"[35] Interestingly, Paul's pronouncements upon reading these samples are similar to those often uttered by the poem's actual reader.

This irreverence provides a rare and unexpected interlude in the poem's otherwise oppressive atmosphere; still, Dr. Paul, while temporarily the advocate of reason, is also a buffoon who describes with warm nostalgia his own earlier career as a poet, when he walked bareheaded in the rain and shook his own fist at heaven while uttering frenzied cries.[36] There is something of the coward about Dr. Paul as well; when Balder's behavior grows more erratic and violent and leads him to threaten Paul's life, the doctor discreetly withdraws, leaving the unfortunate Amy to her fate. More importantly, from a structural standpoint these few lines poking fun at Balder's work are overshadowed by the continual introduction of Balder's longwinded epics. Like Dobell himself, Balder favors a pseudo-Homeric style, in which he portrays "Genius," "Tyranny," "Justice" and even a strange "battle" involving various personifications. In one section he appears to be imitating *Paradise Lost*, comparing himself and Amy to Adam and Eve and mouthing curiously Miltonic lines. As when he invites comparisons with Byron and Coleridge,[37] Balder and Dobell both seem the worse for the comparison.

Because of Dobell's peculiar methods, it is hard to say whether

The Spasmodic Poets

he composed these epics in order to help characterize Balder, or, as Smith is reported to have done while preparing *A Life Drama*, he simply inserted poems he had lying about. In any case, there is really no special voice in these digressive poems that is absent from Dobell's other works—except perhaps that Balder is more metaphysical and more pretentious than even Vittorio Santo in *The Roman*. And there can be little question that the overriding object of *Balder* is the indoctrination of an early Victorian populace eager for an aesthetic leader. Dobell, no less than Balder, aspired to that role. To a greater extreme than Festus, Gerald, and Walter, Balder is the ideal Romantic conception of the Poet, chosen by Nature herself[38] and thus inherently attuned to metaphysical subjects. In an often-cited passage, he describes his calling to poetry in quasi-religious terminology:

> in that hour
> Of young and unforgotten exstacy [*sic*]
> I put my question to the universe,
> And overheard the beech-trees murmured "Yes."
> Therefore I grew up calm like a young god,
> ....
> to pursue
> Amid the crowd a solitary way.[39]

So total is Balder's poetic absorption in Nature that he epitomizes the artist carried away by the pathetic fallacy and wonders, rather madly, if his own "will" dictates its motion or if it and his heart beat as one[40]; already a series of natural omens had advised him that he should begin work on his epic.[41] Balder's status also frustrates him, for Nature seems a mysterious hierarchy in which his own place is agonizingly undefined. Caught, again like Faust, between manhood and godhood, he feels truly welcome in neither.

> My pride
> Hath climbed till I can hardly see the earth
> Beneath me, and from that last possible height
> Looks up with fainting eyeballs to behold
> A heaven no whit nearer. Is there no help?[42]

One can only imagine the potential discomfort of feeling one's eyeballs "faint." Despite his "hunger" for total understanding, which "sucks Creation down, and o'er the void / Still gapes for more," he is forced to wonder, in a titillating metaphor reminiscent of Smith (and perhaps John Donne), how he fares proportionally:

5. "The Unstable Bubble of Inflated Thought"

> Am I but as a fly
> Touching the vestal beauties of a maid
> Unchidden; intimate but by how much inferior?[43]

Since he is determined to complete his epic, Balder fights this insecurity by constantly reminding himself of his favored status as a poet and his special communion with Nature. For this reason his most notable characteristic is his overbearing arrogance. Though "A youth / In years," he is convinced he "hold[s] the weft and woof of age," and the epic he "was born to do" will make him "the King of men."[44] Hand-in-hand with literary zeal goes startling aggression. Not only will Balder be a king, but a tyrant. In the poem's opening speech, he calls his manuscript "my club of war, my staff, my sceptre!"; a few pages later he admits that what he seeks through poetic influence is "Not Fame but Power," except perhaps Fame that will "spread the awe / Of Power among the common herd." He especially savors the potential for mass destruction that will be his:

> Not Fame but Power.
> Power like a god's and wielded as a god!
> I would have been the wind, and unbeheld
> Rase the tall roaring forest, not the flash
> That cannot move unseen; the influence
> Unnamed that finds a city and leaves a tomb....[45]

Balder's megalomania is especially apparent in his scenes with Amy. Clearly, Amy already worships him as if he were a deity, and exercising authority over her provides temporary relief from his cosmic frustration. Seeing her as one who exists in "eternal childhood" (and who is thus especially susceptible to the pull of mythology), he tells her how much more fortunate she is than he "who wrestling would join arms with gods!"[46] Amy, eager to please him, calls him her "dread lord ... / My teacher, friend, and father, all in one, / My poet!" Balder, temporarily soothed by her deference, offers to "do a miracle / To please thee."[47] And, like a heavenly "father," when Balder decides that her life has become a burden to his work, he determines to put an end to her just as he did their daughter. While critics are correct to point to Balder as a continuation of misanthropic Byronic heroes like Manfred (not to mention Heathcliff), Byron's heroes are usually given a single vulnerable point, most often the love of a particular woman. Balder's treatment of Amy, on the other hand, does not permit sympathy on even the barest domestic level, and Victorian audiences were not prepared to forgive infanticide, no matter how great Balder's spiritual reawakening in

The Spasmodic Poets

a future installment. It is little wonder that *Balder* provoked such a violent reaction against the Spasmodics and the entire concept of the contemporary *vates*.

Dobell's apparent lack of judgment in composing *Balder* has been a sore point among his would-be defenders since his own time; as Walker points out, Dobell did "more than any enemy could do to his own hurt"[48] by pursuing his eccentricities so unabashedly. Thale, who favored a Freudian approach to *Balder*, attempted to excuse the poem's erratic structure by suggesting that Dobell's style might have reflected the physical delirium he suffered during his many illnesses, rendering it (like many a gothic production of the eighteenth and early nineteenth century) a kind of fever dream on paper.[49] Alternately, he proposes that *Balder* is an anticipation of *Firmilian*, though in a serious, rather than a satirical, vein: in other words, Dobell was pushing the Spasmodic form, now recognizable but unnamed, to its limits as a kind of poetic commentary.[50] These two possibilities, while intriguing, are ultimately unconvincing. For one thing, they would appear to be mutually exclusive. If Dobell were suffering from an altered perception of reality, it is doubtful he would bother to satirize its artificiality. More importantly, Dobell's peculiar methods of composition must be recognized not as haphazard, but as the faithful rendition of his own poetic theory, preserved in his letters, lectures, and essays.

These documents reveal, not surprisingly, that Dobell wholeheartedly accepted F.D. Maurice and his followers' elevation of the Poet as superhumanly sensitive to the mystical side of existence. Balder confidently acknowledges his own transcendental qualities: though "Man" is his "living moving neighbour," that insipid creature merely represents his "former self."[51] To some extent, readers were not mistaken in attributing these sentiments to author and hero alike. Even Emily Jolly, who in her biography is wholly sympathetic to Dobell, had to admit that in his early life, while he was at work on his most Spasmodic poetry, "Power over the minds of other men was a thing he valued and desired," though mostly "for the sake of the good it would enable him to do."[52] Dobell adapted this concept to incorporate the religious preoccupations of his early life, and came to believe that the perfect and open mind of the poet rendered him, more than other men, a smaller-scale model of God.[53] When Balder asserts "I sat above my work / As God above the new unpeopled world,"[54] he is, notwithstanding the comments later made by Dr. Paul, expressing what Dobell perceived as the proper relationship between the poet and his creations. Again like God, the poet

5. "The Unstable Bubble of Inflated Thought"

(with that word's Classical connotation of "maker" very much intact) reenacts the creation of mankind each time he creates a literary character, since the poet is, in turn, injecting his own consciousness there and living, at least temporarily, within each of his creations.[55]

The written expressions of this godlike being were equally momentous, and Dobell believed the true aim of poetry must be the "elevation of statement into images."[56] For two reasons, then, he considered diffuseness in a poem not as a liability, but actually a boon. First, it allowed for a variety of metaphors, the purpose of poetry in Dobell's view, and second, it recreated Nature in God's own fashion, complex and varied, made up of the beautiful and the ugly alike. Life presents both to the human eye, Dobell felt, and the viewer, like the reader, must focus on what interests him at any given moment. He should investigate each section in turn for meaning, returning to the poem again and again as he might repeatedly examine his physical surroundings in life.

To the extent that *Balder* is intended to exemplify this idea, it is a resounding success. Dobell introduces enough different species of poems on enough different subjects (including a sea shanty, epic personifications, a medieval ballad in the Pre-Raphaelite mode, Amy's songs, and Thomson-like discourses on the seasons) to content readers with virtually any literary preference. What Dobell failed to take into account is the difficulty the reader must necessarily experience in trying to focus on so many detailed digressions patched so closely together without any underlying unity of theme or tone, as well as the dissatisfying effect of inadequate metaphors. Here, Dobell's practice does not exactly correspond to his theory, for he stressed that the poet's "equivalent," or the metaphor, "must truly and essentially correspond to the beautiful or sublime fact for which it stands" since it should preserve the proportional importance of what is represented. If these rules were not violated, he believed, poetic errors such as the pathetic fallacy should not occur. As far as the use of metaphor itself was concerned, *Balder*'s excessive reliance on comparison reflects Dobell's linguistic theory which held that language itself is a series of metaphors, or words standing for things. The poet's duty is to refine that process, and *"and the whole action of his mind in language is therefore to elevate it from the sign towards the metaphor."* The metaphor likewise stands for the characteristics of the poet, for his poem is *"the manifold metaphor of a human mind."*[57] Dobell also believed that one of the poet's primary responsibilities was to create order within his perceptions; the

115

The Spasmodic Poets

lack of any such organization and subordination of parts in *Balder* is conspicuous.

Though *Balder*'s flaws are certainly serious from an aesthetic standpoint, it was less the poem's diffuseness than its presumed moral ambivalence that Victorian audiences and critics found most repulsive. The character of Balder provided the basis for much of the reaction against the poem, and the centrality of so unappealing a figure fueled Aytoun's parody. Balder's identity as a poet—and a presumably Victorian poet at that—dictates the poem's action, and Dobell is more specific even than Byron in asserting that this "great office," rather than some vague Romantic *Weltschmerz*, not only alienates, but presumably absolves the hero from, the compassion required of ordinary (and modern) mortals. Though Balder, enjoying a quiet interlude with Amy, speaks of a plan that the two of them will "save the world,"[58] in the course of the poem we see him murdering his child, attacking his wife, and threatening to hurl Dr. Paul from the tower window, then justifying such cruelty as necessary to his art. To make matters worse, the poems Balder writes, and not infrequently reads aloud, consist largely of bombastic rhetoric and strained personifications which are wearisome to read and seem hardly worth the price of human lives. Even Mrs. Radcliffe, the Brontës, and Browning took the precaution of setting their most grotesque creations in the past and not in readers' contemporary milieu.

The reaction was immediate and severe. Though Dobell hastily prepared a disclaimer for the second edition of *Balder* in order to assert his personal morality, the poem's original audience and the reviewers had access only to the ideas expressed in the text, and they found the implications of those ideas appalling. Without the Preface in which the author disavowed any personal identification with the fictional poet, startled critics and readers alike assumed, on the basis of Balder's centrality in the work, that he was to be taken as an archetype for the neo–Romantic poet who now combined genius with a totalitarian (and psychopathic) strain quite at odds with the ideology of *The Roman*. It seems incredible that Dobell, who had already been cautioned about his tendency to bombast by reviewers of *The Roman*, should have introduced so unpleasant a character without apology, and loaded Balder's speeches with self-aggrandizing rhetoric which, to the Victorian mind at least, verged on the blasphemous. Even Dobell's high-minded choice of a name for his protagonist was unfortunate, as it prompted the obvious joke of adding a single syllable to form the word "balderdash."

5. "The Unstable Bubble of Inflated Thought"

Aytoun and *The New Monthly Magazine*,[59] and no doubt many others, availed themselves of this opportunity.

Though he expressed shock and pique at the public's rejection of his epic, perhaps Dobell had in some sense expected it. He had already exonerated himself from concern about extraneous judgments of his work by deciding that the ultimate test of poetic worth was not objective analysis but merely "whether the poet is moved by his own lines."[60] No doubt this belief helped soften the blow to the author's literary ambitions when *Balder* was received not as the voice of prophecy long overdue, but as an immoral and distasteful collection of ravings; even after the failure of *England in Time of War*, he continued to work on the second *Balder*, and presumably continued to do so until ill health prevented him.[61] His religious sensibilities suffered more acutely. For the first time, the erstwhile heir-apparent to an entire Christian sect was forced to affect overt modesty: when the editor of an American edition of *Poems* defended Dobell with a notice explicitly denying that he was either "a bigot" or "an enthusiast," but merely one for whom "the great object of his life is the introduction, in due season, of a new and nobler organization of Christianity," Dobell felt obligated to protest that "one may desire a reform, without the egotism of desiring to introduce it."[62] How sincere, or how painful, this forced humility was to this former prodigy can only be imagined.

Although Dobell's two subsequent volumes of short lyrics represented an obvious attempt at self-circumscription, they were failures which effectively finished his poetic career along with Alexander Smith's. *Balder* clung to Dobell; years later, even his friends called his home "the Balder-Tower," suggesting that he and his protagonist were still routinely conflated.[63] While the drollness of some of the criticism directed at his more pretentious lapses provokes laughter as surely as *Firmilian* does, the comedy is tinged with the bitter. The hopeful, ambitious young poet who wrote to his sister on the eve of his first fame that he was confident that "a kind of self-reverence—as to an impossible saintdom" was not improper, given the "wider mission and rougher excellence before" him[64] sadly contrasts with the embarrassed dilettante forced to report in April 1854 that "Alexander [Smith] and I seem fated to appear together. There is hardly a week now in which we are not either abused or praised side-by-side" and who cautioned, on behalf of a newly-published friend, that the coming review in Gilfillan's *Eclectic* should be carefully constructed: "the most brilliant essay may be useless to the book from the fact that it has nothing which can thus be made universal and permanent."[65] All that remained for him to do was again to veil his face in ostensible self-satisfaction and hope for posthumous vindication. In 1857, he wrote his father that

> I think the best course is to leave the matter to time. I have just sufficient position in literature now for time necessarily to do all that is desirable.... No one who, a few years hence, looks back to the poetical literature of the past seven years can avoid seeing my name and examining my books. And that examination being inevitable, I have no fear of the result. [I] ... feel perfectly satisfied in leaving [*Balder*] to the first great poetical critic who shall arise in this country.

Of course, the "great critic" who finally did emerge from Dobell's era turned out not to be a man of enlarged, Gilfillan-like sensibilities who attempted to rescue the Spasmodics from obscurity. Instead, it was Arnold himself, who arguably did more even than Aytoun to further immure and discredit them.

Dobell's rapid descent into a life of ignominy, ill health, and disappointment after *Balder* seemed to imitate Spasmodic art to a bathetic degree that might have amused Oscar Wilde. Still, Walter had eventually emerged from despair into national fame and personal enlightenment, magnificent conversions awaited Festus and Balder, and Gerald had escaped into the comfort of death and the promise of posthumous glory. Dobell continued on, like Bailey, the butt of critical jokes and the object of patronizing derision for years to come. When he wrote to the *Athenaeum* to defend Smith from "Z's" charges of plagiarism, for example, his letter was introduced with barely disguised condescension, and the phrases excerpted convey misguided delirium for a long-abandoned cause:

> Among others, we have received a letter from Mr. Sydney Dobell, author of *Balder*, who pleads warmly for his friend Mr. Smith, "whose proud integrity, strong sense and sound unglittering manliness are," he says, "as proverbial as his genius." Mr. Dobell seems to miss the point. The question raised by "Z" is not one of character, but of fact.... Does not Mr. Dobell assume the "genius" which appears to "Z" unproved, and forget the borrowing which *is* proved?[66]

It seems likely that the almost theatrical nature of Dobell's biographical misfortunes still account for most studies' tendency to follow the fortunes of the School to *Balder* and *Firmilian* and scarcely further. Neither of these poems, though, was the final Spasmodic production of the 1850s—leaving aside, for the moment, the vexed issue of Tennyson's *Maud*. In fact, the flowering of what might be called High

5. "The Unstable Bubble of Inflated Thought"

Spasmody, which was also the movement's swan song, occurs in a poem more mentioned than examined in discussions of the Spasmodic phenomenon. John Stanyan Bigg's *Night and the Soul*, which Jerome Thale calls "in some ways the most extravagant of the Spasmodic works"[67] was actually published at the height of Spasmodic controversy, and was released just after the publication of *Firmilian*. Thale's position is eminently defensible, especially since *Night and the Soul* can claim the dubious distinction of exhibiting the highest degree of Spasmodicism with arguably the least contamination by poetic worth.

Anyone familiar with Spasmodic technique can virtually predict the plot of *Night and the Soul*. Bigg's protagonist, Alexis, is a would-be poet who this time shares Shelley's ethereal concerns rather than Keats' sensuality or Byron's aggressiveness, and to further enhance the mysticism of the poem, Bigg employs the unique device of setting all of its scenes at night. Alexis and his closest friend, Ferdinand, spend much time debating with one another the pressing questions of existence, which Ferdinand summarizes at one point as

> The yet stubborn Why? and Wherefore? that are still
> Enscrolled in sunny-pictured hieroglyphs
> Upon the brow of Heaven, and which are stamped
> Upon the earth, and on the souls of man;
> The everlasting interrogatories
> Which all things frame unto the intellect;
> And the unfathomed, and unfathomable,
> And ever-during mysteries of God,—[68]

In the best Spasmodic tradition, Alexis struggles to master these enigmas, and embarks on a quest for both answers and poetic fame. Unfortunately, after repeatedly "plunging in the depths of being," and "tr[ying] in vain to clutch the burning stars," he finds himself so frustrated that he abandons Ferdinand and his betrothed, the devoted Flora, and sinks into a morass of insecurity and spiritual doubt, "disgusted both with [his] pursuits / And with [him]self."[69] As was the case for Walter and Gerald, however, Alexis's soul outlasts its crisis and he eventually returns both to his friends and to God. His art will now be harnessed to a more constructive Christian end.

The poem was announced with the kind of fanfare that had catapulted *Festus* and *A Life-Drama* to popularity. The last page of Bigg's volume was entirely devoted to excerpts from flattering reviews, and the familiar substance of these can also be easily anticipated. A line from *The Bucks Chronicle*, for example, asserts that *Night and the Soul* "at

The Spasmodic Poets

once places Stanyan Bigg in the front rank of English poets," while the *Church of England Quarterly Review*, obviously pleased with the poem's orthodox religious message, goes even further: "Deep in philosophy, splendid in diction, and at once gorgeous and delicate in imagery, it has few compeers.... We rank Stanyan Bigg as *the* poet, *par excellence*, of the rising generation" (emphasis in the original). More important is the almost obligatory, if oddly phrased, endorsement of Gilfillan, who is here identified as author of "The Bards of the Bible" (a work Bigg's publisher offered for sale in the same volume):

> Nowhere out of *Festus* do we find passages which heave and hurry along with a more genuine afflatus than in many of Mr. Bigg's pages. On the future career of such a one there can rest no shadows of uncertainty.

Likewise rescued from these ambiguous "shadows" is the idea that a demonstrable stylistic relationship exists between the poets Gilfillan mentions; Bigg is immediately posited as Bailey's successor, reminding us of Gilfillan's disappointment in *Balder* and suggesting that in Bigg he hoped to find a replacement for his discredited protégés Smith and Dobell.

The Dublin University Magazine also recognized *Night and the Soul* as the latest production of the School and accorded its appearance serious attention. Asserting that "this is no volume to skim lightly over," the reviewer places it in the genre of "'Faust' or 'Festus,' each of which it in part resembles" due to its "psychological and metaphysical" concerns. The biggest difference in Bigg's poem, the reviewer notes, though he might have said the same of *Balder* or *A Life-Drama*, is that here, all the protagonist's "temptations" are "from within; [they are] the trials of his intellect and not of his senses."[70] The Spasmodic protagonist has now, in essence, become both Faust and Mephistopheles, mortal and demon, with only his personal integrity to govern his actions. This represented a step toward the modern conception of the protagonist, not unlike Robert Browning's, however obscured it might be by mechanical deficiencies. The superstitious metaphysics of *Festus* had been left far behind.

Bigg's poem might best be called third generation (and certainly third rate) Spasmodism, a patchwork of ideas culled from Smith and Dobell, who had in turn culled the bulk of theirs from *Festus* and *Gerald*. In some ways, Bigg is less daring than Smith and Dobell; Alexis has moments of agnosticism, misanthropy, and reckless selfishness, but he never descends to the moral depths of forcing his sexual attentions on

5. "The Unstable Bubble of Inflated Thought"

Flora or attempting to murder Ferdinand in order to generate poetic inspiration. Yet the weight of Bigg's borrowing is ponderous. Many familiar-sounding passages may have been intended as homages to the earlier poems; we cannot help but think of *Festus*, for example, when Alexis describes his vision of the end of the world when "the universe [shall] dissolve like wax" and "all the veils of matter shall be rent," or when a group of "ministering spirits" convenes to discuss the preordained triumph of the soul their "evil" counterparts have been given "to torment, / and tempt, and try."[71] From *Gerald*, Bigg poaches a scene in which Alexis and Ferdinand are challenged by a pragmatist with an exasperating empirical frame of mind:

> FERDINAND. Now our friend Anthony would scorn us both;
> Thee for thy musings, and myself for mine.
> All things are made for use, he says; the sun
> Shineth by day to light him to his mill
> ....
> And the great sea rolls endlessly, and pants
> For nothing but earth's ships and argosies;
> And human souls are born into the world
> With all the trappings of eternity
> Still hanging loosely round them, for his use.
>
> ALEXIS. Heaven save me from
> Such moralists as these, who would convert
> Yon infinite expanse into a chart
> Of "ways and means," and turn the universe
> Into a great "Poor Richard's Almanack!"[72]

This passage also recalls Smith's debates between Walter and his anti–Romantic friend, Edward, and the likeness to *A Life-Drama* is reinforced by a scene set at a fashionable literary gathering where the guests take turns reciting. This addition has the benefit of allowing Bigg his own chance to insert some unrelated shorter lyrics. *Night and the Soul* even includes a scene in which Ferdinand and Flora discuss Alexis' despair just as Edward and Charles once did Walter's: Alexis, "Debarr'd of truth, leapt back upon the world / With energies intensified, and saw / Gigantic shapes of wrong upon its thrones,—" then finally "lost faith, lost heart, lost everything," while Walter, "mad and blind, / Threw off the world, God, unclasped pleading arms, / Rushed wild through Pleasure and through Devil-world, / Till he fell down exhausted."[73] Bigg is indebted to Bailey and Smith, too, for *Night and the Soul*'s portrayal of women. Caroline and Flora, like the many mistresses of Festus and Walter, rely on their lovers Ferdinand and Alexis for education in "singing" and astronomy, while the two men rely on them[74] for religious stability and guidance.

Bigg's debt to Dobell and *Balder* is somewhat less obvious, perhaps because Bigg's intent is closer to Smith's. Nevertheless, upon closer examination the influence of Dobell is easily detected. Alexis composes a poem which hails the "mighty soul" which "all men chorus" with the epithet "Poet-King!," a title he explicitly longs to assume himself[75]; Balder's beech-trees murmuring "Yes" to his declaring himself a poet is also echoed, albeit in reversed circumstances, as Alexis invokes the pathetic fallacy to explain his own difficulties in mastering Nature's complexities:

> And I have gone out in the winter's storms,
> And felt the winds all smite me in the face,
> And writhed beneath the buffetings of hail,
> And heard the creaking branches of the trees
> Groan out their "Shame!" upon me as I pass'd.
> And gone home, like a[n] idler, to his meal.[76]

Like Dobell, too, Bigg relies on metaphor and periphrasis to propel his poem's action forward. Describing a cluster of trees, for example, Alexis notes,

> How solemnly this graceful brotherhood
> Of giant trees stand in thick serried lines!
> Like a vast army after victory,
> Waiting the final orders of their king.[77]

Bigg's devotion to depicting the minute features of various landscape recalls Dobell's theoretical basis for poetic digressions into both metaphor and ostensibly inappropriate (or, one might add, unwittingly salacious) detail. Ferdinand explains:

> I love the lowly and the beautiful;—
> The peach, just rounding into ripeness, with
> Its first young blush just spreading o'er its cheek;
> The rain-drops handing on the sturdy arms
> Of wintry thorns, and bearing in their breasts
> A soulless purity, like little Undines....[78]

Like Dobell, Bigg justifies his attention to natural minutiae from his religious conviction that God's mysteries are imbedded in the complex arrangement of the natural elements. This probably accounted for his appeal to reviewers like Gilfillan and the reviewer for the *Church of England Quarterly Review*; it also inspired a curious passage, the

5. "The Unstable Bubble of Inflated Thought"

imagery and diction of which seems to prefigure Gerard Manley Hopkins' "God's Grandeur." Alexis describes Nature as

> The grand repository where he hides
> His mighty thoughts, to be dug out like diamonds;—
> Still is the day irradiate with His glory,
> Flowing in steady, sun-streaked, ocean-gush
> From his transcendent nature,—still at night
> O'er our horizon trail the sable robes
> Of the Eternal One, with all their rich
> Embroidery and blazonment of stars.[79]

Although Bigg certainly lacks Hopkins' technical control, the fleeting resemblance here suggested between the Spasmodic and the canonical cannot help but prompt awareness that the chasm between excess and transcendence need not be unnavigable. Even W.E. Aytoun, while composing his lampoon *Firmilian*, found that some of his hastily-composed passages yielded poetry of surprising quality and could only attribute it to the power of "reckless energy."[80] The *Dublin University Magazine* was painfully aware of this innate conflict in Spasmodic poetry when it commented that Bigg's was "a poem, undoubtedly, of remarkable vigour of thought, and abounding with passages of great poetical power. It has, however, great faults which detract from its merit." These were, not surprisingly, identified as a diffuse structure, bombast, and even occasional "rant."[81]

The internal decay evident in *Night and the Soul* suggests that even without the interference of Aytoun and Arnold, the collapse of the school was imminent. If *Balder* indulged in unintentional self-parody, the flagrant pastiche of *Night and the Soul* might well have eroded Spasmodic integrity to such a degree that, had it not been published almost simultaneously, the only possible successor would still have been the biting satire *Firmilian*. Yet it is impossible to know what might have occurred if Spasmodicism had not been abruptly choked off in its adolescence. Had neoclassical "touchstones" not become widely accepted and prevented the School from attracting newer, and possibly more gifted, adherents, perhaps Spasmodicism really could have reinvigorated Romantic ideals for England's post–Industrial generations. In any case, exclusion from the body of academically sanctioned poetry was inevitable once discussions of *Firmilian* entered the periodicals. Balanced assessments like the *Dublin* reviewer's would all too soon become virtually unknown to discussions concerning the Spasmodics.

6

"All High Poetry Is and Must Be Spasmodic"

The Anti-Spasmodic Reaction

Until the spring of 1854, *Festus*, *The Roman*, and *A Life-Drama* had enjoyed a mostly positive reception from the public and periodicals alike. Some reviewers advised the idealistic and ambitious young authors that certain refinements might improve their poetry, but they nonetheless lauded the innovation and emotional sincerity of all three. Then came *Balder*, awash in stylistic excess and pushing the boundaries of good taste with scenes of infanticide, spousal abuse, and at least attempted murder if not outright homicide. None of these plot devices was unheard of in British fiction, especially the penny dreadfuls, or even poems like Browning's "Porphyria's Lover." However, most authors dabbling in such lurid deeds had taken care to cloak their tales with a historical, foreign, or otherworldly gothic veil. Nor was there any suggestion that the perpetrator was to be regarded as a hero or deserving of admiration. Dobell, like his fellow Spasmodics, had deliberately made Balder a contemporary figure and given the other characters, like Amy and Dr. Paul, recognizably English names; though he intended to reform Balder (and presumably exonerate him of infanticide), he never completed the second part of the story intended to win back sympathy for his protagonist. This was apparently a step too far. Their goodwill stretched nearly to a breaking point, the same critics who had once admired Spasmodic innovation and tolerated its melodrama became restless and uncomfortable.

They began by mildly expressing their discontent with the increasingly extreme Romanticism of Smith, Dobell, and their satellites, but mostly with the intention of elucidating the trend's historical context. *Tait's* speculated that *Balder* was a reactionary gesture arising from the mid-century poetic doldrums, "a time when any new-fangled style is

6. "All High Poetry Is and Must Be Spasmodic"

likely to become 'fashionable'" and owing much to the "diseased softness of Keats." The review remains balanced, observing that although *Balder* provides an easy target, ridicule often stifles "excellence as [well as] mediocrity," and Dobell still possesses much excellence. In fact, the *Tait's* reviewer goes so far as to state that if Dobell would stick to Nature poetry and leave aside philosophy, "we venture to stake the critical reputation of this Magazine upon the prediction that he will prove one in any selection of ten great British poets." Elsewhere, Charles Kingsley compared Smith's wild metaphors and flights of fancy to Pope's plain, old-fashioned good sense, but decided that Smith was guilty only of following the "unmanly" models, like Shelley, then gaining new currency. Smith's lack of artistic discipline was cause for alarm only because it epitomized an age which tended towards chaos: "If the spirit be impatient of all moral rule," Kingsley decided,[1] "its utterance will be equally impatient of all artistic rule."

A few critics began to doubt that the advent of their age's ideal poet, once so eagerly awaited, was at hand after all. *The New Monthly Magazine* condemned the imprudent zeal of the Gilfillan camp, which had led the misguided Dobell into "the rude arena of publicity through a triumphal arch erected in his honour by certain critics of weight.... The Coming Man had long been looked for.... Now he was come. In the author of *The Roman* stood revealed the bard who was not only to grace, but to rule and form the age."[2] Everything afterward, the reviewer implies, has been a sore letdown for all concerned. It seems likely that a good deal of the hostility eventually directed against the Spasmodics resulted from disappointment and embarrassment over this very issue. Even Margaret Oliphant, a staunch Aytoun constituent and a contributor to the conservative *Blackwood's*, admitted in February 1856: "let us labour at it as we will, we cannot make a poet," and lamented that "we wait with equal weariness ... for the Coming Man, who knows neither school nor education ... [to] make the world ring once more with the involuntary outburst of song and youth."[3] The religious terminology used to anticipate the Poet of the Age had been deliberate, and the loss of this particular faith was as bitter and painful for the early Victorians as the spreading malaise of a more general cultural agnosticism.

The Eclectic Review, Hogg's Instructor, and a few other pro–Gilfillan publications remained supportive or impartial during the early stages of the critical reaction to the Spasmodic phenomenon. As late as October 1854, Gerald Massey employed the standard overblown jargon in an issue of *The Eclectic Review* to praise *Balder* as a poem "fitly sung by

The Spasmodic Poets

a company of fire-worshippers when the god of morning was stirring in them," and challenged anyone who disagreed as "not quite of comprehension."[4] Of course, his defensiveness is understandable given that he was a working-class poet who, like Smith, had managed to escape ten-hour workdays in a silk factory; he was for a time promoted by Gilfillan and occasionally classed as a Spasmodic on the basis of both that association and his 1850 volume of poems, rebelliously titled *Voices of Freedom and Lyrics of Love*. Not even this impassioned backing of the yet-unnamed Spasmodics, however, could neutralize a series of fierce blows dealt in quick succession by *Blackwood's Edinburgh Magazine*, then edited by W.E. Aytoun.

The name *Blackwood's* is almost as familiar to modern Victorian scholars as it was to its original readers. "Maga," as it was affectionately known, was a staple in many nineteenth-century households, including that of the Brontës, who admired and were clearly inspired by the gothic tales it frequently published. Maga's writers were also fiercely anti–Romantic and coined the term "Cockney School" to disparage Hunt and Keats. Its chief contributor was John Wilson, who wrote under the name "Christopher North," a well-known figure in his own right. Oxford-educated and fiercely conservative in both his political and literary attitudes, he was also the father-in-law of W.E. Aytoun. Wilson would die in April 1854, just as the Spasmodic controversy was getting underway, and it is tempting to wonder if Aytoun's energetic attack on the young poets was in part fueled by this painful upheaval in his personal life.

As if to challenge (or even taunt) its liberal competitors, *Blackwood's* had already made its anti–Gilfillan stance clear. The March 1854 issue carried two related articles. One was Aytoun's assessment of the relative merits of "The Two Arnolds," Matthew and Edwin (later Sir Edwin; though the two were not related, readers often confused one for the other). Matthew Arnold had just published his 1853 volume with its famous anti–Spasmodic Preface, as well as the conspicuous removal of "Empedocles on Etna," which Arnold felt was too Spasmodic in design and theme.[5] Edwin Arnold, who would in later years earn fame for his works on Indian literature (especially 1879's *The Light of Asia*) was, like Matthew and Aytoun, a Classically-educated scholar who authored another 1853 volume, *Poems Narrative and Lyrical*. "The Two Arnolds" made its chief contribution to the Spasmodic debate by introducing "Guffaw," a flagrant caricature of Gilfillan, and by elevating Matthew Arnold's attention to theme and structure above the Spasmodics'

6. "All High Poetry Is and Must Be Spasmodic"

tendency to "show you a hideous misshapen image, with diamonds for eyes, rubies stuck into the nostrils, and pearls inserted in place of teeth, and ask you to admire it!"[6] While discussing Edwin Arnold, Aytoun could not resist taking a shot at Bailey and Dobell, too: "Let [Edwin Arnold] go on ... eschewing gaudy ornament—and he may hope to win a name which shall be reverenced, when those of the utterers of fustian and balderdash, dear to the heart of Guffaw, are either wholly forgotten, or remembered only with ridicule."[7] "Fustian" and "balderdash" were, of course, Aytoun's pet names for *Festus* and *Balder.*

The review of Alexander Smith's *Poems*, which appeared in the same issue, has been identified by the *Wellesley Index* as the work of E.B. Hamley. Hamley's article is even more disparaging than Aytoun's, both toward Spasmodic technique and Gilfillan. With a patriarchal scowl, Hamley notes that, given the newly literate character of their age, the "demand for excellence in authorship exceeds the supply." Therefore he finds it little wonder that "an absurd monomaniac ... mistaking a dropsical disorder for the divine afflatus ... may, by mere force of impudent pretension, induce a host of ignorant followers to have faith in him." Such a person, he thinks, ought not only to be "exposed and ridiculed," but (rather shockingly) castigated with "the scourge ... till the blood comes."[8] This type of brutal punishment, he notes in a clear allusion to George Gilfillan, has proven effective in curbing his "heir George," who has been spoiled by his grandmother, "a rather silly old woman, much given in her youth to maudlin sentimentalism, and Werterism, and bad forms of Byronism."[9] Hamley depicts Smith as a child throwing a poetic tantrum, but hopes that "the undiscriminating applause he has met with in some quarters" will not prevent him from learning to "mature a worthy leading idea, waiting, watching, fostering it till it is full-grown and symmetrical in its growth"[10]; in short, from approaching his art in a more Arnoldian (both Matthew and Edwin-like) fashion.

The most memorable—and deadly—salvo had yet to be fired, but it was only a few months away and was probably already percolating in Aytoun's mind while he wrote "The Two Arnolds." *Firmilian: A "Spasmodic" Tragedy* appeared first as a mock review in the May 1854 *Blackwood's* (a month after the death of "Christopher North") and then in complete book form that same summer. Aytoun's timing was as well-honed as his wit, and he presented so precise and damning a parody that critics rushed to second Aytoun's condemnation of what was now considered a "School" of inept poet-philosophers given to ludicrous earnestness and hideous verbal excess. Aytoun chose the name

The Spasmodic Poets

of a third-century saint for his protagonist, perhaps to emphasize his character's distinctly un-saintlike behavior and petty, narcissistic personality. *Firmilian* was composed with painstaking detail, nearly every line and scene mimicking another found in a true Spasmodic production—so much so that some readers of the mock review mistook the excerpts for sections of a genuine poem and demanded to see the rest of it.[11] Henceforth, any work even remotely suggesting Spasmodic theory or technique was subjected to vicious critical ridicule, a trend that lasted for years to come.

Aytoun seems to have composed *Firmilian* not out of desire for acclaim as a parodist, which he had already won as co-author of the burlesque "Bon Gaultier's" *Book of Ballads*, but from a sense of moral and aesthetic exasperation. As Chair of Rhetoric and Belles Lettres at Edinburgh University, Aytoun took the writer's duty seriously, and delivered an enormously popular series of lectures on this topic every year from 1845 until 1865, long after the Spasmodics had been driven off the poetic stage. The notes to one such lecture advise that writing "is an art, and as such must be carefully studied"; he then warns students against imagining that they can support themselves by scribbling down their "fancies." Literature, Aytoun stressed, must not become a playground for hacks, but should remain the "higher object" of appreciation and "abstract literary criticism."[12] Unfortunately for these high standards, Aytoun felt, the Romantic influence on younger poets of the time encouraged Byronic melodrama at the expense of Classical unity of time, place, and tone. This was especially true in Spasmodic poetry, where settings switched abruptly from drawing-room soirees to Heaven or Hell, and crude humor alternated jarringly with lofty metaphysics. Tellingly, one of the "Spasmodic" character Firmilian's first actions is to revile Aristotle as a misguided buffoon. Alexander the Great, whom Firmilian sees as a Byronic figure ("The most impulsive and tumultuous sprite / That ever spurned old systems at the heel") rightfully considered his former philosopher-tutor "at twenty, an especial fool."[13]

The aplomb with which the Spasmodic hero flouted conventional morality and decorum also incensed Aytoun, who had long believed that ethical steadfastness was at least as desirable in a poet as technical virtuosity. Like Matthew Arnold, whose views he found congenial, Aytoun believed that both poets and critics should acknowledge the moral dimension of their profession and take seriously their obligation as instructors. Since their characters will be emulated by impressionable readers, poets must create protagonists whose actions

6. "All High Poetry Is and Must Be Spasmodic"

are above reproach and who are guided by a sense of social accountability rather than artistic egotism; in short, they should be as unlike Byronic heroes as possible. Critics must function as guardians of literary taste and expression, curbing radical and irresponsible tendencies in young poets and helping them to direct their talents to higher ends. The Spasmodic hero, to Aytoun's disgust, was usually rewarded, rather than reproved, for his excesses: Festus's promiscuity led God himself to arrange a reunion with his adoring harem in the afterlife, while Walter's egotism and premarital liaison with Violet (possibly amounting to assault) earn not punishment but national fame and her lasting love. *Balder* went further, ending on an ambiguous note that focused attention on the hero's macabre crimes rather than on their consequences.

Finally, and less admirably, Aytoun considered the rise of the working-class Spasmodics an affront to the proper hierarchies that maintained civilization as he knew and preferred it. There can be no doubt that his conservative values supported a clear division between Victorian social strata, especially when it came to university-educated men like himself, his father-in-law "Christopher North," and both Arnolds. His depiction of Alexander Smith as an oafish costermonger in *Firmilian* carried more than a touch of elitist snobbery that modern critics find more repellent than droll. Even less kind is his portrayal of the doddering critic who mistakes his grocery-sales pitch for poetry of the highest vatic order moments before he meets a grotesque end.

The original *Blackwood's* notice began with a mock announcement that the anonymous reviewer had recently "discovered," Gilfillan-style, a poetic drama by a new poet, T. Percy Jones, who may be "that long-expected phenomenon, the coming Poet" of no less than cosmic proportions.[14] The article printed supposed excerpts from the poem with a running commentary by this reviewer (easily identified, even in 1854, as Aytoun by those acquainted with his style). The reviewer maintained a condescending attitude towards Jones but nevertheless elevated his poem above "the tedious drivellings of some other writers of the same school" and supposed that "those who admire spasmodic throes and writings may possibly be inclined to exalt him to a very high pinnacle of fame; for certainly in no modern work of poetry ... have we found so many symptoms of unmistakable lunacy." This was the first use of the word "spasmodic" to identify this supposed school, and it stuck. Once Aytoun's hoax had become public knowledge, such far-reaching and pseudo-religious assertions would provoke laughter from worldly readers, but unfortunately his harsh tone was widely emulated by others

The Spasmodic Poets

eager to be noticed for their own supposed erudition. One particularly vicious (and unsigned) review of Dobell's *England in Time of War*, perhaps thinking of Browning's "Madhouse Cells" of 1842, as well as Aytoun's charge of "lunacy," declared that "out of a madhouse we never met with anything so painfully ludicrous as this" and berates "the idiotic incoherence of the whole."[15] The derivative nature of the sarcasm in this case renders it something less than impressive. Certainly it tells us less about the work being reviewed than about the bias of the reviewer.

The mock *Firmilian* review provided the basic critical vocabulary for every subsequent study of the Spasmodics. Not only did Aytoun introduce the term "Spasmodic" in reference to this particular poetic grouping, but he also produced the first inventory of "Spasmodic" characteristics. First is the supreme egotism and presumed universal importance of the poet-hero. For him, the pursuit of poetic fame dictates that "every social relation, every mundane tie, which can interfere with the bard's development, must be either disregarded or snapped asunder," as are even familial ties in *Balder*. Next is the formlessness of the dramatic structure (Aytoun admits that T.P. Jones may in fact be a little too coherent to prove a true Spasmodic) and unintelligible syntax interspersed with arcane and invented words. Both are intended to mask "poverty of thought" by "blazing away whole rounds of metaphor."[16] Firmilian, according to the review, does all that could be expected of a Spasmodic hero: he digresses for twelve pages on "the glacier theory" even though no other characters are present to hear him, commits several murders and sexual indiscretions for the sake of his art, and conducts himself as his poetic calling dictates, without the slightest attention to ordinary Victorian moral values or personal control.

Still, as annoyed as he was with Smith, Dobell, and their imitators, Aytoun reserved the greatest humiliation in *Firmilian* for Gilfillan. After all, he reasons, the recent "affectation and offensive swaggering of some who may indeed be rhymesters, but who never could be poets" any more than a tavern sign-painter could become a second Raphael, would never have been taken seriously if not for Gilfillan. It is particularly galling when one of these amateurs, relying "on the strength of a trashy duodecimo filled with unintelligible ravings," demands recognition as "a prophet and a teacher" in the language of his mentor.[17] Gilfillan's standards, Aytoun implies, must never be mistaken for those of a person with sense, even if, to his consternation "in the eyes of a considerable body of modern critics, extravagance is regarded as proof of extraordinary genius."[18] Accordingly, one of the review's excerpts details the

6. "All High Poetry Is and Must Be Spasmodic"

absurdities of "Apollodorus," a pompous and inept critic who wanders into the drama infamously wondering

> Why do men call me a presumptuous cur,
> A vaporing blockhead, and a turgid fool,
> A common nuisance, and a charlatan?

He goes on to detail his close relationships with some of the greatest literary minds of the age, most of whom have never heard of him. He also indulges in more than a little self-promotion, as he notes with pride. Aytoun may have been thinking of the defunct magazine *The Palladium*, which was referred to in print as a "mutual admiration society" for the Spasmodics, especially Gilfillan and Dobell:

> I have reviewed myself incessantly—
> Yea, made a contract with a kindred soul
> For mutual interchange of puffery.

Worse, having no real talent himself, he functions less as a critic or mentor than as a kind of literary parasite, choosing younger and more malleable talents as his host:

> I search for genius, having it myself,
> With keen and earnest longings. I survive
> To disentangle, from the imping wings
> Of our young poets, their crustaceous slough,
> I watch them, as the watcher on the brook
> Sees the young salmon wrestling from its egg,
> And revels in its future bright career.[19]

Apollodorus's reverie is interrupted by the market-song of Sancho, a crass vegetable peddler who offers to sell him leeks, onions, or radishes and may even be building up to some sexual innuendo with his conjoined reference to mammary glands and a voluptuous woman named Juanna:

> Down in the garden behind the wall,
> Merrily grows the bright-green leek;
> The old sow grunts as the acorns fall,
> The winds blow heavy, the little pigs squeak.
> One for the litter, and three for the teat.
> Hark to their music, Juanna my sweet![20]

This utterance the eager critic finds wonderfully free of "balanced artifice" and the "coarse conventionalities of rule." Moments later, in the drama's most outrageous (in every sense of the word) scene, the costermonger rebuffs him and Apollodorus forlornly turns skyward. As he begs the heavens for a poet to fall like a "meteor," he is immediately flattened by the poet Haverillo, whom the envious Firmilian has shoved from the top of a Balderesque tower.[21] Since "Apollodorus" was known to be one of Gilfillan's pseudonyms, and this name had also appeared as an imaginary title in the "Guffaw" section of "The Two Arnolds," readers would have had no difficulty identifying Aytoun's (and Haverillo's) target. Aytoun's design, in fact, was to position himself and Gilfillan at opposite critical poles, then leave discerning readers without any doubt as to whom they should trust.

The humor is a good deal less enjoyable, of course, when one considers that Aytoun's slapstick was intended to, and did, wound actual living writers, one of whom had escaped factory toil to become the Registrar of Aytoun's own university. Perhaps Aytoun had a sense of guilt about this after *Firmilian* made Smith the butt of many harsh jokes. This may explain why, although Gilfillan hastily disassociated himself from the Spasmodics once the critical tide had turned, Aytoun approached Alexander Smith after his poetic future had turned to mist and actually offered to secure him an income as a prose writer in *Blackwood's*.[22] Ironically, Aytoun's patronage succeeded where Gilfillan's had proved disastrous, and Smith was finally able to make a modest living as a prose writer.

Aytoun had originally intended to let *Firmilian* rest after the *Blackwood's* review had appeared; however, he found that he had underestimated the public's taste for Spasmody. Several publications, thinking *Firmilian* real, upbraided Aytoun for his harshness (perhaps deservedly) and called for the publication of the entire volume.[23] Deciding to startle the reading public into improving its intellectual standards, Aytoun soon obliged and again set to work, creating the book-length *Firmilian: Or, The Student of Badajoz, A Spasmodic Tragedy*. Less than two months later, a complete drama appeared in print. *Firmilian* was intended as what Weinstein calls "a plea for sanity" on several fronts: religious, artistic, and ethical.[24] Although the satirical intent of the original review was restricted to recent Spasmodic developments, the expanded version included jabs at Catholicism, Gothic fiction, Tennyson (Firmilian's mistresses are ethereal Lilian and Mariana, "The blooming mistress of the moated grange"), Keats' Endymion and Browning's Paracelsus (both of whom are compared to Firmilian). John Ruskin and Thomas Carlyle, whom Aytoun considered a prose Spasmodist, are also (literally) pilloried. At one point, as a character called "Teufelsdröckh" is burnt at the stake by the Inquisition, he delivers a

6. "All High Poetry Is and Must Be Spasmodic"

harangue to the crowd "denounc[ing] all systems, human and divine," though they cannot quite follow his "hideous jargon," and one horrified woman suffers a miscarriage.[25]

That Aytoun was not responding exclusively to Smith, Dobell, and Bailey, but rather to a cultural tendency the Spasmodics exemplified, is apparent in his comparable severity toward the Pre-Raphaelites (whom Aytoun predicted would disappear from critical discourse within three years) and John Ruskin. One month after the mock review of *Firmilian* had appeared, and while the book version was being prepared for the press, Aytoun reviewed Ruskin's *Lectures on Architecture and Painting* for *Blackwood's*. The harsh tone of the article, as well as his explicit comparison between Ruskin and the Spasmodics, reveals Aytoun's exasperation with what he perceived as yet another case of a critic abandoning all artistic sense and decorum. This review also explains the relationship of a seemingly digressive subplot to the whole of *Firmilian*.

Aytoun's review described Ruskin's emotive style as consisting of "a good deal of rubbish, and some unintelligible raving," much like Spasmodic poems. Aytoun was particularly offended by Ruskin's tirade against the architecture of Edinburgh: "Churches, public buildings, streets, private houses—all came within the sweep of his sweeping denunciation."[26] In *Firmilian*, a character known by Ruskin's erstwhile pen-name, "the Graduate," follows a priest through the streets, venting his disdain in the language of Ruskin's book. "Call them not churches, father—call them prisons," he rants. "Beneath the weight of that square-cut weary stone / A thousand workmen's souls are pent alive! / And therefore I declare them all accurs'd." When the priest questions his sanity, "the Graduate" responds, "Do I rave indeed? / So raved Prophets when they told the truth."[27] Aytoun's review impugned Ruskin for "proclaiming himself as an universal regenerator of architecture and painting throughout the universe": since "regeneration" was also a Spasmodic aim, and they too considered themselves prophets of the age, Aytoun sees an obvious correlation.

> [Ruskin] comes forward in the strong power of unproductive genius. If the weakest poet of the new Spasmodic School had, in the preface to his own effusions, declared his conviction that Homer was an ass, and Shakespeare an imposter, this much might be said for him, that he at least challenged comparison. Mr. Ruskin … has nothing whatever of his own to show.[28]

Aytoun here refers to the "new" Spasmodic school because he had himself created this designation only a month earlier in the mock

The Spasmodic Poets

Firmilian review. Presumably the term had already caught on, for he feels no need to mention Dobell, Smith, or Bailey by name. In any case, the "sweep" of Aytoun's own denunciation is here revealed, as he attempts to incorporate everything which, in his mind, had gone wrong with nineteenth-century thought and art. Though he seems to pay the Spasmodics a backhanded compliment in this passage, Aytoun really intended only to expose Ruskin's ludicrous airs. Far from supposing that no Spasmodic poet would really be foolish enough to make such lofty claims for his own art, Aytoun has "T. Percy Jones," the author of *Firmilian*, do exactly that.

The dramatic text of *Firmilian* by itself conveys only a portion of Aytoun's critical message. In order to appreciate all the nuances of the satire, one must consider not only the text of the play, but the Preface, no doubt inspired by Arnold's earnest but somber attempt in 1853, ostensibly written by the Spasmodic poet Jones. As might be expected, Aytoun uses it to attack the naïveté and deluded bravura of the typical Spasmodic poet. "T. Percy Jones" supposedly employs this self-justifying Preface to refute negative critical reactions both real and anticipated, much as Sydney Dobell had in the second edition of the maligned *Balder*. "Jones" is more than a pseudonym or a satirical device. He is as fully realized a character in the drama as Firmilian, and perhaps more so, since he is oddly believable in a way that Firmilian was never intended to be. It is little wonder that some readers assumed the work to be genuine.

As if to defend himself from the jibes of the *Blackwood's* review, Jones first denies, as did Bailey, any affiliation with the Spasmodics, or any other artistic school. He calls himself instead, like the Pre-Raphaelites, a student of "no living master" save "nature," which is patently ridiculous given the drama's melodramatic affectations. Jones invokes all the usual arguments of Spasmodic defenders like Gilfillan and, like Dobell, constructs bizarre theories and comparisons to recast his poetic faults as virtues. Dobell had contended that "poetry is ... the expression of a mind according to its own laws,"[29] and should not be rewritten to placate others, thus vindicating many Spasmodic eccentricities. Firmilian also denies that poets should practice self-criticism, since those who begin their volumes with apologies for their defects are merely being disingenuous. Otherwise, he asks, "how can they expect the public to show them any favor? ... For my part, if I consciously believed that my poetry was not worthy of admiration, I never would commit the impertinence of asking any one to read it." It is also Jones'

6. "All High Poetry Is and Must Be Spasmodic"

"firm opinion that all high poetry is and must be spasmodic"[30] since the contrasts between high and low stylistic devices give a work its artistic peaks. This was also Dobell's belief, but Jones goes further and maintains, as would Gerald Massey, that critics who dislike the unevenness in either Goethe's or his own work should look to the impairment in their own "high imaginative development" for an explanation.[31] Hamley's review of Smith had earlier addressed similar impudence on the part of a supposedly misunderstood young poet: "if an ardent spirit finds the world deaf to his utterances, let him search uncomplainingly for the fault in his own mind, and never rashly conclude that for his fondly believed-in powers of thought and expression there is, as yet, no sympathetic public."[32] In any case, says Jones, even the hostile critics are to be thanked for bringing his work to the public's attention. This was an unavoidable consequence, Aytoun must have wryly realized, of even the most high-minded criticism. Jones' pretentious conclusion resembles passages from Dobell's and Bailey's letters as well as Gilfillan's reviews:

> I am not arrogant enough to assert that this is the finest poem which the age has produced; but I shall feel very much obliged to any gentleman who can make me acquainted with a better.

The Preface announces that *Firmilian* will portray the dilemma of a character who possessed "Intellect without Principle," a decision he goes on to defend in some detail.[33] Here, Aytoun apparently anticipates charges that his venom against *Balder* was misdirected because he, like other hostile critics, did not understand Dobell's purpose. On the contrary, he makes it clear that although a poet and his creation are not necessarily interchangeable, even a Spasmodic must be held responsible for the ideas he presents to the public. Jones' drama focuses on Firmilian's effort to write an epic on Cain; in order to do this, he decides, just as Balder did, to commit murder in order to experience the appropriate sense of remorse. In his original *Blackwood's* review of *Firmilian*, Aytoun noted that this theme should shock no one, for "according to the doctrines of the spasmodic school of poetry, such investigations are not only permitted, but highly laudable."[34] Accordingly, Firmilian's search for a victim is based on entirely practical concerns, and he eventually slaughters half the city before deciding instead to begin the more pleasurable research for an epic on lust.

Firmilian's paradox is that the poet is determined to base his epic on the characteristics that determine one's humanity, namely guilt and remorse, yet "prepares" himself for this task by transgressing every

The Spasmodic Poets

reasonable bound of compassion. In addition to murdering three of his drinking-companions, his rival Haverillo, an entire congregation, and framing "the Graduate," he also impregnates Lilian and, Faust-like, drives her to infanticide. At this point, the *Ignes Fatui* cryptically sing

> Firmilian! Firmilian!
> What have you done to Lilian?
> There's a cry from the grotto, a sob by the stream,
> A woman's loud wailing, a little babe's scream!
> How fared it with Lilian,
> In the pavilion,
> Firmilian, Firmilian?[35]

These lines might also be interpreted to suggest that Lilian has flung herself into the stream along with the child, making Firmilian responsible for two deaths in one blow. Yet all that shames him is his own fleeting pity, which he regards as beneath his intellect and thus not conducive to writing poetry. His attitude is best encapsulated as he recalls an incident involving a blind beggar, an "insect-worm," whom he allowed to fall into a crater as punishment for "destroying a stupendous thought / Just bursting in my mind—a glorious bud / Of poesy, but blasted ere its bloom!"[36] Human contact is unimportant to Firmilian unless it aids the composition of his poetry, and he values, or even recognizes, no emotion which does not provoke a flash of inspiration with all the Byronic trimmings. He envisions "keen-beaked Remorse," for example, as a vulture which "With a shrill scream and flapping of its wings, / ... would settle on my soul." When such a bird does not appear, even after his multiple murders, he refuses to court it further. Aytoun's point is obvious: despite Firmilian's reliance on intense sensation to guide him, it is not necessary for him to "shudder, start, nor scream aloud," nor to "wring [his] fingers from the joints"[37] to experience empathy with other mortals. To the last, Firmilian considers himself god-like, in the manner of Balder, but he would conceivably make an even more malignant deity than Dobell's creation. Musing on his crimes, he asks himself whether, if he were able to undo his deeds and bring his victims back to life, "Would I exert the power?" He immediately decides, "Most surely not."[38]

Balder believed that Nature itself had chosen him as its spokesman and indicated its choice through the whispering beech-trees, and Firmilian's recollection of the moment he became a poet is not dissimilar in either style or substance:

6. "All High Poetry Is and Must Be Spasmodic"

> Then came the voice of universal Pan,
> The dread earth-whisper, booming in mine ear—
> "Rise up, Firmilian—rise in might!" it said;
> "Great youth, baptized to song! Be it thy task,
> Out of the jarring discords of the world,
> To recreate stupendous harmonies
> More grand in diapason than the roll
> Among the mountains of the thunder-psalm!
> Be thou no slave of passion. Let not love,
> Pity, remorse, nor any other thrill
> That sways the actions of ungifted men,
> Affect thy course. Live for thyself alone.
> Let appetite thy ready handmaid be,
> And pluck all fruitage from the tree of life,
> Be it forbidden or no."[39]

Again like Balder (and perhaps like Dobell himself), Firmilian sees himself as specially created to make the "astral brethren quake," but is particularly adamant that he is meant to live "not quite as other men; / My aims are higher, more resolved than theirs." For this reason they hate him and call him a libertine, and like Festus he feels no community with "Uninspired dullards, unpoetic slaves, / The rag, and tag, and bobtail of mankind."[40] The misanthropy fretted over by Gerald, confessed to by Festus, and proudly embraced by Balder here takes an extreme and malignant turn, for Firmilian is selfish to a monstrous, and murderous, degree. It is easy to see why, all humor aside, Aytoun and a good many other Victorian readers would have found this philosophy bone-chilling. Such casual sociopathy would become shockingly commonplace during the modern era, with Balder's (and Firmilian's) crimes against humanity hardly worthy of note when compared to those the world would witness over the next hundred years.

In contrast to the self-serving Firmilian, Aytoun presents his foil in Haverillo, a more conventional and more commercially successful poet. Like Dr. Paul in *Balder* or Edward in *A Life-Drama*, he espouses not only an anti–Spasmodic, but an anti–Romantic, creed. Haverillo is not fiery or passionate about any particular cause, but approaches his art with common sense and critical detachment. He does not consider Firmilian an enemy, and remains unaware that Firmilian seethes with resentment and anger towards him. More than anything, he echoes the disgruntled, but benign, tone of Aytoun's original review when he describes Firmilian as

The Spasmodic Poets

> wayward, doubtless,
> And very often unintelligible,
> But that is held to be a virtue now.
> Critics and poets both (save I, who cling
> To older canons) have discarded sense,
> And meaning's at a discount. Our young spirits,
> Who call themselves the masters of the age,
> Are either robed in philosophic mist,
> And, with an air of grand profundity,
> Talk metaphysics—which, sweet cousin, means
> Nothing but aimless jargon—or they come
> Before us in the broad bombastic vein,
> With spasms, and throes, and transcendental flights,
> And heap hyperbole on metaphor:
> Well! Heaven be with them, for they do small harm;
> And I would no more grudge them their career
> Than I would quarrel with a wanton horse
> That rolls, on Sundays, in a clover-field.[41]

One of *Firmilian*'s hidden messages is that Haverillo would do well to take seriously not only Firmilian's threat to the intellectual, but to the physical well-being of himself and his society. Mariana, one of Firmilian's mistresses, is Haverillo's cousin, and Firmilian eventually lures the well-meaning Haverillo to the top of a tower, as Balder did Dr. Paul, and hurls him to his death.

Firmilian is particularly effective in capturing the peculiarities of Spasmodic style. Aytoun opens his drama just as Smith and Dobell do, with the poet in his study expressing his frustrations with his own limitations, but with a touch of absurdity that makes it difficult to return seriously to Walter or Balder:

> Three hours of study—and what gain thereby?
> My brain is reeling to attach the sense
> Of what I read, as a drunk mariner
> Who, stumbling o'er the bulwark, makes a clutch
> At the wild incongruity of ropes,
> And topples into mud![42]

Aytoun delights in the abundant, and often inappropriate, periphrasis, not to mention the obscure diction favored by the Spasmodics, such as "ichor" for blood—a word that actually does occur in *Balder*.[43] Also employed are the frequent digressions during which the hero relates a tale unconnected to the plot, and the worshipful paeans bestowed upon the poet-hero by a coterie of adoring women. Aytoun is often cheerfully absurd. When Firmilian's necromancy can only raise a

6. "All High Poetry Is and Must Be Spasmodic"

hedgehog (inspiring a bystander to recall a comedic scene in Marlowe's *Doctor Faustus*, simultaneously referencing Bailey), the poet cries out in anguish that his "brain is whirling like a potter's wheel!" or when he and Mariana serenade each other with banal Smithean metaphors perhaps recalling the Orientalist section of *A Life-Drama*:

> MARIANA. O my beautiful!
> My seraph love—my panther of the wild—
> My moon-eyed leopard—my voluptuous lord!
> O, I am sunk within a sea of bliss,
> And find no soundings!
>
> FIRMILIAN. Shall I answer back?
> As the great Earth lies silent all the night,
> And looks with hungry longing on the stars,
> Whilst its huge heart beats on its granite ribs
> With measured pulsings of delirious joy—
> So look I, Mariana, on thine eyes![44]

Aytoun captured the emotive excess of his models, but showed himself more subtle than the real Spasmodics by revealing the duplicitous potential of these techniques. While they may only camouflage the ignorance and empty thoughts of the author, they also promote the abandonment of Christian ethics in the name of art. Firmilian's imagining himself "roll[ing]… / On the fresh carpet of the unsown flowers" only mistakes foolishness for poetic sensibility, but his use of an elaborate floral metaphor to trick Mariana into participating in an orgy with him and his two other mistresses is actually sinister. "[T]here's a moral in't," he assures her regarding his arrangement of the flowers, but it is clearly not one Aytoun intended his audience to condone. Mariana's response, as a squirming Firmilian hastily attempts to reassure her of his mission's profundity, seems entirely justified: "You nasty thing!" she reviles him, "Is this your poetry—/ Your high soul-scheming and philosophy?"[45] Significantly, Firmilian experiences an actual "spasm," supposedly prompted by his "better genius," at the moment of his most dramatic murder, when he uses explosives to terminate the Cathedral service.[46] Spasmody, Aytoun implies, is a euphemism for anarchy.

Ultimately, even Aytoun the parodist could not bear to leave so repulsive a hero unpunished at the end of his tale. In allegorical fashion, the Classical *Ignes Fatui* appear just ahead of the Inquisition to run the Romantic Firmilian into the same crater that claimed the blind beggar. They catalogue his sins in a song (although they do acknowledge that "One good deed he has done in his days; / Chaunt it, and sing it, and tell it in chorus—/ He has flattened the coxcomb of Apollodorus!"), and finally proclaim what could serve as an epitaph for the entire Spasmodic movement: "There's a pit before, and a pit behind, / And the seeing man walks in the path of the blind!"[47] By the time Firmilian plunges to his deservedly violent end, Aytoun no doubt expected his readers finally to appreciate the original review's plea:

> Seriously, it is full time that the prurient and indecent tone which has liberally manifested itself in the writings of the young spasmodic poets should be checked. It is so far from occasional, that it has become a main feature of their school; and in one production of the kind [*Festus*], most shamefully bepuffed, the hero was represented as carrying on an intrigue with the kept-mistress of Lucifer! If we do not comment upon more recent instances of marked impurity, it is because we hope the offense will not be repeated.[48]

Firmilian, which was widely circulated, did indeed prove more effective than Aytoun's insular *Blackwood's* assaults. Within a few months he had the satisfaction of seeing his views upheld after a storm of debate about the Spasmodics and the direction of modern poetry. Nearly every British periodical, it appeared, had an opinion on the relative merits of the Spasmodics, and most were resoundingly negative.

Some cautious reviewers focused their comments on the text of *Firmilian*, referring to the Spasmodic school only tangentially. As might be expected, the organ in which Gilfillan's "Apollodorus" pen name frequently appeared failed to see the humor in "Fermilian's" [sic] excesses. *The Eclectic Review* groused, "the afterthoughts are saddening, like those of the reveller's next morning." This critic compared Aytoun to Gifford, who had savaged Keats, and again lamented early Victorian literature's lack of "lofty religious earnestness."[49] *The Dublin University Magazine* found the entire production laughable, though not in the way Aytoun hoped, noting T. Percy Jones's arrogance in believing that "by the spasmodic energy of his genius he can ... 'pile the agony' to any height ever attained by mortal inspiration." Although the reviewer suspected a hoax, he took the precaution of declaring that he nonetheless considered *Firmilian* "to border upon the profane and vulgar,"[50] especially given the protagonist's professed hatred of schoolmasters and instruction.

More curious is the review in *Tait's*, the magazine that in January of 1854 had dubiously rejected Matthew Arnold's insistence on "finding an excellent action as the basis of a poem," since "against such a law the greatest objection to be urged is, that it would condemn half the poetic faculty in the world to silence."[51] Two months after the appearance of

6. "All High Poetry Is and Must Be Spasmodic"

Firmilian, the *Tait's* reviewer attempted to imitate Aytoun's sardonic tone, but added considerable bitterness. Recently, he notes, "a certain poet [Bailey] … became stellatic, and bit several young men while in that state: by which the disease has become propogated" using sentimental women and youthful readers as carriers. Now the rabid Spasmodics "dare talk of life and love as quivering sense, of Nature as their concubine, and God as their familiar." Of "Jones," whom the reviewer treats as a genuine member of this company, he can only grudgingly admit that "the Infinite hath taught him all its oaths.… With the ripe Strength of Genuis he hath rent the bowels of Inspiration, and hath ta'en its mighty heart for dinner … but prythee, Percy, be more blasphemous!"[52]

Other reviewers, especially after "Jones" was unmasked, hurried to condemn the Spasmodic phenomenon. *The Spectator* wryly observed that Dobell belonged to "the class of poets who seem to think that not to write prose is certainly to write poetry," while *Chambers' Journal* sadly noted that "the poets of the rising generation are going sadly astray … we have little else save mist and moonshine" which fail to address "the heart of ordinary humanity."[53] J.S. Bigg's *Night and the Soul*, previously little noticed, was pilloried for its resemblance to other Spasmodic productions: *The Athenaeum* ridiculed Bigg as "all spurt, and fizz, and crack, and blaze.… He is far gone in poetical epilepsy … it is on the stars, already sufficiently treated by Mr. Bailey and mal-treated by Mr. Smith, that Mr. Bigg plays the wildest of his fantasies."[54] The reviewer goes on to note sourly that it is "the peculiarity of this race of poets that they are always calling themselves shrivelled weeds on the world's wheels, and are for ever holding coroner's inquests on themselves.… How long are we to hear men raving of 'clasping the infinity' whose minds cannot embrace the first elements of logic?" *The New Quarterly Review*, which became increasingly savage towards Dobell in particular, concurred that any educated man could write verse, but not necessarily poetry; *Balder* represents "an egregious example of that daring style of modern poetry which consists in putting words together pell-mell, and trusting to the reader to give them a meaning … no obscure or mystic poet ever did or ever will live beyond his own age." By 1858, the same publication used Arnold's *Merope*, deliberately composed as an antidote to Spasmodic poetic dramas by using a Greek model, to stress the importance of "Idea, Plan, and Execution," all of which are conspicuously absent from the works of "the 'spasmodic' school, [which is] chiefly remarkable for excelling in the ornaments of poetry.… We lose sight of the principal idea in the multitude and richness of its decorations."[55]

The Spasmodic Poets

As this article, with its revealing title "The Anti-Spasmodic School of Poetry" demonstrates, Matthew Arnold's strictures regarding the appropriate relationship between form and content were increasingly invoked as standards against which the Spasmodics were found to be hopelessly incompetent. Gilfillan, likewise, became a critical example to be avoided at all costs, if not actually ridiculed.[56] In October 1854, *The North American Review* examined an edition of Edward Young's eighteenth-century *Night Thoughts* edited by Gilfillan. The reviewer makes clear his attitude not only towards Young's work, but towards Gilfillan's critical qualifications:

> Mr. Nichol of Edinburgh [the publisher] was by no means fortunate ... when he selected this gentleman to preface every volume with 'a critical dissertation.' He is well known as ... a sort of literary conjurer in the sober walks of criticism, who never appears without a blaze of fireworks about his head. He carries what is called fine writing to an excess which quite outdistances the usual range of sophomoric effort in that direction.... His metaphors are entirely out of proportion with the necessities and fitnesses of his subjects.... We see the prettiness, and admire the sparkle, but think the display too extensive to be real.[57]

Although Gilfillan ineffectually denounced Aytoun, he soon lost his literary credibility. Though he continued to write biographies and prefaces for other poets like Burns and Thomas Percy, he abandoned his campaign to discover and promote the Poet of the Age. Soon he was forgotten along with the young poets he had once championed so ardently.

Aytoun's victory, and the eruption of the Spasmodic controversy itself, should not be underestimated as a hub in literary criticism and practice. Although the neo–Romantic camp had seemed for a time victorious, the anti–Romantic strain quickly took precedence and within three years established its tenets as the only logical and responsible direction for aspiring Victorian poets. While many agreed that the Spasmodics' missteps might not have been entirely of their own doing, no one came forward to suggest that they might actually have laid the foundations for a new, freer poetry which might mature along the same emotive lines and that of Shelley or Keats. Instead, reviewers were unanimous in suggesting that young poets given to Spasmody would do well to rethink their techniques and, in essence, begin again. "J.W.'s" letter to *The Athenaeum*, quoted above, is typical: "Mr. Smith ... must learn to renounce his love for 'spasm' and mere idle image-making" and learn "that true passion is not violence of language" but is better expressed through decorous restraint.

6. "All High Poetry Is and Must Be Spasmodic"

Even occasional dissenters from the critical onslaught were only moderate in their defense. *The British Quarterly Review*'s *Balder* article of January 1855, for example, reiterated that Dobell's intended, but often misunderstood, theme was "genius without faith," and admired the psychological insight evinced in the depiction of Balder's madness as a subtler touch than any found in *The Roman*. Yet even this reviewer could not refrain from the pessimistic concession that "in our day, there is a morbid craving for intellectual gifts, as though they were the highest," and admitted that modern art tended "to subordinate the higher moral ambition to the lower aesthetic one."[58]

The effect of these new strictures on the bewildered Smith and Dobell was profound. At first, Dobell was inclined to see the humor in what he described as "a happy burlesque of Alexander and me."[59] He may have even felt a touch of flattery in serving as the inspiration for such a lively and undeniably entertaining pastiche. Later, when things began to spiral out of control, to his credit Dobell continued to conduct himself with dignity in literary circles. One curious anecdote in a letter to his parents, however, suggests that he viewed himself as a wronged Byronic hero and had to struggle to keep his angry resentment in check. Meeting Aytoun on the road, Dobell attempted to clear up a misunderstanding involving an anonymous attack on Aytoun, and informed him that "'if I should ever find it my duty to attack you, it will be in an open field and with the weapons of a gentleman' [and thus I] made him distinctly aware ... that I might, if necessary, use other modes of warfare." Apparently Aytoun responded to this strange address by looking dumbfounded. Later that evening, the two ended up seated side by side at a Thackeray lecture, which Dobell confessed was an "odd conjunction."[60] Rather than attempting to defend Spasmodic technique in the press, Dobell and Smith began new works in which they struggled against their own Spasmodic instincts by paying more attention to characterization and form.

It is no accident that their joint volume of 1855 consists entirely of tightly structured sonnets depicting conventional Crimean War scenarios; to their mortification, *Sonnets on the War* was immediately treated as yet another ridiculous Spasmodic production. *Blackwood's* cheerfully added fuel to the conflagration, ridiculing the entire book as unintelligible rant. Aytoun's "Poetry of the War," published in *Blackwood's* in 1855, singles out one admittedly unfortunate line, "A whirlwind whirled across the whirling land," and notes that "after this we closed our eyes for a minute or two, under the impression that the centrifugal force had suddenly got it all its own way, and we had gone blundering off into space among the planets"; of another sonnet, he declares "If Mr. Smith wrote this, we should say he never wrote anything approaching nearer to rant; if it was the other gentleman, we would say to him, in the words of Cedric the Saxon, 'Down, Balder, down! I am not in the humour for foolery!'"[61] Other magazines praised the volume only insofar as it differed from the two authors' earlier productions. Sales were disappointing and the critical drubbing must have been even more so for the two ambitious authors.

Dobell quickly released a similar volume made up only of his own sonnets, *England in Time of War*, only to have the *National Review* declare "we must confess we have little patience with the whole school of which Mr. Dobell is one of the most prominent members" and denounce the very "Raggedness, want of finish, and exaggeration,"[62] he had studiously attempted to avoid. Smith released two more collections of poetry, *City Poems* and *Edwin of Deira*, which were also intended to be as unlike *A Life-Drama* as possible. *Edwin* utilizes historical Scottish subject-matter in a highly serious, almost Arnoldian, fashion; *City Poems*, which contains the excellent and much-anthologized "Glasgow," was immediately denounced by *The Athenaeum* as plagiarism, and "Z" provided his readers with several columns of examples of other poets' works "so turned, and padded, and tagged to breadths of homespun inanity, that we scarcely know whether to be amazed at the impudence or to pity the poverty which makes such an attempt to cover its own nakedness."[63] Unable to counter the increasing vehemence of these attacks, Smith and Dobell withdrew from the poetic arena entirely. J.S. Bigg brought out one more book of poetry in 1862 before turning, like Smith, to prose, and Bailey contented himself with revising and expanding *Festus* for the remainder of his long life.

Since identifiably Spasmodic writings were no longer current after 1854, critics and periodical reviewers quickly returned to their original course and attempted to place the phenomenon into historical perspective. In 1857, while reviewing Smith's new work *City Poems*, *The Athenaeum* described the movement which had produced it as the "strange poetical propaganda" of the "Apollodorus poets," who were "by birth flighty, by education ungrammatical, by transmutation poets.... They saw strange visions and dreamt impossible similitudes."[64] Other articles were perceptive enough, even without the benefit of several years' hindsight, to recognize Spasmody as a transitional phase connecting the imaginative excess of Romanticism and

6. "All High Poetry Is and Must Be Spasmodic"

the Byron craze with the more restrained lyricism of Tennyson and his imitators.

One of the first, Margaret Oliphant's *Blackwood's* essay of February 1856, signaled the demise of the Romantic view of the divinely sanctioned poet. She ridiculed the vision of this "separated creature, garlanded and crowned for the sacrifice" whose "smallest actions are noteworthy ... his very bread and cheese symbolical" and instead underscored the successful poet's need for professionalism and objectivity. Greater poets in earlier eras, she asserts, eschewed personal aggrandizement and thus produced poetry which was lasting and meaningful; the reading population has "that great poetic rebel, Wordsworth" to thank for the more recent idea that "the poet in these days is to be regarded as a delicate monster, a creature who lives not life but poetry, a being withdrawn out of the common existence, and seeing events only in the magic mirror of its own consciousness." She credits this idea with producing neo–Romantics like Dobell who propagate self-serving rant, metaphorical acrobatics, and loathsome poet-heroes like Balder. Now, "when we hear a man declaring his sublime superiority, we are puzzled, and pause, and smile, and try to make it out a burlesque or an irony," in the wake of *Firmilian*.[65] Anticipating a famous Dorothy Parker quip, Oliphant says Balder's egotism provoked her to the extent that she was ready to hurl Dobell's book out the window Haverillo-style.

Gerald Massey's more comprehensive article in *The North British Review* exactly two years later concurred that the Spasmodics had grown from a Wordsworthian edict, namely that the poet be "a man speaking to men," but asserted that they had fallen short of producing great poetry because they had forgotten the related requirement that the artist interpret the "realities" around him rather than manufacture false beauty from personal idiosyncrasies. The reviewer further identifies much that is "Spasmodic" in Byron and Keats.[66] Both this piece and Oliphant's agree that Tennyson represents a stronger model for a singer in an increasingly bewildering age, who must approach a myriad of questions regarding man's place and goals with steadying dignity and inspiring piety.

It is now routine to identify these conscientious and decorous qualities as Victorian, and to recognize their opposition to the individual expressiveness that the Spasmodics, like the Romantics, valued in life and poetry. If one now agrees automatically that Spasmodic verses "do little more than incessantly contradict the right definition of poetry," as Coventry Patmore, best known as the author of the cloyingly sentimental and astonishingly patriarchal "Angel in the House," put it in 1856,[67] it is really because this definition had changed so drastically between the publication of *Festus* and *Firmilian*. The idea that there could be only one "right" poetry, as far as the needs of Victorian society were concerned, is itself a product of this particular debate. In *A Look Round Literature*, Robert Buchanan demonstrates the extent of the change which took place by fervently defending his friend Dobell and the other Spasmodics with a warning that

> those who underrate that school know little what real poetry is. It was a chaos, granted; but a chaos capable, under certain conditions, of being shaped into such creations as would put to shame many makers of our modern verse. As it is, we may discover in the writings of Sydney Dobell and his circle solid lumps of pure poetic ore, a quality scarcely discoverable in modern literature this side of the Elizabethan period.[68]

If Buchanan's plea sounds like the prattle of a crank today, it is because another result of the Spasmodic catastrophe was the appropriation of authority by a particular critical strain which deemed itself qualified to construct the "right definition." Sentimental adulation was steadily replaced by supposedly objective analysis, such as Arnold's "touchstones," as the appropriate content for critical evaluation. Woolford points out that articles like Oliphant's, which presents the Spasmodics as little boys, where "Mr. Dobell is the sulky boy" and "Mr. Smith the younger brother, desperately bent on being even with the firstborn" (to say nothing of those advocating that the poets be whipped like naughty children), had the simultaneous effect of "shrink[ing] serious points into a squeaking chorus of juveniles" while elevating the critic in comparison.[69] The paternal role of the critic, proposed by Matthew Arnold and endorsed by Aytoun and his colleagues Hamley and Oliphant, among many others, was increasingly taken for granted in the Victorian periodical press. Like the Classically dominated English canon these same attitudes helped shape, this representation of the gravely serious, moralistic and uncompromisingly masculine critic would go on, at least for a few decades, to become a twentieth-century commonplace.

7

"A Cloud of Poisonous Flies"
After the Spasmodics

In 1856, a year after Smith and Dobell's joint *Sonnets on the War*, publishers Parker and Son brought out a modest volume titled *Pinocchi* (illustrated on the title page with pine-cones) by an anonymous author since identified as Thomas Brinsley Norton, Lord Grantley. In most of the poems, the average length of which was four or five pages, the author reflects upon various Italian landscapes, abstract topics, and melodramatic characters such as "A Dying Atheist" or "The Neglected Poet." All are unmistakably Romantic in tone and intent, with a distinctly Keatsian flavor reinforced by the frequent use of medieval spellings and antiquated words and syntax. A fairly typical example of *Pinocchi*'s contents is a selection called "Capri (Midsummer)":

> E'en now I see the plain-like deep,
> Where couchant as a stately pard,
> With gules and yellow quaintly barred,
> You're stretched in softly-gleaming sleep.
>
> From molten depths of azure steel,
> They rise, praerupt and devious heights,
> With zigzag shadows, zigzag lights,
> Grots that with crannied echoes peal....[1]

At times, *Pinocchi*'s author strays into the Gothic mode, encountering a few lamenting Roman ghosts and detailing with peculiar relish the imagined scenario of the emperor Tiberius shoving his enemies off a notorious cliff into the sea:

> Oh me! To think how thick they spun,
> The mangled bodies eddying fast
> That into daggered depths were cast—
> Rocks daubed and fleshed steamed in the sun.[2]

The Spasmodic Poets

A similar luridness informs even his more introspective attempts, as when the dying atheist is compared to a "wheel-crushed" dog "whose head the heavy tire has mashed." While such descriptions may not strike one as particularly tasteful or intellectually illuminating, they may be understood as the excesses of an amateur, hinting perhaps of Decadent works, such as Baudelaire's *Fleurs du Mal* and Wilde's *Salome* yet to come in 1857 and 1893, respectively. Moreover, the work was apparently not widely read and would by now have been forgotten if not for its mention in John Woolford's article in Shattock's anthology. Tellingly, Woolford mistakenly calls the author of *Pinocchi* "one Percy Jones"[3] (even though this name appears nowhere in the volume) and uses an excerpt from a scalding review to demonstrate the savage criticism of the 1850s, which was prone to lump authors together for derision and express paranoid outrage at the mere suggestion that any "new school" of poetry may be forming. Lord Grantley was briefly associated with the Pre-Raphaelites,[4] but unfortunately for *Pinocchi*, a number of reviews pilloried its creator as a member of the Spasmodic School.

One such review appeared in *Fraser's* in 1856, two years after the *Firmilian* debacle. The reviewer begins by speculating on the advantages anonymity might afford a poet, particularly if that poet has already gained a reputation through previous publications and wishes to attempt a new style of expression. Since anonymity was hardly unusual at the time, and in fact was almost always the practice of the periodicals themselves, this discussion seems oddly superfluous. It is tempting to speculate whether the reviewer suspected that *Pinocchi* had been written by one of the better-known Spasmodics who feared a biased reception for his new work (as had happened with both Smith and Dobell's Crimean War volumes), or perhaps that a known author was attempting a Spasmodic revival and wished to protect his reputation until the critical verdict was in. Whatever the case, the reviewer attributes to the unknown author many Spasmodic characteristics: one cannot help but think of Smith when the reviewer asserts that the *Pinocchi* poet "is young, impassioned, and exercised in premature misfortunes," and is also Byronic in that he "labours, in a morbid spirit, under the wrongs and neglects which may perhaps be delusive."[5] The reviewer was correct in guessing at Lord Grantley's youth, though at 25 he was slightly older than Alexander Smith had been at the time of Gilfillan's most energetic promotion. Unlike Smith, however, he hailed from an aristocratic as well as a literary family. His great-grandfather was the Restoration playwright Richard Brinsley Sheridan,[6] and his mother, Caroline

7. "A Cloud of Poisonous Flies"

Elizabeth Norton, was a published novelist nicknamed "the Byron of poetesses."[7]

The review also questions whether the poet actually visited the exotic landscapes of which he writes. He suggests that doubts arose because the descriptions in the book seem idiosyncratic rather than natural, a charge often levelled against Smith, whose working-class origins precluded him from attempting other than purely imaginative descriptions. These, too, are criticized for Spasmodic excesses such as "incoherent ornaments and imagery" and abrupt switches in tone: from "soaring flights [the poet] is apt to descend to a grovelling minuteness." Although the reviewer does not specifically mention Bailey or Dobell, also notorious for both tendencies, he does concede that "dangerous models" followed "in an undiscriminating spirit" are largely to blame for *Pinocchi*'s failures.

The review most resembles those written about the Spasmodics in that it cautions the "mystic" poet to avoid a "recondite and affected manner" and "forswear all conceits and rarities" in composition. It also assumes a tone of resigned disappointment that "we are not very hopeful that these friendly words are addressed to a patient ear.... The cruel skill of a Gifford and a Jeffrey would be wasted on the insensibility, and defeated by the arrogance of the rising generation in rhyme [who] now smile upon their impotent reviewers" and continue blithely in the same vein as before.[8] In this observation, the reviewer could only have been thinking of the Spasmodics, who had become known (the poets perhaps being unfairly conflated with their protagonists) for their supposed indifference to criticism and their air of superiority towards those lesser mortals who had not been born poets. With these words, the *Fraser's* review helps chart the waning of the Spasmodic School. Clearly, this critic's conception of a group of "impotent reviewers" protesting poetic excess without effect suggests that *Firmilian* did not instantly extinguish Spasmody's influence, as has been generally assumed. Rather, it was still an active force in literature in 1856, two years after Aytoun's parody appeared, and might have been capable, as *Fraser's* supposes, of seducing a better-known author into its ranks.

Even more scathing and direct in its accusations of Spasmody was the example quoted in Woolford's essay, an attack on *Pinocchi* by the notoriously elitist *Saturday Review* in February of the same year. Entitling his notice "Poetical Nuisances," the reviewer complains that "a new poetical school is springing up, which ought to be brought under the Nuisances Removal Act," and impatiently declares that

The Spasmodic Poets

the day has gone by for dallying with the present race of rhyming offenders. Here is a writer who ... is as dull as Bailey, and as sensual as Alexander Smith. ... We have had more than enough of mystics and spasmodics; but this writer, in his spasmodics, only rises into a gibber, and his mysticism is but unmitigated nonsense. He not only has no meaning, but affects none.

The reviewer goes on to prepare a thorough list of peculiar, Smithean epithets for ridicule, among them "luskish health," "wire-worms in oaken peach-orbs coiled," and "pollard-visaged youth," as well as the more sensuous "topaz-fountain of her hair" and "throbless Aeons of superbient joy." Without hesitation, he condemns the entire volume as "stark, staring, unmitigated folly and idiotic raving."[9] One can only imagine the aristocratic and well-educated Lord Grantley's reaction to these charges. It is doubtful he remained as silent and patient as his less-privileged Spasmodic predecessors had to be.

Pinocchi is not usually encountered in discussions of the Spasmodic movement. However, the charges brought against it would seem to warrant a closer examination to determine whether it should be included as at least a peripheral Spasmodic work. There can be no question that the author indulged in wild verbal excess, and perhaps exceeded the bounds of taste with some of his more gruesome, though realistic, descriptions. A line from *Sonnets on the War*, "the raven croaking at [the fallen soldier's] carrion ear," called by *Blackwood's* "altogether vile," seems tame in contrast to, for example, *Pinocchi*'s "smooth limbs / all torture-bruised and crushed."[10] In terms of subject matter, two poems are deeply informed by Spasmodic tenets with regard to the poet's deified status, and in fact recall the short poems discussing literary fame and ambition appended to *A Life-Drama*.

"The Neglected Poet" in particular may have prompted the *Fraser's* critic to doubt the author's respect for critical judgment. As a member of a group "who gaze inwardly on glorious scenes, / Who have strange alchemy within our minds" and who "can outstrip the ebon seeds of death," the speaker-poet depicts himself battling against critical injustices perpetrated by petty dilettantes.

> When great and good
> Are followed by a crowd of fashion's urchins,
> And tittered, pelted, starved to death, I rear
> An Ajax shield against these pigmy darts,
> And, reining in my arm to its full might,
> Launch a huge spear amongst their waspish ranks.

7. *"A Cloud of Poisonous Flies"*

After all, he asks, "How shall a world whose fruit is mediocrity / Judge of the mighty?" and evokes Dante as a proto–Romantic who enjoyed both Classical and religious sanctions: "Dante, / The supernatural, the Virgil-crowned, / Taught—that A POET IS THE NEXT TO GOD."[11] None of these sentiments would seem at all out of place in the speeches of Balder, Walter, or even Festus. The *Saturday Review* critic makes it plain that *Pinocchi*'s Spasmodic impertinence, rather than its artistic blunders, is what has finally taxed his patience beyond the limits: "All this intolerable babbling might be dismissed as what it is," that is, pedestrian and inconsequential, save for one fact: namely, that "the writer ... writes in this fashion because he feels that he has a mission."[12] For these reasons, quite apart from its critical drubbing, *Pinocchi* could be ranked as a Spasmodic volume even more readily than *Maud* or Smith's own *City Poems*.

The fear expressed by *Fraser's* that Spasmodic excess might seduce and corrupt established authors was not a novel concept. Tennyson's *Maud* and Browning's *Men and Women* had both appeared the year before, and critics were still indignant about what they considered their Laureate's desertion to the Spasmodic camp and the possibility that Browning might usher in a second phase of Spasmody. *Fraser's* ventured that the *Pinocchi* poet "applied himself to the oracles of Keats and Tennyson in their darkest and quaintest temper,"[13] and the vituperative *Saturday Review* critic complained that *Pinocchi* "combine[d] the uglier metrical peculiarities of Tennyson with the inverted gibberish of Browning."[14] Margaret Oliphant's *Blackwood's* article, portraying them as members of an eccentric family, appeared that same month:

> Mr. Tennyson is the eldest of the group, and they all take after him; but they are true brothers.... Mr. Dobell is the sulky boy—Mr. Browning the boisterous one—Mr. Smith the younger brother, desperately bent on being even with the firstborn, and owning no claim of birthright.[15]

Clearly, critical paranoia regarding a possible Romantic revival had by 1856 reached a feverish pitch, and every effort was being made to shame and harass it from print. Spasmodic influence had become so integral to the poetic fabric of the time that what we now consider the three major poetic voices of the Victorian age were profoundly affected: Arnold fretted about *Empedocles on Etna*'s unintentionally Spasmodic traits,[16] and swapped it for his anti–Spasmodic Preface of 1853; recognition of Robert Browning's genius was impeded by accusations of Spasmody; and Tennyson, rocked by the vicious critical reception of *Maud*,

The Spasmodic Poets

decided to forego contemporary themes and retreated to the Arthurian age for his next major works.[17] His *Idylls of the King*, a celebration of traditional respectable English masculinity and poesy, appeared in 1859.

Because of the charges levelled against it by Tennyson's contemporaries, and the reiteration of those charges by modern commentators, *Maud* is often considered a Spasmodic work. It even inspired a *Firmilian*-type lampoon, W.C. Bennet's *Anti-Maud*, published in pamphlet form in 1855. Some critics, such as Joseph Collins, have taken issue with this classification, arguing instead that the Spasmodics were indebted to Tennyson's earlier works and that their poetry and *Maud* are independent outgrowths of a common neo–Romantic tradition.[18] Of course, only an analysis of *Maud* itself can satisfactorily determine its relationship to Spasmodic technique, but there can be little question that, to its original reviewers, it was sufficiently similar to *Balder* and *A Life-Drama* that one's reaction to it largely depended on one's estimation of these earlier productions. As far as the public was concerned, within three months *Maud* had sold eight thousand copies and was apparently a popular success.[19] It is important to remember that, despite the condemnations of reviewers, other Spasmodic works, particularly *A Life-Drama* and *Festus*, also enjoyed excellent sales, indicating that the same characteristics which offended critics actually appealed to many readers.

Maud seems to have been the product of twin influences, biographical and poetic. Its portrayal of thwarted love and mental aberration are supposed to have been inspired by Tennyson's hopeless love for Rosa Baring, a woman socially inaccessible to him, along with melancholia and alcoholism in his father, who suffered financial embarrassment as did the father of *Maud*'s protagonist. There is also speculation that the class issues portrayed in *Maud* are expressions of Tennyson's own ambiguous relationship to the Victorian aristocracy.[20] On the other hand, the poem is Byronic to a degree suggesting either that Tennyson was imitating poets he was known to have read, in particular Bailey and Dobell, or that he was simply moving in the same direction because of his own inherent Romanticism. As Margaret Oliphant observed, Balder and the protagonist of *Maud* are equally the descendants of Wordsworth's Recluse, like him "living a long life for Self and Poetry," even though they take the less healthy step of appearing to promote insanity as a heroic virtue. Bryant quotes one reviewer as charging, "If an author pipe adultery, fornication, murder, and suicide, set him down as the practiser of these crimes." Tennyson supposedly replied, "Adulterer

7. "A Cloud of Poisonous Flies"

I may be, fornicator I may be, murderer I may be, suicide I am not yet." Certainly this recalls Dobell's pain at being "morally misunderstood."[21]

In a sense, these two influences are not entirely separate. It was a Romantic, and especially a Spasmodic, belief that the self and its individual passions were the best subject for poetic expression, and Tennyson seemed to espouse this creed in *Maud*. Though most critics may not have known of the biographical details which influenced *Maud*, they assumed that *Maud*'s first-person narrator expressed at least some of the poet's own opinions, if not his moral failings, ranging from fornication to murder, and was attempting to justify them in verse. In his own review,[22] Aytoun grumbles that "Mr. Tennyson has written a mad passage, but we must needs say that he had better have spared himself the trouble.... The case is bad enough when young poetasters essay to gain a hearing by dint of maniacal howls; but it is far worse when we find a man of undoubted genius and widespread reputation, demeaning himself by putting his name to such absolute nonsense." Elsewhere, he condemns the portrayal of the protagonist's language when he is carried away with love for Maud, insisting that "there must be a limit somewhere." Unfortunately for Tennyson, the form in which he presented *Maud* provided little evidence to the contrary, since the story is told from the unnamed protagonist's point of view and even the smallest details in the story are presented through his idiosyncratic vision. Few of *Maud*'s detractors bothered to consider that the poem was in fact a *tour de force* of characterization. The lines that to them smacked most of Spasmodic wildness, both in content and form, were intended to reveal the protagonist's madness without using an external narrative voice—the same mistake, in fact, that misled critics of *Balder*. Even those who recognized and understood Tennyson's method, including Aytoun, considered it unacceptable for serious poetry and thus unbecoming to the Laureate. According to Aytoun, during the days of Byron and Scott, readers "had hardly devoured one dish fit for a banquet of the gods, before we were ready for another," but now a discouraged public has only the kind of poem "so spasmodic that it reminds you of the writhing of a knot of worms."[23] Today it is easy to see that *Maud* prefigured the type of psychological poem central to the modern era; this flavor, however, is not to Aytoun's liking in the least.

By far the most common note in the negative criticism of *Maud* is disappointment in Tennyson's character, amounting at times to wails of personal betrayal. Despite the bids of lesser talents and the skepticism

The Spasmodic Poets

of weary critics, many readers had begun (ironically enough) to believe that he was, in fact, the *vates* or poet-philosopher of the age. By the mid–1850s, he had come to be regarded as a teacher as well as a source of literary entertainment. As Victorian values demanded, both his subject matter and mode of expression caused him to appear morally impeccable and thus fit for ubiquitous social consumption. He was certainly preferable to the Romantic poets, with their unsettling forays into libertinism, sexual license, and atheism. The Spasmodics had dabbled in all but the last, making them for a time a source of titillation to the reading public, but the fact that they never gained the prophetic status hoped for by Gilfillan prevented their excesses from threatening complacency. Tennyson carried no such embarrassing baggage. Though critics were not unanimously approving of his work, they found nothing in his biography or work that would bring the proverbial blush to a young person's cheek.

Maud's appearance therefore proved something of a shock. Aytoun's review is particularly bitter, charging that serious readers eager for their Laureate's new work had been slapped across the face by this travesty, and a good many others shared his dismay. Margaret Oliphant's "Modern Light Literature—Poetry," laments that "ours is only a twilight kind of radiance, however much we may make of it. It differs sadly from the full unclouded shining of that Day of the Poets which is past."[24] Gerard Manley Hopkins' 1879 pronouncement that "*Maud* is an ungentlemanly row"[25] displays a mildness of hindsight that Walter Bagehot could not quite share in 1859:

> The subject [of *Maud*] was calculated to call out the unhealthier sort of youthful imaginations.... The hero of *Maud* is a young man who lives very much out of the world, who has no definite duties or intelligible occupations ... it was inevitable, too, that this taint should be rather agreeable than otherwise to many of the poet's warmest admirers. The Tennysonians, as we have said, were young men; and youth is the season of semi-diseased feeling.

Even more startling, Bagehot notes, was the fact that Tennyson "seemed to agree" with his hero's "odd invectives" and was "not severe on melancholy vanity."[26]

The uneasiness caused by this supposition was a long time fading. Likewise, the apparent jingoism of *Maud*'s conclusion was considered offensive not necessarily because it expressed warmongering, but because the poem's protagonist, and Tennyson, seemed to regard the fighting not as patriotism but as an extension of, and a cure for, poisonous self-absorption. The Crimean conflict serves, one critic notes,

7. "A Cloud of Poisonous Flies"

as "an external sensation ... where an internal effort is the obvious and the true cure" (curiously, the same had been said of Dobell and Smith's Crimean War volumes). He goes on to remind Tennyson that "the manhood of a poet ... must be redeemed, not by talking lightly of blood, but by true tenderness, self-control, obedience to the moral law, and fidelity to the end of his mission,"[27] suggesting that at least some of Tennyson's admirers considered their poet in need of such a corrective. To them, *Maud* seemed social blasphemy that had, astonishingly, come from the very pen that had framed the Victorian creed, the last lines of "Ulysses" with their firm promotion of duty and personal industry: "Made weak by time and fate, but strong in will / To strive, to seek, to find, and not to yield." Aytoun warned Tennyson that he was "seriously imperilling his fame by issuing poems so ill considered, crude, tawdry, and objectionable as this,"[28] although he expresses the by-now familiar doubts that his advice will be taken seriously,

There can be little question that *Maud*'s perceived similarity to Spasmodic works has affected even modern assessments. Whether or not calling it a Spasmodic work is justified is another matter. Certainly even at the time of its original release, Tennyson recognized its Spasmodic elements, especially the excessively Byronic qualities of his misanthropic yet lovelorn protagonist. He had considered the possibility that others would, too, for he was said to be particularly nervous about the appearance of W.E. Aytoun's review. His dread of being classified as one of the Spasmodics is suggested by the vehemence of his friend F.G. Tuckerman's reassurances that Aytoun had not the power to reverse the tide of Tennyson's fame.[29] No doubt both correspondents recalled how Aytoun had done just that to Smith and Dobell the year before. Nor were the periodical critics alone in noticing the similarities between *Maud* and Spasmodic works. Dante Gabriel Rossetti, although an ardent admirer of Tennyson, admitted that "the story throughout, from the 'flattened' father onward, seems worthy rather of Alex[ander] Smith than Tennyson." Rossetti also gives a detailed account of Tennyson's embittered "groanings and horrors" over the storm of negative criticism and even hate mail he received following *Maud*'s publication. "His conversation was really one perpetual groan," he notes.[30] Tennyson's portrayal of an aberrant mental state was also as deliberate as Dobell's in *Balder*; he had initially intended to call it *Maud or the Madness*. The mad scene was at the time particularly congenial to his talents, for he claimed to have written it in twenty minutes. *Maud* was completed in January 1855, approximately six months after the release

The Spasmodic Poets

of *Firmilian*, making it unlikely that the discussions, assessments, and reprinted sections of recent Spasmodic works were not fresh in Tennyson's mind.

Several aspects of *Maud*'s content, form, and style appear to justify the charge of Spasmody. *Maud*, especially in its first edition, resembles a Spasmodic poem in that the details of the plot are only vaguely recounted and must be pieced together by the reader from clues dropped during the narrator's ranting. *Balder* and *A Life-Drama* were similarly elusive, for example regarding the death of Balder's daughter and the circumstances of Walter's separation from Violet. Tennyson seems to have recognized this likeness himself: when he revised *Maud* in 1856, he paid particular attention to delineating the plot more sharply and adding passages[31] to explain those previously thought obscure.

Like *A Life-Drama*, Tennyson's poem is divided into scenes between which unspecified amounts of time have passed and circumstances have changed in ways not always readily apparent to the reader. One example of this technique may have been responsible for some of the outrage against *Maud*. The possibility that Maud and the narrator may have enjoyed a sexual consummation between Cantos XVII and XVIII is still debated by modern critics. This interpretation was apparently suggested by a sudden burst of what one critic calls "Elizabethan sexual imagery"[32] at this point in the poem, and may have prompted some of the charges of immorality against Tennyson and his hero, much as Walter's ambiguous seduction (or possibly rape) of Violet in *A Life-Drama* had cast aspersions on Smith's character. Certainly, after a similar break between scenes in Smith's poem, Walter is found lamenting his trespass to a prostitute, so it is likely that this passage in *Maud* reminded some readers, even subconsciously, of this universally deplored passage in the earlier poem. Otherwise it is hard to understand the vehemence with which Tennyson was accused of promoting adultery and fornication.

Although William Buckler contends that *Maud* had "no model or paradigm" and was a "leap into a distinctively new form,"[33] A. Dwight Culler has shown that it lies structurally between the monodrama of the early Romantic period and the dramatic monologue as perfected by Browning.[34] Though Culler does not consider the Spasmodics in his discussion, their style of poetic drama, which focuses exclusively on the hero's moods and ideas and consists mostly of monologues, is obviously similar to *Maud* although their works might be called less extreme in

7. "A Cloud of Poisonous Flies"

that other characters, however poorly drawn, do appear and do speak directly to Walter, Festus, and Balder.

Maud seems to have been most influenced by the three major Spasmodic poems in its internal variety of styles, ranging from short songs and lyrics to longer, more elaborate descriptions as dictated by the speaker's moods. Here, Tennyson's technical virtuosity clearly outclasses the Spasmodics, but to Victorian critics this amalgamation of styles was as choppy, amateurish, and cryptic as theirs had been. Aytoun's *Blackwood's* review (rather histrionically) raged at *Maud's* experimental form, calling it a "positively hideous cacophony" which had been "set to a metre which has the string-halt, without even the advantage of regularity in its hobble" and, worst of all, was "studded all over with those metaphors, strange epithets, and conceits which are the disfigurement of modern poetry."[35] Within *Maud's* impassioned lines are imbedded many of the Spasmodic, and particularly Smithean, epithets condemned by Aytoun, who picked out just a few to demonstrate that Tennyson had apparently "become addicted to exaggeration, and an unnecessary use of very strong language": among these are "daffodil skies," "gross mud-honey," "ashen-grey delights," and, perhaps most shockingly of all, "the delicate Arab arch" of a woman's foot, displaying what Victorians would have considered indelicate anatomical precision. Aytoun offers all of this as evidence to support his claim concerning *Maud's* "*singular* resemblance to fustian."[36] "Fustian," it will be recalled, was Aytoun's favorite name for "Festus."

Occasionally, the narrator of *Maud* resorts to another favorite Spasmodic device, the digression. As in *Balder*, digressions in *Maud* take two forms. One involves a complete break in the action during which the speaker discourses at length about some philosophical topic. In *Maud* these are almost all concerned with social evils brought on by human greed and complacency. The other occurs when the speaker pauses to notice some small physical object or detail which prompts an intricate description. Balder noticed the wood in his floor, and *Maud's* protagonist remarks on "a lovely shell, / Small and pure as pearl, / Lying close to my foot" for approximately thirty lines.[37] That these digressions are far more germane to the movement of the poem as a whole than in *Balder* does not negate the resemblance.

In matters of diction, *Maud* often utilizes the exaggerated, even morbid tendencies of Walter's speeches. This is apparent in *Maud's* opening lines:

The Spasmodic Poets

> I hate the dreadful hollow behind the little wood,
> Its lips in the field above are dabbled with blood-red heath,
> The red-ribbed ledges drip with a silent horror of blood,
> And Echo there, whatever is asked her, answers "Death."[38]

Other lines ring even more shrilly with Spasmodic sensationalism, such as "And my pulses closed their gates with a shock on my heart as I heard / The shrill-edged shriek of a mother divide the shuddering night," "Now to the scream of a maddened beach dragged down by the wave," and "As [Mars] glowed like a ruddy shield on the Lion's breast."[39] Even a random selection of lines from one of Walter's self-flagellating speeches at the beginning of *A Life-Drama* bears a telling resemblance to many in *Maud*:

> We find our aspirations quenched in tears,
> The tears of impotence, and self-contempt,
> That loathsome weed, up-springing in the heart,
> Like nightshade 'mong the ruins of a shrine;
> I am so cursed, and wear within my soul
> A pang as fierce as Dives, drowsed with wine,
> Lipping his leman in luxurious dreams;
> Waked by a fiend in hell!
> ....
> Naught for me
> But to creep quietly into my grave;
> Or calm and tame the swelling of my heart
> With this foul lie, painted as sweet as truth.[40]

Due largely to *Firmilian* and the well-orchestrated *Blackwood's* campaign, Aytoun's colleagues arranged their discussions around the same Spasmodic blemishes he had trained them to spot. Yet it is possible to make a case against viewing *Maud* as a quasi-Spasmodic poem, and not all of *Maud*'s commentators were prepared to side with Aytoun. While the reaction against *Maud* swelled, a few critics attempted to assess its relation to the Spasmodic School more objectively. George Brimley, whose remarks on *Maud* earned the poet's endorsement, recognized the common elements in *Maud* and the Spasmodic poems, but asserted that Tennyson and his work were of a different order and that the Spasmodics deserved commiseration rather than ridicule. He gives as earlier examples of the type Keats, Shelley, and Chatterton:

> You see, God makes these morbid, hysterical, and spasmodic individuals occasionally, and they have various fates ... and somehow, for their sake the class becomes interesting, and we are at times inclined to measure the spiritual capacity of an age by its treatment of these weak souls.

7. "A Cloud of Poisonous Flies"

The poem's narrator, not Tennyson, is the "spasmodic" in *Maud*'s case, and he is essentially too noble and sensitive, rather than amoral and selfish, to survive in his world of "social evils." In essence, Brimley believed Tennyson was creating a dramatic portrait of the tragic individual found in, and even created by, their own century.[41] Later, in 1870, Alfred Austin attempted to separate Tennyson from lesser, imitative talents, who "squander their lives in trying to attain the impossible, exhaust themselves in poetical spasms, and illustrate Alexander Smith's simile:—'O Poesy! thou art a rock; / I, a weak wave, would break on thee, and die.'" He speculates that these men might have been considered fine poets in a more receptive age, but considers them distinct from Tennyson and "very much his inferiors."[42] The Spasmodic elements in *Maud* are here considered products of the stylistic experimentation of the age, and the hero perhaps a conscious parody of a typical Spasmodic poet. Tennyson was assumed to be responding to an observed trend, not partaking in it.

The text of *Maud* also provides evidence exonerating itself of Spasmody. Its form may resemble works like *A Life-Drama*, but it has the advantage of being a good deal shorter, more concise, and thematically unified. Tennyson's intention had originally been to portray a character suffering from mental instability, which the poem's various moods and tones exhibit, whereas Smith's Walter is a wooden figure whose spiritual and artistic crises take place off-stage, precluding genuine dramatic tension. A. Dwight Culler also demonstrates that Tennyson had more control over his chosen form than was at first recognized, for *Maud* does indeed meet the demands of the monodrama as it was developed by Goethe and Rousseau and modified in England by the Gothic novelist Matthew "Monk" Lewis. Elements we might call Spasmodic were common to this genre, which was originally intended for the stage, and dictated *Maud*'s bloodthirsty finale.[43] Even the hero is explained by the monodrama's Romantic origins; Walter and the narrator resemble one another in temperament, but they are cousins rather than brothers. As far as Balder is concerned, while it is true that both he and *Maud*'s narrator commit homicide, the murder in *Maud* occurs in a suitably Byronic duel, while Balder's main crimes, against an infant and a hopelessly insane young wife, are those of a sadistic coward. Thus, of the two, *Maud*'s narrator is the more truly Byronic in a strictly literary sense.

Maud's narrator also differs in a crucial point, as even Margaret Oliphant noticed in her otherwise condemnatory article. While he may be possessed of a morbidly sensitive temperament, he "does not think

The Spasmodic Poets

himself a divinity; he has not a manuscript at hand to draw forth and gaze upon with delighted eyes; he is not—let us be grateful—a poet." *Maud* is therefore free of "the solemn foolery of its much-pretending contemporaries, the lauds of the self-worshipping man, or the rhapsodies of the self-admiring youth."[44] Nor does he express any desire for literary fame or social domination as did the Spasmodic heroes; even Festus had composed an epic which he displays to his followers with false modesty to earn their adulation. *Maud*'s protagonist comments on the social issues of his day rather than explaining universal law or religious doctrine, and the fact that his comments are not directed towards any identifiable listener indicate that they are musings which he does not expect his contemporaries to take seriously. If anything, he would lead

> a philosopher's life in the quiet woodland ways,
> Where if I cannot be gay let a passionless peace be my lot,
> Far-off from the clamour of liars belied in the hubbub of lies;
> From the long-necked geese of the world that are ever hissing dispraise
> Because their natures are little, and whether he heed it or not,
> Where each man walks with his head in a cloud of poisonous flies.[45]

While this misanthropy, and the language in which it is expressed, would not seem anomalous in a Spasmodic hero, Tennyson makes no effort to portray his protagonist as a genius among men, whose inherently superior nature excuses him from the constraints of morality. In fact, the narrator himself behaves as though his head is wrapped in "poisonous flies" in his outbursts of hatred toward Maud's domineering brother and father, emotions more contained and particular than any that ever troubled a Spasmodic hero, and in his misguided perception that the physical world is entirely in tune with his emotions. Whereas the stars stirred Walter to rhapsodic frenzies, to *Maud*'s narrator they are only "tyrants in [their] iron skies" reminding him of man's "nothingness."[46] His isolation from others adds to his frustration, making his madness more dramatically convincing. It is also difficult to imagine the self-satisfied Balder or Festus lamenting, "And ah for a man to arise in me, / That the man I am may cease to be!"[47]

Taken as a whole, therefore, *Maud* does share several features with the genuine Spasmodic poems, but it is not accurate to call it a Spasmodic poem. Though P.J. Bailey repeatedly denied any affiliation with the Spasmodics, the internal evidence found in *Festus* makes such claims superfluous, whereas the opposite holds true for Tennyson. Perhaps more secure in his status as Laureate, Tennyson made no attempt

7. "A Cloud of Poisonous Flies"

to condemn or disassociate himself from the Spasmodics beyond editing out a few of *Maud*'s more Spasmodic traits for its second edition. As textual analysis shows, *Maud* is exactly what Tennyson claimed it was, a monodrama that adhered to that Romantic formula and thus is only incidentally Spasmodic. Ultimately, the ongoing debate about *Maud* reveals less about the poem itself than about the increasing disgrace attached to the Spasmodic label, and indicates just how intense the battle between the anti–Romantics and the neo–Romantic poets had grown. Only a shift in poetical tactics allowed Tennyson to re-emerge as the Victorian spokesman.

Robert Browning's assimilation was, if inevitable, for a time less certain. In his 1929 assessment of Robert Browning's literary reputation and fame, D.C. Somervell remarked that maintaining faith in Browning was like playing the stock market: Browning shares sold cheap early in the nineteenth century but paid off well by its end.[48] "Shareholders" who stood by the poet (among them Dante Gabriel Rossetti and the Oxford Brotherhood, all of whom had supported Smith and Dobell in the *Oxford and Cambridge Magazine*) would have experienced some precarious moments at the height of the Spasmodic backlash, when Browning's poetic career seemed likely to be extinguished along with Smith's and Dobell's. In 1863, Lovell Reeve recalled when Browning was "denounced" as a spasmodist, and reviews of the time support his claim: *The Saturday Review* classed his 1855 *Men and Women* with the work of Bailey, *The Literary Gazette* declared it was "marked" by the obscurity and "crudeness" of the "spasmodic school,"[49] and in 1858 Gerald Massey called Browning "one of the greatest Spasmodists,"[50] a sentiment echoed in 1939 by Lionel Trilling.

Both Brownings, in fact, were accused of membership in the waning school, although evidence of their actual involvement with its members is circumstantial at best. All that is certain is that at one time both had admired *Festus*, and their discussions with "Orion" Horne contributed much to his chapter on Bailey in his book *A New Spirit of the Age*. As far as Smith is concerned, Elizabeth mentioned reading reviews of his poetry "and some MSS.," but her husband's involvement in this activity can only be inferred; there is no proof at all that either was familiar with Dobell's poetry.[51] Actual proximity to fellow Spasmodics had, however, never been a requirement as far as the critics were concerned, and the tenuous association with Bailey proved sufficient. As early as the 1840s, W.E. Aytoun had postulated a yet-unnamed school containing both Brownings, Horne, and Bailey, known for its mysticism

The Spasmodic Poets

and unique methods of versification. The reference comes from an unpublished lecture of Aytoun's from the mid–1840s, in which he says the school "is founded on deliberate mystery, professes strange metaphysical and aesthetical views [and] adopts new methods and theories of versification...."[52] As the Spasmodic controversy swelled, it seemed, any poem accused of sharing these traits could be labelled "Spasmodic" and made an object of ridicule. George Brimley was not far wrong when he speculated that even the works of Shakespeare could be twisted to fit the "Spasmodic" label[53] if a critic tried hard enough. As with *Maud*, it is only fair to look beyond the reviewers' rather transparent intentions to expose and embarrass "Spasmodics" and examine those aspects of both Brownings' poetry that might suggest their influence.

Mrs. Browning's *Aurora Leigh* was pilloried as Spasmodic by Aytoun himself in *Blackwood's* in 1857. His review took issue with her depiction of the poet and the "coarseness of language throughout,"[54] but Weinstein admits that the article's main thrust was to characterize yet again what Aytoun considered unhealthy, which is to say overly Romantic, poetic practices (as a social and religious conservative, he would been offended by the poem's liberal and feminist themes as well). *Aurora Leigh* itself was practically forgotten as Aytoun attacked the general faults of mid-century British poetry with the usual fervor applied to "Spasmodic" poems. *Men and Women* fell victim to this same practice: *The Saturday Review* readily admitted that its "main object" was to check "the false teachings of a perverted school of art" by "us[ing] this book of Mr. Browning's chiefly as a means of showing the extravagant lengths of absurdity to which the tenets of that school can lead a man of admitted powers." Likewise, a hostile *Athenaeum* reviewer switched immediately into the plural when he pointed out that "some among the poets ... have relied on the sympathy of the interpreter" to give sense to their verse, and therefore new "artists show themselves, by their exigencies, to be less masterly than the artists of old."[55] *Men and Women*, which contains many of what are now considered Browning's finest poems, was tainted by the association and thus denied the benefit of objective assessment and was kicked callously aside. It did not even reach a second edition.[56] This fact was no doubt particularly distressing to Browning, since *A Life-Drama*, *Balder*, and even Smith's later *Edwin of Deira* all went into second editions.

Aytoun's charge against *Aurora Leigh* was only loosely supported to begin with, and aside from the poem's portrayal of an individual's poetic development, accompanied by an occasional impassioned outburst

7. "A Cloud of Poisonous Flies"

from its heroine, it has little in common with the works of Smith or Dobell. The fact that it centers around a female poet is actually difference enough to exclude it, for the women in the more traditional Spasmodic schemes are mere ciphers whose primary function is to worship the male poet. Though Aurora does occasionally suffer from Spasmodic angst about having her poetry taken seriously, the reader (especially in the modern era) understands that it is sexism, and not narcissism, that oppresses her. The underlying feminist theme of *Aurora Leigh* automatically renders her a more sympathetic figure than the privileged Walter or the vicious Balder. Aurora's poetic quest, which leads her to crown herself with ivy in an admittedly Spasmodic fashion, is motivated less by smug self-regard than by a desire to use poetry to better the world. The rest of the poem, especially Aurora's attempt to rescue an abused seamstress and her unfortunate son, reveals more social conscience than the rest of the Spasmodic canon put together.

The case of Robert Browning is more complex, since his early works, particularly *Sordello*, *Paracelsus*, and to some extent *Pauline*, do seem Spasmodic in some aspects of form and technique. Browning's approach to his art was from the beginning colored by the same Romantic assumptions that had produced the Spasmodics. In 1863, as he looked back on *Sordello*, he commented in a letter that "my stress lay on the incidents in the development of a soul: little else is worth study. I, at least have always thought so"[57] and this emphasis led Arnold to devalue Browning for the same reasons he devalued the Spasmodics and Keats. Browning was also identified with neo–Romantic forces in Horne's *A New Spirit of the Age*, which linked him to J. Westland Marston, and Browning openly shared Horne's enthusiasm for supposedly revolutionary, emotive poetry like *Festus*. It is not then surprising that *Pauline* and *Paracelsus* are cast in dramatic form, and that they deal with, respectively, a young man's description of intellectual and spiritual progress and a Faust-like 15th-century alchemist.[58] *Sordello* went even further, taking the form of a monologue. Browning intended to show the development of a poet's soul,[59] with the attendant problems of his social and philosophical duty. Despite the theme he shared with Smith and Dobell, however, Browning's poetry and dramatic talent clearly developed much more rapidly than the Spasmodics'. By the time he completed the poems featured in *Men and Women*, his portraits of artists had matured and deepened, producing balanced and ironic depictions such as those in his dramatic monologues. "Andrea del Sarto" and "Fra Lippo Lippi," for example, contain characterizations far subtler than those of Smith,

The Spasmodic Poets

Bailey, or Dobell. Unfortunately, both his subject matter and his unique, difficult treatment obstructed critical recognition of the volume's merits for nearly a decade after its release.

Stylistically, Browning also shared the supposed fault of obscurity with the Spasmodics from the beginning of his poetic career. Negative reviews of *Men and Women* acknowledged that a certain murkiness of diction was a pre-existing flaw of Browning's.[60] It was a serious flaw to Victorian taste, nonetheless, and *Sordello* (1840) particularly offended its readers. Tennyson himself commented that he understood only the first and last lines of the poem, which promised that Sordello's story would be and had been told, and that both were lies. Thereafter it acquired a reputation as "the least comprehensible poem written in the English language," much to Browning's detriment.[61] When he was, perhaps inevitably, compared to the Spasmodics in this regard, it was his idiosyncratic technique reviewers focused on. "Balder and the Harbingers" commented that Amy, Balder's wife, sounded a good deal like Browning in her mad ravings, and a review of *Maud* accused Tennyson of speaking "Browningese" in that poem,[62] much to the consternation of his readers.

Still, some critics understood that the comparison was not quite fair, and they believed that Browning's apparent ramblings had more substance behind them than the Spasmodics' even looser digressions. Patmore defined Browning's particular form of "spasmody" as consisting of "a wilful delight in remote and involved thinking, abrupt, and jerking mental movements, and 'pernickitieness' of expression," none of which are bad in themselves, and all of which are informed by "genius" in Browning's case. Margaret Oliphant, who had few kind words either for the Spasmodics or *Maud*, admitted that Browning, despite his occasional spasms, "works like the old primitive painters, with little command of his tools, but something genuine in his mind, which comes out ... ugly, yet somehow true." "Balder and the Harbingers" stated that Browning was rivalled only by Tennyson with respect to "real poetic furor" and talent. Their main difference was, to this critic, Browning's propensity for "too often" heading "up to the clouds"[63] whereas Tennyson's feet were more firmly planted on the ground.

Once the Spasmodic controversy had grown stale, the "multitudinousness" of Browning, which Arnold had originally deprecated as masking a poverty of genuine intellectual content,[64] was gradually recognized as a distinctive and appropriate model for a lively intellect. Within thirty years, Browning's reputation had soared. Though he was

7. "A Cloud of Poisonous Flies"

described in terms that seem startlingly irrelevant and insensitive by today's standards, they are exactly the reverse of those originally used to degrade him and his supposed colleagues, the Spasmodics, by referring to them as diseased, effeminate, and mystical:

> Of all poets Mr. Browning is the healthiest and manliest. The most subtle of minds, his is the least sickly ... and when once Browning's method has ceased to surprise, no one will object to the corresponding excrescence in poetry.[65]

Arthur Symons' 1880 assessment is not merely rhetorical, but touches on what is actually the primary difference between his poetry and the Spasmodics'. Browning's poems are difficult to read, peculiar in their syntax and arrangement, and utilize eccentric subject-matter. Yet even those with the potential to become lurid or exaggerated, such as "Porphyria's Lover," the theme of which can be compared to that of *Balder*, remain controlled by the complex irony of Browning's ventriloquism. Obscurity and intricacy are intentional, and reward the critic patient enough to unravel their meaning. Granted, much is extraneous in Browning; some of his poems were "one hundred per cent too long," as Somervell wryly remarked. Yet, he asks, once the many examples of this "too-much-ness" are disregarded, "what remains? Surely a great deal."[66] By the time Somervell published his article in 1929, the critical tide had fully turned against the Spasmodic poets. They were dismissed as dull, pedestrian, and devoid of original ideas in spite of an occasional clever turn of phrase.

This fact illustrates the major split between Browning and the Spasmodics: whereas Browning took Romanticism as his starting point but eventually moved away from its restricting solipsism,[67] the Spasmodics became prematurely confident that they had harnessed the ideal medium for poetic expression, and failed to perceive their hyper-Romanticism's limitations in the changing Victorian world. Though Browning, like most other aspiring poets of his generation, passed through a Romantic phase, he was only accidentally classed as a Spasmodic. Leaving aside all questions of the relative quality of his works and theirs, his different intentions and informing artistic principles are enough to set him apart.

The story of the Spasmodic poets ends, of necessity, in 1874, with the death of Sydney Dobell at the age of fifty. His anti–Spasmodic campaign accomplished, W.E. Aytoun had died a decade earlier, in 1864; J.S. Bigg followed in 1865, Alexander Smith in 1867. Though Bailey

The Spasmodic Poets

survived until 1902, his poetic career perished with his post–*Festus* failures. Despite the initial critical panic, Browning and Tennyson soon proved that they had been mistakenly labelled Spasmodics, and no other *Pinocchi*-style attack appeared. The Spasmodic School was written about, when it was mentioned at all, as an unfortunate episode of the past which had, as William Michael Rossetti acknowledged in 1876, "to all practical purposes" been "extinguished."[68] Hugh Walker was even more pessimistic in 1913 when he declared that the Spasmodics had left behind no issue. "The Spasmodic School died with Dobell," he writes, because he "and Smith transmitted their beauties to no one; perhaps because those beauties were too fragmentary and too closely associated with imperfection to be transmissible." Of the mid-nineteenth century Romantics, only the Pre-Raphaelites and a post–*Maud* Tennyson remained and "jointly molded poetry in the sixties and seventies."[69] Walker is correct in that specific acknowledgments of Spasmodic inspiration are, not surprisingly, lacking, and all critical discussions recalling them are patronizing. However, it should seem peculiar that poems so widely discussed, and widely read, would have failed to leave some impression on subsequent poetic productions. Indeed, it is not in individual poets, but in the poetic trends of the second half of the Victorian age, that the Spasmodics' legacy can be glimpsed.

Walker and others refer to the Spasmodics as the less gifted and therefore less fortunate relations of the Pre-Raphaelites. As we have seen, the comparison between the two groups is valid despite the Pre-Raphaelites' greater awareness that they constituted a movement, and their greater patience as they successfully weathered of an initial gale of adverse reaction. Eventually, they were able to garner what the Spasmodics could not, critical support and thus eventual legitimacy. By the late 1850s their status as artistic rebels had been replaced by respectability, their more mature brand of Romanticism modified to suit a now recognizably Victorian audience. What Welby tellingly called the "spasmodic assaults" on "the established order" of society and art were left to late-comers to Pre-Raphaelitism like Swinburne,[70] who certainly shared some traits with the Spasmodics but eventually broke away to follow his own eccentric path.

As had been the case at the close of the original Romantic period in the 1830s, a period of drabness and complacency followed the fresh burst of color the Pre-Raphaelites, along with Tennyson and to a lesser extent Browning and the Spasmodics, had represented. Buckley describes an 1880s movement to restore the decorum and understatement of the

7. "A Cloud of Poisonous Flies"

eighteenth century to Victorian taste,[71] and Robert Buchanan, admirer of Dobell and enemy of Pre-Raphaelitism, bitterly complained in 1887 of the "present dead swoon" and "utter sterility of passion and hopeless stagnation of sentiment nowadays."[72] The lamentable result of this aridity, Buchanan believed, was the sudden idolization of Gautier, or in other words the shading of the Aesthetic movement, spearheaded by the Pre-Raphaelites, into Decadence. If the Spasmodic movement shared a common origin with the Pre-Raphaelites, then Decadence is to an equal degree its evolutionary product. The Decadents were what the Pre-Raphaelites and other Aesthetic factions could no longer be: unassimilated, proudly outcast heretics. They represented a next step in artistic iconoclasm, separated from the pious Spasmodics by the more tentatively Bohemian Pre-Raphaelites.

The parallels between the Decadent and Spasmodic movements were obvious, even in their own time. *Blackwood's* itself compared the rise of a Decadent poet, Stephen Phillips, to that of Alexander Smith while asserting, strangely heedless of past lessons, that Phillips' genius was genuine whereas Smith's had not been. Both Phillips' method, combining "the epic manner of Milton" with "the opulence of Tennyson" and his fate, "tragic oblivion,"[73] also recall Smith. The Decadents were prepared to worship detail and the poetic soul with as much fervor and extravagance as the Spasmodics; Dorian Gray's quest for aesthetic stimulation within the cult of artifice is obviously related to Balder's and Walter's.

Decadence also shared the same touch of melodrama, perhaps unexpectedly informed by the hoped-for revelation of a moral absolute like that reflected in the disfigurement of Dorian's portrait. Since Life was cultivated to imitate Art in the absence of any such intervening force, those qualities that made Walter and Balder exasperating were now cheerfully adopted by living poets:

> The staidest of Nonconformist circles begot strange, pale youths with abundant hair, whose abandoned thoughts expressed themselves in "purple patches" of prose, and whose sole aim in life was to live "passionately" in a succession of "scarlet moments." Life-tasting was the fashion....[74]

This description might as well apply to a Spasmodic, too, especially "the minor poet [who] … always contrived to clothe his verse in most gracious language which had full power to charm by its ingenuity and beauty…. Fancy and Prettiness never sought to dethrone Imagination and Beauty, but to support and serve them like good courtiers."[75]

The Spasmodic Poets

Characteristics like self-centeredness, amorality, artificiality, and even prurience and effeminacy, which had once mortified the Spasmodics, were cheerfully accepted and even cultivated by the Decadents. Kingsley's 1857 caricature in *Two Years Ago*, Elsley Vavasour, is a transitional figure between the two eras. By the time he completes his aesthetic transformation, he has taken on a new identity as well as a fraudulent name.

The Decadents sometimes appear to be Spasmodic successors afflicted with a *fin-de-siècle* lassitude, just as the Spasmodics were Romantic successors infected by the excesses of that period. If the opponents of the Decadent movement looked to England's judicial code rather than the periodical review columns to dismantle Wilde in the 1890s, it was because the forty intervening years had done so much to crush the vision of the artist as an exalted figure who lived apart from his fellow mortals. He was now regarded as securely bound by the same social and moral constraints as the Philistine beside him; any deviation would bring punishment as swiftly, perhaps even more so. The late Victorians had finally, and with no little pain, given up the belief that a *vates* would appear to instruct and unite the increasingly divided appendages of their Post-Industrial society. The failure of the Spasmodics to fulfill this expectation was instrumental in preparing both the critics and consumers of literature for this shift to what we would now call the modern sensibility (and the ascendance of the novel). It is perhaps not ironic at all that they were swiftly forgotten, for they quickly became remnants of an early Victorian innocence which had itself died after a series of humiliating and disillusioning spasms.

Epilogue:
"Vast Displays of Critic Wit"
The Future of the Spasmodic School

> *There have been vast displays of critic wit*
> *O'er those who vainly flutter feeble wings,*
> *Nor rise an inch 'bove ground,—weak Poetlings!*
> *And on them to the death men's brows are knit.*
> —Alexander Smith

In her 2001 study, *The Brontë Myth*, Lucasta Miller demonstrates that each succeeding generation of readers, critics, and scholars reinterprets the dramatic story of Haworth's most famous family according to their own social milieu.[1] The sisters and their works morph according not only to their audiences' intellectual, but emotional needs. Shifting attitudes and definitions of class, feminism, and religion, among other topics, continually alter our understanding of the Brontës until the underlying reality of even mundane biographical details becomes hazy and politically fraught. Though they will obviously never achieve the literary significance of the Brontës, and almost no one reads their works for pleasure, the Spasmodic poets have also served as cultural mirrors for those who study and write about them.

Both the history and the current trajectory of Spasmodic criticism bubbles with passion both positive and negative. Not only the poets and poems, but the context of the group's implosion has provided much grist for the critical mill for over a hundred and seventy years. As is the case with Charlotte and Emily, and to a lesser extent Anne and Branwell, scholars who have waded into the churning Spasmodic waters soon start to identify with some aspect of their earnest ambition and subsequent (and public) embarrassment. As was the case in the original Victorian setting, some commentators have focused on these youthful

Epilogue

poets' technical missteps, either as a way to establish their own superior taste (like Arnold and Aytoun) or in an effort to praise them for daring to challenge poetic and social norms. Others have focused on the Spasmodics' earnest struggle to overcome class-based prejudice and educational deprivation, sympathizing with their inability to triumph as artists in a hostile environment dominated by pretentious Oxbridge standards. Yet another group has returned to the Spasmodic texts themselves, applying close readings and cross-referencing to refute their supposed literary inferiority. The Spasmodic soil is rich enough that many of these approaches can be simultaneously applied; few are mutually exclusive.

Of course, one problem has always been the scarcity and isolated nature of Spasmodic criticism. Until recently, rounding up Victorian periodical articles, many available only on microfiche or in rare book rooms, was a formidable task for even the most painstaking researcher. Consulting unpublished dissertations, such as Alan D. McKillop's seminal Spasmodic study in 1920, might involve anything from travel to university archives or physical shipments through interlibrary loans. It is little wonder that the most easily accessed and well-known works that deal with the Spasmodics, such as Lionel Trilling's *Matthew Arnold* (1939) and Jerome Buckley's *The Victorian Temper: A Study in Literary Culture* (1951), along with Mark Weinstein's *William Edmondstoune Aytoun and the Spasmodic Controversy* (1968), shaped much of the twentieth century's attitude toward the Spasmodics. Most students of Victorian literature first met the Spasmodics through one of these works, all of which were at best ambivalent and at worst dismissive of Bailey, Dobell, Smith, and their satellites. Arnold's conservative critical voice, as well as the traditional (and some might argue, narrow) nineteenth-century canon, set the tone for the occasional dissertation or article that did mention the so-called School. Even scholars who championed Dobell or Smith, such as Martha Westwater[2] and Mary Jane Scott,[3] tended to begin from a defensive position. Their bibliographies tended to overlap considerably, too.

All that has changed. Current scholars of the Spasmodic School have an advantage their academic predecessors never imagined. The age of the internet has yielded a treasure trove of digitized manuscripts, articles, and books long out of print, many of which can be downloaded instantly and for free. Their digital format also allows quick textual searches and other forms of computerized analysis. Many previously unpublished or even unknown doctoral dissertations and

"Vast displays of critic wit"

Masters' theses about the Spasmodics have also surfaced, including Jerome Thale's *Sydney Dobell: A Spasmodic Poet*[4] and even one on the seldom-discussed Ebenezer Jones.[5]

Internet searches have also increased the visibility of books about the Spasmodics, enabling researchers to move beyond the ubiquitous triad of Trilling, Buckley, and Weinstein. Martha Westwater's 1992 book on Dobell makes a convincing case for viewing him as a feminist author as well as an insightful theorist.[6] Simon Berry's 2013 biography of Alexander Smith, *Applauding Thunder*, presents a sympathetic view of Smith's difficult life and career,[7] as well as his importance to Scottish literary history. Both of these books provide a different perspective than the earlier works, which viewed the Spasmodics through the eyes of their harshest detractors, Arnold and Aytoun.

Journal articles about the Spasmodics, too, have increased in frequency and widened in perspective. Modern forays into Spasmodic scholarship have dealt with Dobell and Smith's attitude toward the Crimean War,[8] Smith's importance as the voice of working-class Glasgow,[9] and Gilfillan's role as agent and victim of the increasingly powerful Victorian periodical press.[10]

Of particular significance was the release of a special issue of *Victorian Poetry* in Winter 2004, which celebrated the one hundred and fiftieth anniversary of Smith's controversial arrival on the literary scene by devoting an entire issue to a re-examination of the Spasmodic School and its members' contribution to nineteenth-century thought and poesy. Several articles deal boldly with the class issues and intellectual snobbery (not to mention some outright verbal cruelty) that incinerated the fledgling movement and the once-promising careers of Smith and Dobell, not to mention the well-meaning and fair-minded Gilfillan. Other articles present surprising new readings of the Spasmodic poems' explorations of gender, sexuality, and spirituality. One promising direction has been to reexamine the literary appropriation of the medical term "Spasmodic" itself,[11] which suggests a yet-unexplored connection between the physical (including the aural) and metaphorical qualities of poetics. It seems reasonable to assume that each new generation of scholars will continue to build on the critical innovations of the last.

Not so long ago, the Spasmodic poets seemed a group without a future. Their "school" was a phantasm created as a tool for ridicule, their poetry dismissed as ephemera bound for well-deserved oblivion. Yet, like the Brontë sisters, the group has undergone a kind of metamorphosis that has restored them to a position of relevance and even

Epilogue

respectability. The Spasmodics continue to inspire scholarly articles and increasingly appear in encyclopedia-type compendiums of Victorian lore and literature (though there is still some doubt as to which category they more accurately fall under).

It is doubtful that *Festus*, *Balder*, or *A Life-Drama* will ever claim a place among canonical Victorian works, though Dobell and Smith, at least, did demonstrate flashes of superior talent and even greatness. However, twenty-first century academics have embraced the field of cultural studies as an indispensable component of literary analysis. With its unflinching examination of class-based prejudice and the politics of canon formation, this approach has led to a more sympathetic and balanced view of the Spasmodics. There is no doubt that their story and their writings will continue to engage scholars of Victorian life and literature.

A Spasmodic Timeline

1802   Richard H. Horne born on 31 December

1813   George Gilfillan, the Spasmodic mentor, born on January 30

       William Edmondstoune Aytoun, satirist and critic, born on June 21

1816   Philip James Bailey, author of *Festus*, born on April 22

1819   John Westland Marston, author of *Gerald*, born on January 30

1820   Ebenezer Jones, author of *Studies of Sensation and Event*, born on January 20

1822   Matthew Arnold, poet and critic, born on December 24

1824   Sydney Dobell, author of *Balder*, born on April 5

1828   Gerald Massey, author of *Voices of Freedom and Lyrics of Love*, born May 29

       John Stanyan Bigg, author of *Night and the Soul*, born on July 14

1829   Alexander Smith, author of *A Life-Drama*, born on December 31

1837   Algernon Charles Swinburne, author of *Poems and Ballads*, born on April 5

       Queen Victoria ascends the throne June 20, beginning the Victorian era

1839   Philip James Bailey publishes first edition of *Festus*

1841   Thomas Carlyle publishes *Heroes, Hero-Worship, and The Heroic in History*, based on a series of six lectures given in May 1840

1842   John Westland Marston, publishes *Gerald*

A Spasmodic Timeline

1843 Richard H. Horne publishes *Orion*

Ebenezer Jones publishes *Studies of Sensation and Event*

1844 Richard H. Horne publishes *A New Spirit of the Age*

1846 Sydney Dobell reviews *Poems by Currer, Ellis, and Acton Bell* (the Brontë sisters) in the July 4 edition of *The Athenaeum*

1850 Gerald Massey publishes *Voices of Freedom and Lyrics of Love*

Sydney Dobell publishes *The Roman*

Sydney Dobell publishes "Currer Bell" in the September issue of *The Palladium*, prompting a correspondence with Charlotte Brontë (1816–1855)

1851 George Gilfillan introduces Alexander Smith's "A Life Fragment" to the public in the October issue of *The Eclectic Review*

1853 Alexander Smith publishes *A Life-Drama*

Matthew Arnold publishes *Poems*, adding his anti–Spasmodic Preface and removing "Empedocles on Etna"

Crimean War begins in October

1854 Sydney Dobell publishes *Balder*; the first periodical reviews appear in January

William Edmondstoune Aytoun's mock review of "Firmilian" appears in the May issue of *Blackwood's Edinburgh Magazine*; he publishes *Firmilian: a Spasmodic Tragedy* later that summer

1855 Alexander Smith and Sydney Dobell publish their collaboration, *Sonnets on the War*

Tennyson publishes *Maud*

1856 Sydney Dobell publishes his second Crimean War volume, *England in Time of War*

Crimean War ends in February

1857 Alexander Smith publishes *City Poems*

Elizabeth Barrett Browning publishes *Aurora Leigh*, possibly the last Spasmodic epic

A Spasmodic Timeline

1860 Ebenezer Jones, author of Studies *of Sensation and Event*, dies September 14

1865 John Stanyan Bigg, author of *Night and the Soul*, dies May 19

William Edmondstoune Aytoun, satirist and critic, dies August 4

1867 Alexander Smith, author of *A Life-Drama*, dies January 5

1874 Sydney Dobell, author of *Balder*, dies August 22

1878 George Gilfillan, the Spasmodic mentor, dies August 13

1884 Richard H. Horne, author of *Orion*, dies March 13

1888 Matthew Arnold, poet and critic, dies April 15

1890 John Westland Marston, author of *Gerald*, dies January 5

1901 Queen Victoria dies January 22, ending the Victorian era

1902 Philip James Bailey, author of *Festus*, dies November 6

1907 Gerald Massey, author of *Voices of Freedom and Lyrics of Love*, dies October 29

1909 Algernon Charles Swinburne, author of *Poems and Ballads*, dies April 10

Chapter Notes

Introduction

1. Lionel Trilling, *Matthew Arnold* (New York: Meridian, 1955), 136.
2. Jerome Buckley, *The Victorian Temper* (New York: Vintage, 1951), 42–43.
3. Buckley, 42.
4. Trilling, 136; cf. Donnelly's article on "Philistine taste" among the Victorian public with respect to their embrace of the Spasmodics.
5. Jason R. Rudy, "Rhythmic Intimacy, Spasmodic Epistemology," *Victorian Poetry* 42, no. 4 (2004): 466.
6. Lori A. Paige, "Charlotte Brontë and the Spasmodic School," *Brontë Society Transactions* 21, no. 3 (1994): 63–69.
7. See, for example, www. https://effectiviology.com/sturgeons-law/ for a more complete (and illuminating) explanation.
8. Linda K. Hughes, "Alexander Smith and the Bisexual Poetics of *A Life-Drama*," *Victorian Poetry* 42, no. 4 (2004): 491–508.
9. Robert Buchanan, in fact, retaliated against the charges of Spasmody made against him and Sydney Dobell, whom he admired, by pointing out the Pre-Raphaelites' "spasmodic ramifications in the erotic direction." See Robert Buchanan, *A Look Round Literature* (London: Ward and Downey, 1887), 888. Browning and Tennyson also embarrassedly shook off the association after critics bombarded them with similar accusations in 1855.
10. Martha Westwater, *The Spasmodic Career of Sydney Dobell* (Lanham, MD: University Press of America, 1992), 112. In fact, Rossetti ranked Dobell's poem "A Nuptial Eve" as a masterpiece on the same level as Keats' "La Belle Dame Sans Merci."

Chapter 1

1. Florence S. Boos, "'Spasm' and Class: W.E. Aytoun, George Gilfillan, Sydney Dobell, and Alexander Smith," *Victorian Poetry* 42, no. 4 (2004): 588.
2. Boos, 561–563.
3. Richard Garnett, "Sydney Dobell," in *The Poets and Poetry of the Century*, vol. 5, *Charles Kingsley to James Thomson*, ed. Alfred H. Miles (London: Hutchinson, 1898), 179.
4. Garnett, "Sydney Dobell," in *The Poets and Poetry of the Century*, ed. Alfred H. Miles (London: Hutchinson, 1898), 179.
5. Robert Chambers, ed., *Chambers's Cyclopædia of English Literature: A History, Critical and Biographical, of Authors in the English Tongue from the Earliest Times Till the Present Day, with Specimens of Their Writings*, New ed., vol. 3 (Philadelphia: J.B. Lippincott, 1910), 527. The author of this section is identified as W. Robertson Nicoll.
6. John Bulloch, ed., "A Bibliography of Edinburgh Periodical Literature," in *Scottish Notes and Queries*, vol. 3, 2nd series (Aberdeen: Rosemount, 1905), 166. W.J. Couper contributed this section.
7. Dobell was identified as the reviewer by Anne Passel in *Charlotte and Emily Brontë: An Annotated Bibliography* (New York: Garland, 1979).
8. E[mily] J[olly], *The Life and Letters of Sydney Dobell*, vol. 1 (London: Smith and Elder, 1878), 165.

Notes—Chapter 1

9. See, for example, Lucasta Miller, *The Brontë Myth* (New York: Anchor, 2007), 21–23.

10. Clement Shorter went so far as to assert that Dobell founded the Emily "cult." For a more detailed discussion of the Spasmodic connection to Charlotte Brontë, see Lori A. Paige, "Charlotte Brontë and the Spasmodic School," *Brontë Society Transactions* 21, no. 3 (1994): 63–69.

11. Southey's letter to Charlotte Brontë can be found at https://www.bl.uk/collection-items/letter-from-robert-southey-to-charlotte-Brontë-12-march-1837. It is one of the more satisfying ironies of literary history that Charlotte Brontë has become a household name, while Southey is nearly forgotten outside of academics.

12. Matthew Arnold to A.H. Clough, 21 March 1853, *The Letters of Matthew Arnold*, ed. Cecil Y. Lang, 6 vols. (Charlottesville: University of Virginia Press, 2001), 1:258; qtd. in many sources, not to Arnold's credit.

13. Boos, 572.

14. Hughes, "Alexander Smith and the Bisexual Poetics of *A Life-Drama*," passim.

15. Trilling, *Matthew Arnold*, 133–135.

16. Florence Boos argues that Gilfillan's praise was not as untempered as W.E. Aytoun's merciless lampoon has led history to believe; she views his critiques as more akin to the suggestions of a modern college professor or dissertation advisor (564).

17. Charles LaPorte, "Spasmodic Poetics and Clough's Apostasies," *Victorian Poetry* 42, no. 4 (2004): 531.

18. LaPorte, 532.

19. Boos, 555.

20. Boos, 576.

21. J[olly], 2:33. In 1854, just before the publication of *Firmilian*, Dobell found himself forced to "g[i]ve extempore lectures" on Smith's poetry to defend him from "immorality" and earn him a secretarial post at the University of Edinburgh.

22. J[olly], 1:335. By 1856, Smith had married and turned to prose to support his new wife and growing family. In 1857, the accusation of plagiarism, apparently motivated purely by spite, brought Dobell to his defense again.

23. Aytoun died in 1865; the first edition of Smith's book of essays, *Last Leaves*, appeared in 1868.

24. Alexander Smith, *Last Leaves: Sketches and Criticisms* (Edinburgh: Nimmo, 1869), 173, 175.

25. Buckley, *The Victorian Temper*, 61.

26. Andrew Rutherford, *Lord Byron: The Critical Heritage* (London: Routledge, 2013), 492.

27. David DeLaura, "Robert Browning the Spasmodic," *Studies in Browning and His Circle* 2 (1974): 56–57.

28. [Charles Kingsley], "Thoughts on Shelley and Byron," *Fraser's* 48 (1853): 573–574. This and the other uses of "spasmodic" are quoted and discussed fully in DeLaura 57–59. Martha Westwater's *Spasmodic Career of Sydney Dobell* playfully suggests that Robert and Elizabeth Barrett Browning, who mentored R.H. Horne and admired P.J. Bailey, should actually be considered "the parents of Spasmodicism" (Westwater, 7).

29. George Brimley, *Essays* (New York: Rudd and Carleton, 1861), 41, 75.

30. Brimley, 81.

31. Rudy, "Rhythmic Intimacy, Spasmodic Epistemology," 453–4. According to Rudy, the word carried particular resonance during the era of *A Life-Drama*, *Balder*, and *Firmilian*; a deadly epidemic known as "Spasmodic Cholera" had ravaged Britain in the 1830s and again in 1853–1854; the word also appears in *Jane Eyre* (1847) and Elizabeth Gaskell's *Ruth* (1853), in both cases describing a bodily reaction to dramatic plot twists.

32. The frequent references to bodily shaking in Spasmodic poems, both abstract and physical, are discussed in Kirstie Blair, "Spasmodic Affections: Poetry, Pathology, and the Spasmodic Hero," *Victorian Poetry* 42, no. 4 (2004): 184 and passim.

33. Rudy explains that Dobell's use of metrical spasms was deliberate, perhaps akin to Coleridge's description of the Aeolian Harp; Dobell believed that the effect of verbal messages could and should result in "vibrations of the human

body." See Rudy, "Rhythmic Intimacy, Spasmodic Epistemology," 457–459 and 453.

34. Blair, "Spasmodic Affections," 474.

35. Martha Westwater, *The Spasmodic Career of Sydney Dobell* (New York: University Press of America, 1992), 6.

36. Nick J. Watson, "Muscular Christianity in the Modern Age," *Sport and Spirituality* (London: Taylor and Francis, 2007), 81–82.

37. J.C. Hawley, "Charles Kingsley and Literary Theory of the 1850s," *Victorian Literature and Culture* 19 (1992): 171; Tennyson was apparently outraged when he mistakenly believed he was the model for Vavasour, lending credence to his self-identification with the Spasmodics.

38. Dobell's essays were collected in a posthumous volume edited by his admirer John Nichol, and will be dealt with in the chapter on Dobell.

39. Rutherford, 291.

40. Isobel Armstrong, *Victorian Scrutinies: Reviews of Poetry 1830–1870* (London: Athlone, 1972), 125.

41. "Alexander Smith's Poems," *Blackwood's Edinburgh Magazine* 75 (1854): 346.

42. See, for example, Kirstie Blair, "Swinburne's Spasms: *Poems and Ballads* and the Spasmodic School," *Yearbook of English Studies* 36, no. 2 (2006): 180–196. As noted, the Pre-Raphaelite "School" drew together a variety of poets and artists with sometimes incompatible tastes and methods in much the same way the Spasmodic movement did. Despite this, the Spasmodics, like the Pre-Raphaelites, shared a common agenda of revitalizing poetry via an infusion of extreme Romanticism. Dante Gabriel Rossetti, as we have seen, was an admirer of Dobell, as were other members of his circle. In particular, William Morris and Edward Burne-Jones' organ, *The Oxford and Cambridge Magazine*, enabled the iconoclastic Oxford Brotherhood to champion various Spasmodic productions.

43. Complete bibliographical citations for all of the anthologies containing Spasmodic poems mentioned here can be found in the supplementary bibliography.

44. Laura Riding and Robert Graves, *A Pamphlet Against Anthologies* (New York: AMS, 1970), 44.

45. Gerald Graff, *Professing Literature: An Institutional History* (Chicago: Chicago University Press, 1987), 99–100. Almost concurrently, the canon utilized by American schools was born in response to entrance standards developed in 1894 by representatives for the new National Conference on Uniform Entrance Requirements.

46. W. Davenport Adams, *Dictionary of English Literature*, 1880 ed.

47. Riding and Graves, 123, 125–6.

48. W.H. Auden, ed., *Nineteenth Century Minor Poets* (New York: Delacorte,1966), 15–16.

49. John Ruskin, *Modern Painters*, https://www.gutenberg.org/files/44329/44329-h/44329-h.htm.

Chapter 2

1. Richard D. Altick, *The English Common Reader* (Chicago: University of Chicago Press, 1957), 257.

2. Lowry, Howard Foster, ed., *The Letters of Matthew Arnold to Arthur Hugh Clough* (London: Oxford University Press, 1932), 136.

3. Altick, *English Common Reader*, 243, 390.

4. Louis James, *English Popular Literature 1819–1851* (New York: Columbia University Press, 1976), 18–21. James discusses in detail the effects increased literacy had on English society in the early nineteenth century, including turning popular consciousness from superstition towards the beginnings of rationality and even political awareness.

5. Walter E. Houghton, "Victorian Periodical Literature and the Articulate Classes," *Victorian Studies* 22, no. 4 (1979): 389.

6. Caley Ehnes, *Victorian Poetry and the Poetics of the Literary Periodical* (Edinburgh University Press, 2018), 2.

7. Richard D. Altick, *Writers, Readers, and Occasions: Selected Essays on Victorian Literature and Life* (Columbus: Ohio State University Press, 1989), 144, 146.

8. Dalziel, Margaret. *Popular Fiction*

Notes—Chapter 2

One Hundred Years Ago (London: Cohen and West, 1957), 2. Even in the most lurid tale of homicide, Dalziel notes, as in a gothic romance, "the heroine's feelings were as prominent as the murder" (16).

9. Altick, *The English Common Reader*, 249. Alexander Smith, as will be seen, was said to have indulged both in reading and writing while supposedly at work in a muslin factory.

10. Altick, *The English Common Reader*, 290; see also James, *English Popular Literature 1819–1851*, 38–39. One penny novel-publisher admonished his staff illustrators to make the eyes of the characters larger and to depict "more blood" (Dalziel, 20). Dalziel also notes that the diction of the characters resembles that of the staged melodrama, filled with soliloquy and mechanical rhetorical flourishes (17).

11. Altick, *English Common Reader*, 287.

12. A good many of these are reproduced in James, 248–53.

13. Reproduced in James, 251.

14. James, 86. James suggests that the blending of melodrama and art was far less unsettling to the Victorians than to us: at the time, "melodrama ... with its roots in tradition and the sensibility of the people, but with its dynamic of emotional conflict and change, became a natural stylistic mode for the period" (87). Certainly the Spasmodics, who grew up in the workaday world, would have accepted melodramatic conventions as common and acceptable modes of expression.

15. Buckley, *The Victorian Temper*, 57; this line, due to the wide exposure it received in Buckley's book, has unfortunately become the best-known Spasmodic quote.

16. Altick suggests that illiterate lovers of books may have paid others to read to them, and that groups of laborers commonly did so to stifle the boredom of long hours (*English Common Reader*, 250). The Spasmodics, coming from laboring backgrounds, would surely have been aware of this and may well have taken it into account when composing their most impassioned passages.

17. Altick *English Common Reader*, 248–49.

18. [Hamley, E.B.], "Alexander Smith's Poems," *Blackwood's Edinburgh Magazine* 75 (1854): 346.

19. Trilling, for example, asserts that for the most part "the British public admired genius—and rather preferred it raw, like Alexander Smith's ... the idea of genius was attractive to the middle class: a genius was an absolute success and he had won his way *all by himself*" (*Matthew Arnold*, 181, emphasis Trilling's).

20. Altick, *English Common Reader* describes that "era's sentimental adulation of the low-born poet" and names a few examples, all of whom are now forgotten with the exception of Burns (241).

21. Merle Mowbray Bevington, *The Saturday Review: 1855–1868* (New York: AMS, 1966), 229; Altick (*English Common Reader*, 387) claims that by 1866 Tupper had sold no less than 200,000 copies; these numbers become more meaningful when contrasted to Tennyson's collected works, which according to Altick's calculations on the same page would have sold about 100,000 between 1885 and 1891.

22. Ward and Waller, *The Cambridge History of English Literature* Vol. 12, Part 2 (New York: Putnam, 1917), 167.

23. Bevington, 230.

24. Ralf Buchman, *Martin F. Tupper and the Victorian Middle Class Mind* (Bern: Verlag A. Francke, 1941), 29; Buchman regards this curious stance as "a true Victorian compromise!"

25. Buchman, 14, 43, 36.

26. Edmund Gosse, *Portraits and Sketches* (London: Heinemann, 1912), 104. In 1834, Ragg apparently published an ambitious work called "The Deity," which earned him a brief fame.

27. See, for example, Trilling, *Matthew Arnold*, 136: "The very great popularity of the Spasmodics may be accounted for easily enough: they were intense yet pious; they made a fine show of rushing out to meet the problems of modern life but their endowment was limited enough to keep them safe and platitudinous." Likewise, he sees Smith as having "received part of his acclaim

Notes—Chapter 2

on the ground of being a poet of the people. He had been a mechanic [in the sense of one who labors with his hands, i.e., a factory worker] and this seems to have induced Citizen Clough to read into his pretentious work a democratic significance which was simply not there." Clough's article in *The North American Review*, in which he compared Smith unfavorably to Arnold, had aided Smith's reputation immensely, although it enraged Arnold.

28. Walter Houghton, *The Victorian Frame of Mind* (New Haven: Yale University Press, 1957), 140–141.

29. David Perkins, "The Construction of 'The Romantic Movement' as a Literary Classification," *Nineteenth-Century Literature* 45 (1990): 136–37. Only after the publication of Walter Pater's "Romanticism" in 1876 does the label and concept of "a Romantic School," comprising most or all of the poets we now classify as Romantics, appear in a critical discussion.

30. [Charles Kingsley], "Thoughts on Byron and Shelley," 571–72. Many of Kingsley's contemporaries, inspired by his dedication to the cause of Christian Socialism, suggested that he should become "a Poet of the People" himself; however, Kingsley chose to advance his cause through novels instead (Hawley, *Charles Kingsley and Literary Theory of the 1850s*, 169, 177.

31. William K. Wimsatt and Cleanth Brooks, *Literary Criticism* (New York: Knopf, 1959), 435–36.

32. J.S. Mill, "What Is Poetry?" *Victorians on Literature and Art*, ed. Robert Peters (New York: Appleton, 1961), 91.

33. Leslie A. Marchand, *The Athenaeum: A Mirror of Victorian Culture* (Chapel Hill: University of North Carolina Press, 1941), 232.

34. Marchand, 244.

35. Marchand, 233.

36. [Kingsley], "Thoughts" 568.

37. "Keats and His School," *Fraser's Magazine for Town and Country* 38 (1848): 496.

38. "Keats and His School," 496.

39. Walter Houghton, *The Victorian Frame of Mind*, 155.

40. D. Masson, "Theories of Poetry and a New Poet," in Armstrong, *Victorian Scrutinies*, 331.

41. Sydney Dobell, *Balder: Part the First* (London: Smith, Elder, 1854), 86, 188.

42. T. Percy Jones [W.E. Aytoun], *Firmilian* (Edinburgh: Blackwood, 1854), 139.

43. Arnold's exasperation, which at times borders upon the paranoid, is reflected, for example, in his rant against the "touch of grossness in our race" as shown in working-class names like Wragg, Stiggins, and Bugg, in "The Function of Criticism at the Present Time." One can certainly hear the echo of real-life working-class poets Thomas Ragg and J.S. Bigg in them, whether intentional or not.

44. R.G. Cox, "Victorian Criticism of Poetry: The Minority Tradition," *Scrutiny* 18 (1951): 2–17.

45. Amy Cruse notes, however, that in spite of their rejection of Byron, people who had moved on "looked back on their youthful extravagances with pride rather than with shame." See *The Victorians and Their Reading* (Boston: Houghton-Mifflin, 1935), 174.

46. George Saintsbury, "On Byron's Second Rateness," in Rutherford, *Byron: The Critical Heritage*, 478–79.

47. Carlyle, "Burns," rpt. in Rutherford, 290.

48. Again, Carlyle seems to be speaking of Byron himself in *Past and Present* when he declares the "endless significance" of "Work," and implies the utter waste of superior personal ability as the "English lord" merely "works weakly ... sitting in sunny Italy, in his coach-and-four [and] writes, over many reams of paper, the following sentence, with variations: *Saw ever the world one greater or unhappier?*" He warns: "This was a sham strong man," and demands of the reader, "Choose ye—" (Rutherford, 292).

49. [Kingsley], "Thoughts," 570.

50. Samuel Chew, *Byron in England: His Fame and After-Fame* (New York: Russell and Russell, 1965), 259.

51. Mark A. Weinstein, *William*

Notes—Chapter 3

Edmundstoune Aytoun and the Spasmodic Controversy (New Haven: Yale University Press, 1969), 68.

52. [Kingsley], "Thoughts," 576.
53. Henry Taylor, Preface to *Philip von Artevelde*, rpt. in Rutherford, 329.
54. qtd. in Cox, 6–9.
55. Rutherford, 326–327.
56. Rutherford, 329.
57. Gosse, *Portraits and Sketches*, 67–69.
58. Tennyson, embarrassed, replied to the young man's sincere effusion with a curt "Don't talk such damned nonsense." The anecdote is related in (among others) Jerome Thale, *Sydney Dobell: A Spasmodic Poet* (Ph.D. Diss., Northwestern University, 1953), 145. Its veracity is doubted by Gosse, and Weinstein concurs that the date of Tennyson's introduction to Dobell makes it unlikely to have happened as related (Weinstein, *William Edmundstoune Aytoun and the Spasmodic Controversy*, 173).
59. Byron, a baron, towered socially over the working-class Keats. His work was also free of the subversive politics found in Shelley poems like "England in 1819" and "Song to the Men of England."
60. "Keats and His School," 495.
61. Edmund Gosse, *A Short History of Modern English Literature* (New York: Appleton, 1900), 364.
62. J.A. Pyre, "Byron in Our Day," rpt. in Rutherford, 492.
63. "Keats and His School," 496.
64. [Kingsley], "Thoughts on Byron and Shelley," 575.
65. Bernard Richards, *English Poetry of the Victorian Period 1830–1890* (London: Longman, 1988), 13–14.
66. [Peter Bayne?], Rev. of Smith's *Poems, Tait's Edinburgh Magazine* 20 (1853): 303.
67. As Geoffrey Tillotson puts it (*Criticism and the Nineteenth Century* [Hamden, CT: Archon, 1967], 48), seeing the need for "practical morality" among the newly empowered middle class, Arnold "set himself the task of refining that class … [by] endowing it with 'culture' and by transferring onto poetry the traditional role of religion in shaping ethics." George Ford (*Keats and the Victorians* [Hamden, CT: Archon, 1962], 55) agrees that "Arnold felt the need for some sustaining forces to replace the crumbling masonry of the old order…. Thus he asserts in 'The Study of Poetry': 'most of what now passes … for religion and philosophy will be replaced by poetry.'"
68. Cruse, 180. Thackeray and Ainsworth were also Bailey's champions. Ainsworth declared, again in the familiar vein, that Bailey's "place will be among the first, if not the first, of our native poets" (Weinstein, 74).
69. Rev. of *The Roman*, by Sydney Dobell, *Literary Gazette* 35, no. 1775 (1851): 63.
70. Rev. of *The Roman*, by Sydney Dobell, *The Athenaeum* 1172 (1850): 398.
71. [George Gilfillan], Rev. of *The Roman*, by Sydney Dobell, *The Eclectic Review* 101 (1850): 672.
72. [Gilfillan], Rev. of *The Roman*, 677.
73. [Gilfillan], Rev. of *The Roman*, 677–78. Gilfillan does not, however, see the irony in his declaring this perfect Christian poet the potential "Magnus Apollo of our present age."
74. [Gilfillan], Rev. of *The Roman*, 678–79.
75. [Gilfillan], Rev. of *The Roman*, 684.
76. [George Gilfillan], Rev. of *Poems*, by Alexander Smith, *The Eclectic Review* 6 (1853): 541–44.
77. [Gilfillan], Rev. of *Poems*, 550.
78. [W.E. Aytoun], "The Two Arnolds," *Blackwood's Edinburgh Magazine* 75 (1854): 304.
79. See, for example, Hawley, *Charles Kingsley and Literary Theory of the 1850s*, 167–68.
80. [Hamley], "Alexander Smith's Poems," 347.

Chapter 3

1. Robert Chambers, ed., *Chambers's Cyclopædia of English Literature: A History, Critical and Biographical, of Authors in the English Tongue from the Earliest Times Till the Present Day, with Specimens of Their Writings*, New ed., vol. 3 (Philadelphia: J.B. Lippincott, 1910),

Notes—Chapter 3

507. James Douglas is identified as the author of this entry.

2. Westwater, *The Spasmodic Career of Sydney Dobell*, 6.

3. LaPorte, "Spasmodic Poetics and Clough's Apostasies," 524.

4. Edmund Gosse, *Portraits and Sketches*, 61, 62..

5. Cornelius Weygandt, *The Time of Tennyson: English Victorian Poetry as It Affected America* (New York: Appleton, 1936), 277. This same commentator goes on to note that "if only the verse of Philip James Bailey ... were as poetical as his appearance in old age he would have been a great poet indeed."

6. Gosse, *Portraits and Sketches*, 63.

7. Robert Birley, *Sunk Without Trace: Some Forgotten Masterpieces Reconsidered* (Westport, CT: Greenwood, 1962), 206–207.

8. James Douglas, in *Chambers's Cyclopædia of English Literature*, 508. See also Westwater, 6. Bailey had been favorably compared with Tennyson, Browning, and even Milton by a number of nineteenth-century critics.

9. *Chambers's Cyclopædia of English Literature*, 508.

10. *Chambers's Cyclopædia of English Literature*, 507.

11. George Saintsbury in A.W. Ward and A.R. Waller, *The Cambridge History of English Literature*, 172.

12. Weygandt, *The Time of Tennyson*, 278–79.

13. Greta A. Black, "P.J. Bailey's Debt to Goethe's *Faust* in His *Festus*," *MLR* 28 (1933): 167.

14. According to Weinstein, Thackeray called Bailey "an author of much merit and genius," while Ainsworth declared that "his place will be among the first, if not the first, of our native poets" (74). Tennyson recommended *Festus* to FitzGerald in 1846 with the following warning: "Order it and read: you will most likely find it a great bore, but there are really very grand things in *Festus*" (Edith Batho and Bonamy Dobree, *The Victorians and After: 1830–1914* [New York: McBride 1938], 233). Birley (187) also speculates that Tennyson echoed some of Bailey's lines in *In Memoriam*.

15. Birley, 173–75.

16. George Gilfillan, *Modern Literature and Literary Men: Being a Second Gallery of Literary Portraits* (New York: Appleton, 1850), 340, 341.

17. The preceding biographical information is from Hallman B. Bryant, *The Spasmodic School: A Study of a Victorian Literary Phenomenon* (Diss., Vanderbilt University, 1968), 51–60.

18. W. Robertson Nicoll and Thomas J. Wise, *Literary Anecdotes of the Nineteenth Century: Contributions Towards a Literary History of the Period* (London: Hodder and Stoughton, 1896), Vol. 1, 413–14.

19. Hugh Walker, *The Literature of the Victorian Era* (Cambridge: Cambridge University Press, 1913), 349. Of course, Smith and Dobell also rejected the idea of belonging to a particular "School" and were embarrassed by the label "Spasmodic."

20. W.M. Rossetti, "William Bell Scott and Modern British Poetry," *Macmillan's* 33 (1876): 427.

21. Ward and Waller, 173.

22. *Chambers's Cyclopædia of English Literature*, 507.

23. Richard Hengist Horne, *A New Spirit of the Age* (1844; London: Oxford University Press, 1907), 468, 470. Cf. Festus 130, in which a "Student" declares:

For well we know that, properly prepared,
Souls self-adapted knowledge to receive
Are by the truth desired, illumined; man's
Spirit, extolled, dilated, clarified,
By holy meditation and divine
Lore, fits him to convene with purer powers...

24. Horne 453, 469. As Weinstein elaborates, "Bailey soared and sunk into Heaven, Hell, Everywhere, and Nowhere" and thus "ardent young spirits [among them Elizabeth Barrett Browning], feeling a sense of liberation, tended to confuse its merit with its intent" (Weinstein 75).

25. Birley, 173.

26. Black, 167.

27. *Chambers's Cyclopædia of English Literature*, 507, 510.

28. See Gosse, *Portraits and Sketches*, 73–74 for a catalogue of similarities.

Notes—Chapter 3

Gosse also notes that, as subsequent editions of *Festus* appeared, Bailey tried to minimize his poem's resemblance to Goethe's.

29. P.J. Bailey, *Festus: A Poem* (1839; New York: Knox, 1885), 17; Byron, *Cain, Lord Byron: Selected Poems and Letters*, ed. William H. Marshall (Boston: Houghton Mifflin, 1968), I.i.1–8. Since the lines are not numbered in Bailey's *Festus*, all references to its contents will be to page numbers.

30. Byron, *Cain*, II.i.22–25; Bailey, *Festus*, 36.

31. Bailey, *Festus*, 34; Byron, *Cain*, I.i.180, 213–215.

32. As far as Black was able to discover, "the doctrine of Universalism had never been introduced into poetry, and in that respect *Festus* was different from anything that had previously appeared" (Black, 168).

33. John Gross, *The Rise and Fall of the Man of Letters* (London: Weidenfeld, 1969), 191. Gross calls Gilfillan "the MacGonigall of criticism," referring to a particularly inept but beloved popular poet, who was "throbb[ing] with the libertarian idealism of the Mazzini-Kossuth epoch" (this accounted, obviously, for his enthusiasm for Dobell's *The Roman*) who "refused to be intimidated by great names when his beliefs were at stake" (190).

34. Westwater, 4.

35. Gosse, *Portraits and Sketches*, 92.

36. Weygandt, 278

37. *Chambers's Cyclopædia of English Literature*, 507.

38. Hugh Walker, *The Age of Tennyson* (London, Bell, 1914), 64.

39. Martin Farquhar Tupper, *Proverbial Philosophy: A Book of Thoughts and Arguments, Originally Treated* (New York: Wiley and Putnam, 1846), 1st Series, 31. Since Tupper's lines are not numbered, all references to *Proverbial Philosophy* will be to series and page number.

40. Tupper, 1st Series, 36.

41. Bailey, *Festus*, 63–64.

42. This aspect of *Festus* is thoroughly discussed in Birley, 184–87.

43. Birley, 177.

44. Walker, *Literature of the Victorian Era*, 346. In Bailey's own words, "when I dismissed the piece [*Festus*] it seemed to me perfect." See Alan McKillop, "A Victorian Faust," *PMLA* 40 (1925): 743.

45. McKillop, 745. Cf. Westwater's discussion of Dobell's solitary education (23).

46. Cf. also Gerald's initial revulsion from the common people of his village, for which his love Edith rebukes him: "Bethink thee, love! they are thy fellow men" (J.W. Marston, *Gerald* [London: Mitchell, 1842], 14).

47. Bailey, *Festus*, 7, 391.

48. Walker, *Literature of the Victorian Era*, 349, 347.

49. Bailey, *Festus*, 132; 376.

50. Bailey, *Festus*, 96.

51. Byron, *Cain*, II.ii.285.

52. Bailey, *Festus*, 295–96.

53. Tupper, 1st Series, 64–65.

54. Bailey, *Festus*, 304–307.

55. Black, 173.

56. Byron, *Cain*, I.i.558–60.

57. Bailey, *Festus*, 20.

58. Bailey, *Festus*, 280.

59. Bailey himself seemed to be unhappy with the weak characterization in this section, and he tried repeatedly to rectify it by adding more lines contributing to Elissa's development (see Birley, 200–201).

60. Bailey, *Festus*, 34–35. Cf. 46: "Oh! if God hates the flesh, why made He it / So beautiful that e'en its semblance maddens?"; 57: "But I cannot live unless I love and am loved; / Unless I have the young and beautiful / Bound up like pictures in my book of life"; 324: "What can we do but love? It is our cup"; and 332: "The cold calm kiss which cometh as a gift, / Not a necessity, is not for me, / Whose bliss, whose woe, whose life, whose all is love."

61. Bailey, *Festus*, 71.

62. See, for example, Bailey, *Festus*, 64–65, 340, and Marian's charge, so similar to Amy's in *Balder* that Festus' main purpose "'tis to sue—to gain—deceive—/ To tire of—to neglect—and leave" (181).

63. Bailey, *Festus*, 34.

64. Bailey, *Festus*, 133.

65. Bailey, *Festus*, 30, 39.

66. Bailey does, unlike his successors,

see a certain humor in Festus' interstellar preoccupations: at one point (192), Lucifer is exasperated enough to chide Festus that "thou art ever prating of the stars / Like an old soldier of his wars; / Thou shouldst have been a starling, friend, / And not an earthling: end!"

67. Bailey, *Festus*, 333.
68. J[olly], 1:182.
69. Bailey, *Festus*, 205. Bryant (*The Spasmodic School*, 83) suggests that Bailey is actually inverting the Neoplatonic "ladder of love" by which man proceeds from sensual to divine love.
70. Bailey, *Festus*, 291.
71. Bailey, *Festus*, 87, 96.
72. Bailey, *Festus*, 146.
73. These digressions occur, respectively, in Bailey, *Festus*, 113, 94, and 106–107.
74. Bailey, *Festus*, 272–73. For evidence relating to the Byronic identity of the friend, see Bryant, 94.
75. Ward and Waller, 173.
76. Bryant, 102–5.
77. Gosse, *Portraits and Sketches*, ix. Gosse goes on to note that, sadly, "those who had an opportunity of conversing with these interesting and pathetic figures in their old age are growing rare, while no life of either of them has appeared." Horne died in 1884, like Bailey reaching his eighties.
78. *Chambers's Cyclopædia of English Literature*, 413.
79. Gosse, *Portraits and Sketches*, 103.
80. [William Henry Smith], "Festus," *Blackwood's Edinburgh Magazine* 67 (1850): 416.
81. [Smith], 429.

Chapter 4

1. Thomas Carlyle, *On Heroes, Hero-Worship, and The Heroic in History*, Lecture 3, http://www.gutenberg.org/files/1091/1091-h/1091-h.htm.
2. Buckley, *The Victorian Temper*, 47.
3. See Lionel Stevenson, *The Pre-Raphaelite Poets* (Chapel Hill: University of North Carolina Press, 1972), 299, for a discussion of P.B. Marston's involvement in the third phase of Rossetti's movement.
4. James Vinson, "John Westland Marston," *Great Writers of the English Language: Poets* (New York: Palgrave Macmillan, 1979), 656–58.
5. Horne, *A New Spirit of the Age*, 359.
6. For a further explication of Horne's meaning and this passage's effect on Browning, see DeLaura, "Robert Browning the Spasmodic," 57–58. Famously, Lionel Trilling pronounced Browning "a Spasmodic poet who managed to be good" (*Matthew Arnold*, 136).
7. Horne, *A New Spirit of the Age*, 357–58.
8. Horne, 368, 364.
9. Wimsatt and Brooks, *Literary Criticism*, 436.
10. Horne, 369–70.
11. Horne, 365, 368 (emphasis Horne's).
12. John Westland Marston, *Gerald: A Dramatic Poem and Other Poems*, v–vii (emphasis Marston's).
13. Marston, *Gerald*, 23n.
14. Marston, *Gerald*, 45, 64, 43. Since the poem's lines are not numbered, all subsequent references to it will be to page numbers only.
15. Marston, *Gerald*, 9, 47.
16. Marston, *Gerald*, 112.
17. Marston, *Gerald*, 6–7 (emphasis Marston's).
18. Marston, *Gerald*, 14, 98.
19. Marston, *Gerald*, 24 (emphasis Marston's); cf. the unintentionally amusing speech by Edith, so similar to several spoken by Amy in *Balder*:

   Ah! mine own!
   There is a title that I covet more
   Than any thou hast given me.
   ...
   The simple one of—*Woman* [5].

20. Joseph Bristow, ed., *The Victorian Poet: Poetics and Persona* (London: Croom Helm, 1987), 51–52. The emphasis is Smith's. See also M.H. Abrams, *The Mirror and the Lamp: Romantic Theory and the Critical Tradition* (London: Oxford University Press, 1971), 148–155, for more information on Smith of Banff and his critical views.
21. Nigel Cross, *The Common Writer: Life in Eighteenth-Century Grub Street*

Notes—Chapter 4

(Cambridge: Cambridge University Press, 1985), 128.

22. Alexander Smith, *Poems* (1853; Boston: Ticknor and Fields, 1855), 109, 183. This volume contains the full text of *A Life-Drama*. Since *A Life-Drama*'s lines are not numbered, all references will be to the poem's title and its page numbers only.

23. Richard Cronin, *A Companion to Victorian Poetry* (New York: Wiley, 2008), 294.

24. Boos, "'Spasm' and Class," 561. In contrast, Boos (not without justification) casts Aytoun as a near-villain, who indulges in an almost "perverse ... attempt to convict [Smith's] pensive soul of 'gross sensuality'" (575).

25. [George Gilfillan], "Recent Poetry," *The Eclectic Review* 2 (1851): 458–59. According to Bryant, the readers responded as Gilfillan hoped; letters of "warm congratulation" to Smith flowed from both England and Scotland even before the publication of his first volume (Bryant, *The Spasmodic School*, 122).

26. [Gilfillan], "Recent Poetry" 461–62; Weinstein also attributes the Smith phenomenon to the fact that Smith "seemed to be a new Keats at a time when Keats had become extremely popular" (92).

27. Smith, *A Life-Drama*, 19, 32.

28. Armstrong, *Victorian Scrutinies*, 154.

29. While Cronin has attempted to exonerate Gilfillan from blame regarding the poem's uncalled-for expansion ("Alexander Smith and the Poetry of Displacement," 134), Weinstein (87) has no qualms about attributing the ill-advised padding of the "Fragment" to him. Evidence suggests that the revising went on for no less than two full years until *Poems* appeared in 1853.

30. [Gilfillan], "Recent Poetry," 459. Ironically, the *Festus*-like preoccupation with imagery was to result in one of the most severe blows of Smith's career, the charges of plagiarism in *The Athenaeum*.

31. Hughes, "Alexander Smith and the Bisexual Poetics of A Life-Drama," passim.

32. Bryant, *The Spasmodic School*, 147.

33. Armstrong, 163.

34. Armstrong, 155–56.

35. Armstrong, 157. Earlier, Clough had openly declared that Smith's lowly vocational status "does add to [his poems'] external interest, and perhaps also their intrinsic merit," not least because they provide a "grateful contrast to the ordinary languid *collectanea* published by young men of literary habits" (154). His ensuing comments regarding his friend Arnold's social privileges leaves his real purpose in contrasting these two poets all too obvious.

36. Armstrong, 159. While Arnold's 1853 Preface is commonly regarded as his rejection of Clough's Romantic agenda for poetry, to some extent Arnold did agree that some of his poetry did resemble mere exercises in prosody at the expense of moral instruction. Hence his famous removal of "Empedocles on Etna" from the volume's next edition. Unlike Clough, Arnold continued to believe that the Spasmodics, and other neo-Romantic poets, offered no such guidance in an uncertain age and was apparently determined not to be so classed himself.

37. To answer Bayne's question about Smith's nickname, it was "Aleck" according to Simon Berry, *Applauding Thunder* (Inverness: FTRR, 2013), 1.

38. [Peter Bayne?], Rev. of Smith's *Poems*, 302–303. In spite of this flattery, Bayne did recognize small flaws in Smith's technique, prompting him to issue some gentle *caveats* concerning putting more thought into his composition and toning down his rampant imagery (cf. Armstrong, 168–70). These strongly resembled those given Dobell upon publication of the flawed *Roman*. As Cox notes, *The Spectator* likewise warned Smith to "learn more about facts, care more about what objects are in themselves and less about the amount of pleasure they are capable of giving him" (Cox 9).

39. Smith, *A Life-Drama*, 85.

40. Smith, *A Life-Drama*, 10–11.

41. Smith, *A Life-Drama*, 101–102.

42. Smith, *A Life-Drama*, 88.

43. Smith, *A Life-Drama*, 159. Cf. 85, where Walter declares that "to set this

Notes—Chapter 4

Age to music [is] the great work / Before the Poet now..."

44. This device had, of course, been exploited in *Festus* (346): "I had / A friend with whom, in boyhood, I was wont / To learn, think, laugh, weep, strive, and love, together..."

45. Smith, *Poems*, 180.

46. [Peter Bayne?], Rev. of "Poems," 305.

47. Smith, *A Life-Drama*, 5–6.

48. Smith, *A Life-Drama* 9. Cf. Walter's later "A Passion has grown up to be a King, / Ruling my being [like a] mad sun on prostrate desert" (33) and his friend Edward's observation that

Walter's love-sick for Fame:
A haughty mistress! How this mad old world
Reels to its burning grave, shouting forth names,
Like a wild drunkard at his frenzy's height,
And they who bear them deem such shouting *Fame*,
And, smiling, die content [83].

49. Smith, *A Life-Drama*, 11, 59; cf. [Gilfillan], Rev. of *The Roman* 398.

50. Smith, *A Life-Drama*, 17–18; The remainder of this passage is cited by Bryant as a prime example of Smith's overreaching and muddled image-making:

Most souls are shut
By sense from grandeur, as a man who snores
Night-capped and wrapped in blankets to the nose,
Is shut out from the night, which, like a sea
Breaketh forever on a strand of stars.

The incongruity and lack of "hard intellectual content," he notes, cause "Smith's images [to] roll and jerk about in a kind of mental void" (147).

51. Smith, *A Life-Drama*, 155. Walter's Keatsian mentor similarly "Came with all his youth and unblown hopes / On the world's heart, and touched it into tears" (33), a passage which again helps to convince us that Smith himself is a second Keats.

52. Smith, *A Life-Drama*, 51.

53. Smith, *A Life-Drama*, 131. Earlier in the same scene, Walter has managed to evoke one of his ubiquitous astral images by imploring Violet to

Bend over me, my Beautiful, my Own.
O, I could lie with face upturned forever,
And on thy beauty feed as on a star! [130].

54. Smith, *A Life-Drama*, 134–35.

55. Buckley, *The Victorian Temper*, 54.

56. Smith, *Last Leaves*, 127. Cf. 131, which declares, in appropriately metaphoric form, that "style preserves [the textual idea] as balsams preserve Pharaoh. Fine phrases are, after all, the most valuable things... The enamel of style is the only thing that can defy the work of time."

57. Smith, *Last Leaves*, 132–33.

58. Smith, *Last Leaves*, 179–82.

59. For example, both poems open, as did *Faust*, with the hero brooding in his study, concerned with the prophetic role he feels obliged to assume. At one point, Walter wishes for necromantic power: "Would I could raise the dead!" (93). Both preoccupations, as will be shown, will concern Balder as well. Likewise, Balder's famous speech (Dobell, *Balder*, 10) which concludes,

I put my question to the universe,
And overhead the beech-trees murmured "Yes."
Therefore I grew up like a young god
...
To feel me not as others, to pursue
Amid the crowd a solitary way...

bears more than a passing resemblance to Walter's declaration (117) that

I have a work—
The finger of my soul doth point it out;
I trust God's finger points it also out...

Another point of comparison is that Walter's various female companions all sound at times like Amy, Balder's worshipful helpmeet.

60. "Z," "The Last New Poet," *Athenaeum* 3 Jan. 1857: 17. The anonymous reviewer is careful to note that he, for one, had never been taken in by Gilfillan's celestial introductions to his new-found prophet, for although Smith has been called "the last new poet," "Z" asserts that he is "too old to run after new lights, and Mr. Smith's former rockets had scaled the sky in vain for me." Further, once he recognized Smith's plagiarism for what it was, "the whole mysteries

of the new poetic system of composition stood revealed.... I found the new poesy quite familiar" (16).

61. Richard Cronin, "Alexander Smith and the Poetry of Displacement," *Victorian Poetry* 28 (1990): 136–37.

62. P.G. Scott, "Alexander Smith's Glasgow Miscellany and Robert Burns," *Studies in Scottish Literature* 16 (1981): 101.

63. Cross, 126–27. Cross notes that in this respect, English custom was even more rigid than Scottish, but working-class authors were willing to conform for the sake of possibly escaping crushing vocational toil and entering a higher social class they could not afford to embarrass. Interestingly, Ebenezer Elliot, an unrepentant radical who penned *Corn Law Rhymes* in the 1820s, was one of Alexander Smith's literary icons (Cronin, "Alexander Smith and the Poetry of Displacement," 132).

64. Cronin sees Walter as Smith's wealthier English alter-ego, in a sense; not until he commits what Cronin considers the rape of Violet does Smith's repressed social anger find metaphorical vent ("Alexander Smith and the Poetry of Displacement," 133).

65. J[olly], 1:335.

66. Smith, *Last Leaves*, 134–35.

67. For a discussion of Smith's novels, see Maurice Lindsay, *History of Scottish Literature* (London: Hale, 1977) who compares Smith's novels with those of Sydney Dobell's admirer Buchanan, sometimes referred to as a Spasmodic himself. He calls both Smith's *Alfred Hagart's Household*, popular in its day, and Robert Buchanan's *The Shadow of the Sword* (1876) and *God and The Man* (1881) "swaggering" and "unreadable." Perhaps not too surprisingly, Lindsay finds Smith's "narration fulsome and overblown."

68. Weinstein, 88.

69. Westwater, *The Spasmodic Career of Sydney Dobell*, 105.

70. Trilling, *Matthew Arnold*, 135.

71. Mary Jane W. Scott, "Alexander Smith: Poet of Victorian Scotland," *Studies in Scottish Literature* 14, no. 1 (1979): 98.

72. Smith, *A Life-Drama*, 68.

Chapter 5

1. Westwater, *The Spasmodic Career of Sydney Dobell*, 115.

2. "Introductory Memoir" to *The Poems of Sydney Dobell (Selected)*, ed. John Nichol (London: Scott, 1887), xv.

3. Robert Buchanan, *A Look Round Literature*, 187–90. Buchanan likewise considers Alexander Smith a sacrifice to bloodthirsty critics, and in even more explicitly evangelical language: "The story of Smith's martyrdom has yet to be told—nay, never can be told this side of the grave. But let this suffice—it *was* a martyrdom and a tragedy. How tranquilly, how beautifully, Smith took the injustice and the cruelty of the world, many of us know." Buchanan's idolatry of the Spasmodics, and of the sensuous Smith in particular, is curious in light of the viciousness with which he attacked the Pre-Raphaelites for faults which were in some ways similar.

4. Malcolm Pittock, "Dobell, *Balder*, and Post-Romanticism," *Essays in Criticism* 42 (1992): 238 n17; Martha Westwater, 13.

5. As Walker puts it (*Literature of the Victorian Era*, 515), "At an early age young Dobell gave evidence of remarkable [intellectual] powers, and, to his misfortune, he was looked upon as a rising apostle of his grandfather's church." When Dobell eventually decided to break with the sect in favor of more conventional Protestantism, the strain of his family's disapproval caused him an emotional breakdown (see Thale, *Sydney Dobell*, 47).

6. Bryant, *The Spasmodic School*, 181.

7. J[olly], *Life and Letters*, 2: 280.

8. J[olly], 1:286. For Jolly's comment regarding the young poets' asking for aid, see 126.

9. See, for example, Dobell's assertion to Richard Glover that if he were to attempt "to acknowledge all the kind things that have been said and written about me for the last two months" he would have no time to fulfill these kind "oracles" of success by continuing to write at all (J[olly], 1:132).

Notes—Chapter 5

10. Rev. of *The Roman*, *Chambers's Edinburgh Journal* 21 Sept. 1850: 187.
11. Rev. of *The Roman*, *Chambers's*, 189.
12. As it turns out, Santo (in the guise of a monk) has merely used this startling statement as a rhetorical introduction to another long-winded speech on the tyranny of Austria. As Bryant wryly notes, Santo certainly "has a way of starting a conversation" (190).
13. Thale, *Sydney Dobell*, 5.
14. Westwater, 112.
15. Related in J[olly] 1:198.
16. Buckley, *The Victorian Temper*, 40–42. In an often-reproduced comment, Buckley uses Dobell's fall as a metaphor both for Dobell's misguided Byronic aspirations (albeit "saintlier" than his model's) and the "high aspiration and descent to oblivion of the poetic group to which he belonged." The fall also had tragic, and again ironic, consequences for the hapless Dobell: having suffered spinal cord injuries and probably brain damage, he was afterwards subject to epileptic seizures and literal, physical "spasms" that no doubt hastened his death (Thale, *Sydney Dobell*, 425).
17. Rev. of *The Roman*, *Chambers's*, 188. When one of Dobell's friends, Dr. Samuel Brown, was honest enough to point out the poem's flawed structure and unity, the poet took the critique as a personal injury and turned instead to the lavish praise others had offered him (J[olly], 1: 139). As he told Brown, "I care one jot for the literary opinions of the very fewest" (1:136). One of these select few was Gilfillan; however, by the time *Balder* was composed Dobell had also ceased to listen to his mentor's caveats. Gilfillan was privately far from satisfied with *Balder* upon its publication (Thale, *Sydney Dobell*, 171).
18. J[olly], 1:104–105.
19. Heather O'Donoghue, *English Poetry and Old Norse Myth: A History* (London: Oxford University Press, 2014), 160–164.
20. Thale, *Sydney Dobell*, 167.
21. J[olly], 1:295.
22. Bryant, *The Spasmodic School*, 199.
23. See, for example, Emma Mason, "Rhythmic Numinousness: Sydney Dobell and the Church," *Victorian Poetry* 42, no. 4 (2004): 537–552.
24. Rev. of *Balder*, *Chambers's Edinburgh Journal*, July 8 (1854): 27.
25. Poe's description of the crazed artist in "The Oval Portrait" could almost serve as a stage direction for Balder: "And he was a passionate, and wild, and moody man, who became lost in reveries; so that he would not see that the light which fell so ghastly in that lone turret withered the health and the spirits of his bride, who pined visibly to all but him."
26. Dobell, *Balder*, 230–31. Since the lines in *Balder* are not numbered, all references to the text will be to pages numbers only.
27. John Nichol, ed., *Thoughts on Art, Philosophy, and Religion: Selected from the Unpublished Papers of Sydney Dobell* (London: Smith and Elder, 1876), 256, 340.
28. Dobell, *Balder*, 24.
29. Dobell, *Balder*, 73–74.
30. See Weinstein, 97.
31. Dobell, *Balder*, 6, 5.
32. Dobell, *Balder*, 122.
33. Dobell, *Balder*, 59, 81, 250; Buckley quotes the "ah" line in *The Victorian Temper* (57), rendering it Dobell's best-known line. Arnold's 1858 verse-drama *Merope*, probably not coincidentally, made a point of including a single "ah" in several places, meant to convey a variety of ideas and emotion in a single syllable. At one point Merope utters three "ahs" in succession. Ironically, Arthur Quiller-Couch (who was apparently not familiar with *Balder*) wryly noted, "We suppose that no English poet before or since has so cruelly overworked the interjection 'Ah!' But far worse than any number of 'ah!s' is Arnold's trick of italic type" (*Studies in Literature* [Urbana-Champaign: University of Illinois Press, 1924], 227).
34. Dobell, *Balder*, 194.
35. Dobell, *Balder*, 98, 108, 107, 111.
36. Dobell, *Balder*, 87.
37. See Walker, *Literature of the Victorian Era*, 522 for examples.
38. As Balder puts it (11),

Notes—Chapter 5

Nature from my birth
Confessed me, as who in a multitude
Confesseth her beloved and makes no sign;
...
or as a sage amid
His pupils in the peopled portico
Denotes the favoured scholar from the crowd;...

39. Dobell, *Balder*, 10.
40. Dobell, *Balder*, 64.
41. Dobell, *Balder*, 12.
42. Dobell, *Balder*, 222.
43. Dobell, *Balder*, 3,4.
44. Dobell, *Balder*, 9, 10. Cf. 17: "I do think / My throne is set!"
45. Dobell, *Balder*, 15–16.
46. Dobell, *Balder*, 154.
47. Dobell, *Balder*, 165. Elsewhere, Amy admiringly muses, "Husband, to be born to feel / As no man felt before thee!" (161) and asks Balder to "take the worlds and bowl them round about me, / For well I think thou canst" (157). That she fully accepts his professed communion with heaven is nowhere more apparent than in her description of how she fell in love with him:

Oh, was I not a floweret in thine hand
When thou didst stand upon the peak of thought
Gazing to heaven, which with a thunder-shock
Rolled back, and angels came to thee, and thou
Didst stretch to them thine open hands uplift
In welcome, and I fell to where I am. [27]

Biographically, Dobell seems to have taken the role of the poet's wife equally seriously. Upon hearing of Alexander Smith's engagement, he remarked that "report speaks well of [Flora MacDonald], but it is no ordinary 'well' that should qualify her for a poet's wife" (J[olly], 2:33).

48. Walker, *Literature of the Victorian Era*, 522.
49. Thale, *Sydney Dobell*, 45.
50. Thale, *Sydney Dobell*, 339.
51. Dobell, *Balder*, 20.
52. J[olly], 1: 117.
53. For a discussion of this aspect of Dobell's theory see Bryant, *The Spasmodic School*, 239–40. Dobell also believed that appropriate inspiration effected a complete "mental transformation" due to the poet's special susceptibility and that "no imperfect Man can be a great Poet without possessing" this. Moreover, the change "transfigures the mind towards Perfection—approaching the perfect state in proportion to its own power in the given mind ... in this state the Poem is designed" (Dobell in Bristow, 77).
54. Dobell, *Balder*, 19.
55. Dobell in Bristow, 78. Dobell states that the degree of transference from the poet's mentality to the characters marks the difference between the epic and the Drama, two forms which interact both literally and symbolically in *Balder*.
56. Bryant, 242; for a useful explication of Dobell's poetic theory, see Westwater, 115–132.
57. Dobell in Bristow, 80, 82–83; emphasis Dobell's.
58. Dobell, *Balder*, 142; likewise, he asserts elsewhere that as "King of the world" he would "on the inform / And perishable substance of Time / Beget a better world" (10) once his epic is complete.
59. Rev. of *Balder*, *New Monthly Magazine* 100 (March 1854): 296; see also Weinstein, 118. Weinstein adds that Aytoun's favorite word for *Festus* was "fustian," in its sense of "pompous and insipid speech."
60. Bryant, 241. Cf. Jolly's statement concerning the intense spiritual experience poetry was to Dobell: "the making of poetry, as of prayer, was a thing between a man and his God, a thing, like the deeper sorrows and joys of the heart, with which the stranger intermeddleth not" (1:115). Seen in this light, his disdain for the adverse criticism of mere mortals becomes more understandable and perhaps even inevitable. Dobell also believed that writing criticism was damaging to one's poetic powers, since it detracted from the close and immediate connection with God it provided: "A critique once or twice a year is therefore all I shall allow myself," he told Samuel Brown in 1850 (J[olly], 1:138).
61. J[olly], 2:40.

Notes—Chapter 6

62. J[olly], 2:139.
63. J[olly], 2:139.
64. J[olly], 1:351, 385–86.
65. J[olly], 2:105.
66. "Our Weekly Gossip," *Athenaeum* (Jan. 17, 1857): 84.
67. Thale, *Sydney Dobell*, 311.
68. John Stanyan Bigg, *Night and the Soul: A Dramatic Poem* (London: Groombridge, 1854), 5. Since the poem's lines are not numbered, all references will be to page numbers only.
69. Rev. of *Night and the Soul*, by J.S. Bigg, *The Dublin University Magazine* 212 (October 1854): 479–80.
70. Bigg, *Night and the Soul*, 48, 77.
71. Bigg, *Night and the Soul*, 7.
72. Bigg, *Night and the Soul*, 154; *A Life-Drama*, 148. In both poems, of course, one of the interlocutors remains convinced that the poet will yet be converted: "I do believe he will be brought to God," Flora states, truthfully (155), while Edward insists that Walter "will return to the old faith he learned / Beside his mother's knee" (149).
73. Bigg, *Night and the Soul*, 27; see also the scenes in which Caroline urges, "Nay, ever trust in God, my Ferdinand" (148) and Flora's belief that "when woman loses faith in him she loves / There is no other comforter but God" (161). Accordingly she has "sigh'd," "wept," and "pray'd" for the lost Alexis, "And would have died for thee, believing thee as worthy of my life as of my love!"
74. Bigg, *Night and the Soul*, 170, 130.
75. Bigg, *Night and the Soul*, 89.
76. Bigg, *Night and the Soul*, 1.
77. Bigg, *Night and the Soul*, 6.
78. Bigg, *Night and the Soul*, 10.
79. Aytoun confided to a friend that it was "very curious, when you sit down to write this sort of thing, to find how very closely some of the passages approximate to good poetry" (Weinstein, 123).
80.
81. Rev. of *Night and the Soul*, *Dublin University Magazine* 212 (1854): 482.

Chapter 6

1. [Peter Bayne?], "Balder and the Harbingers," *Tait's Edinburgh Magazine* 21 (1854): 168, 171, 169; [Charles Kingsley], "Alexander Smith and Alexander Pope," *Fraser's Magazine for Town and Country* 48 (1853): 456, 464.
2. Rev. of *Balder*, *The New Monthly Magazine*, 292.
3. [Margaret Oliphant], "Modern Light Literature—Poetry," *Blackwood's Edinburgh Magazine* 79 (1856): 125–26.
4. [Gerald Massey], Rev. of *Balder*, *The Eclectic Review* ns 8 (1854): 429, 434. The identification of the writer as Massey is from *The Wellesley Index*.
5. The central image of the volcano in "Empedocles on Etna" may have been a particular sticking point for Arnold, for volcanoes came to be so closely associated with Spasmodic poets that they "quickly became the quintessential metaphor of the Spasmodic movement" (LaPorte, "Spasmodic Poetics and Clough's Apostasies," 529).
6. [W.E. Aytoun], "The Two Arnolds," 306.
7. [Aytoun], "The Two Arnolds," 314.
8. [E.B. Hamley], "Alexander Smith's *Poems*," 346.
9. [Hamley], "Alexander Smith's *Poems*," 350.
10. [Hamley], "Alexander Smith's *Poems*," 351, 349.
11. Westwater, *The Spasmodic Career of Sydney Dobell*, 91. Westwater thinks that at this point Aytoun became "carried away by his own wit" and took his joke to "cruel" excess, destroying Smith, Dobell, and Gilfillan in one blow.
12. Andrea A. Lunsford, "A Bibliographical Note on William Edmondstoune Aytoun's Manuscript: Lectures on Rhetoric and Belles Lettres," *Rhetoric Society Quarterly* 16 (1986): 334.
13. T. Percy Jones, [W.E. Aytoun], *Firmilian: Or, The Student of Badajoz, A Spasmodic Tragedy*, 14. Since *Firmilian*'s lines are not numbered, all references will be to page numbers only.
14. [W. E. Aytoun], Rev. of *Firmilian: A Spasmodic Tragedy*, by T. Percy Jones. *Blackwood's Edinburgh Magazine* 75 (May 1854): 533.
15. Rev. of *England in Time of War*, *New Quarterly Review* 5 (1856): 433, 420.

Notes—Chapter 6

16. [Aytoun], Rev. of *Firmilian*, 534, 551.
17. [Aytoun], Rev. of *Firmilian*, 534.
18. [Aytoun], Rev. of *Firmilian*, 551.
19. T. Percy Jones, [W.E. Aytoun], *Firmilian*, 111.
20. T. Percy Jones, [W.E. Aytoun], *Firmilian*, 112.
21. [Aytoun], Rev. of *Firmilian*, 543–44. Many modern critics, notably Frances Boos, find little more than snobbery and even "displaced self-loathing in this oddly grotesque cartoon." Smith's modern biographer, Simon Berry, concurs (87).
22. Weinstein, *William Edmundstoune Aytoun*, 162.
23. Weinstein, 124–25.
24. Weinstein, 125.
25. T. Percy Jones, [W.E. Aytoun], *Firmilian*, 121. The references to Mariana, Endymion, and Paracelsus occur on 21, 24, and 130, respectively.
26. [W.E. Aytoun], "Ruskin on Architecture and Painting," *Blackwood's Edinburgh Magazine* 75 (1854): 740. The prediction concerning the Pre-Raphaelites occurs on 756. While there is yet hope for Millais, Aytoun states, "Mr. Hunt we take to be incorrigible, and consign him to the company of Mr. Ruskin."
27. T. Percy Jones, [W.E. Aytoun], *Firmilian*, 63–64. Later, when the Graduate [Ruskin] is burnt at the stake along with "Teufelsdröckh" [Carlyle], an onlooker reports, in the language of Aytoun's review, that

He curs'd the city, and he curs'd the church;
He curs'd the houses, and he curs'd their stones.
He cursed, in short, in such miraculous wise,
That nothing was exempted from his ban.

The crowd responds by throwing live cats at him (119).
28. [Aytoun], "Ruskin on Architecture and Painting," 744–45.
29. Dobell, "Lecture on Poetry," qtd. in Thale, *Sydney Dobell*, 343.
30. T. Percy Jones, [W.E. Aytoun], Preface to *Firmilian*, iv–v.
31. T. Percy Jones, [W.E. Aytoun], Preface to *Firmilian*, vii–ix.
32. [Hamley], "Alexander Smith's *Poems*," 346.
33. T. Percy Jones, [W.E. Aytoun], Preface to *Firmilian*, vi.
34. [Aytoun], Rev. of *Firmilian*, 534.
35. T. Percy Jones, [W.E. Aytoun], *Firmilian* 164.
36. [Aytoun], *Firmilian*, 76, 159–60.
37. [Aytoun], *Firmilian*, 61–62.
38. [Aytoun], *Firmilian*, 141.
39. [Aytoun], *Firmilian*, 17–18. It is precisely this speech that Firmilian unsuccessfully tries to emulate for the benefit of the enraged Mariana (158).
40. [Aytoun], *Firmilian*, 25, 38, 100.
41. [Aytoun], *Firmilian*, 26.
42. [Aytoun], *Firmilian*, 13.
43. [Aytoun], *Firmilian*, 58.
44. [Aytoun], *Firmilian*, 162, 151.
45. [Aytoun], *Firmilian*, 149, 150–54. Another device Aytoun borrows from both *Festus* and *A Life-Drama* is that in which the hero muses on a lost friend, also a poet. Firmilian does this as well, though his intention is to flaunt his libido: the poet he knew "made pale Eros veil his face with grief" and was as "amorous as a crocodile / In the spring season." He also "had a soul beyond the vulgar reach" and so is entitled to his promiscuity, unlike lesser men (47).
46. [Aytoun], *Firmilian*, 78.
47. [Aytoun], *Firmilian*, 163–65.
48. [Aytoun], Rev. of *Firmilian*, 545.
49. [Aytoun], Rev. of *Firmilian*, 44–45.
50. [Aytoun], Rev. of *Firmilian*, 488–89.
51. [Horatio Mansfield], Rev. of *Poems*, by Matthew Arnold, *Tait's Edinburgh Magazine* 21 (1854): 59.
52. [Peter Bayne?], "The Last Spasm," *Tait's Edinburgh Magazine* 21 (1854): 557, 561.
53. Thale, *Sydney Dobell*, 395; "The Month, The Library, and The Studio," *Chambers's Edinburgh Journal* (25 Feb. 1854): 126. A complete discussion of many other negative reviews in this vein may be found in Weinstein's chapter on the subject.
54. Rev. of *Night and the Soul*, *Athenaeum* 28 Oct. 1854: 1296.
55. "Retrospect of the Literature of the Quarter IV," *New Quarterly Review*

Notes—Chapter 7

4 (1855): 6; "Retrospect of the Literature of the Quarter," *New Quarterly Review* 3 (1854): 129, 131; "The Anti-Spasmodic School of Poetry, *New Quarterly Review* 7 (1858): 124.

56. Weinstein, 156–58.

57. "Edward Young," *North American Review* 165 (1854): 270.

58. Rev. of *Balder, The British Quarterly Review* 19 (1854): 570.

59. Westwater, 89. Dobell, appearing to be a good sport about the whole thing, reported in a letter that he "laughed more, on first reading it ... than at anything I have read lately."

60. J[olly], *Life and Letters* 2: 50–51; curiously, another *Blackwood's* writer had killed John Scott, editor of the *London Magazine*, in a duel over a literary dispute in 1821 (see http://www.lordbyron.org/archives.php?choose=Scott Blckwd).

61. [Aytoun, W.E.] "Poetry of the War," *Blackwood's Edinburgh Magazine* 77 (1855): 533–534.

62. Thale, *Sydney Dobell*, 392.

63. "Our Library Table," *Athenaeum* August 22, 1857: 1056.

64. "Our Library Table," 1055–56.

65. [Margaret Oliphant], "Modern Light Literature—Poetry," 126–28, 134.

66. [Gerald Massey], "Poetry—The Spasmodists" *North British Review* 28 (1858): 231, 240.

67. [Coventry Patmore], "New Poets," *Edinburgh Review* 104 (1856): 339.

68. Buchanan, 189.

69. John Woolford in Joanne Shattock and Michael Wolff, eds. *The Victorian Periodical Press: Samplings and Soundings* (Toronto: University of Toronto Press, 1982), 113.

Chapter 7

1. [Thomas Brinsley Norton, Lord Grantley], *Pinocchi* (London: Parker, 1856), 3. Since individual lines in this volume are not numbered, all references to its poems will be to individual title and page.

2. [Norton, Lord Grantley], *Pinocchi*, 12 (The poem is called "Two Night Visions of Capri").

3. John Woolford, "Periodicals and the Practice of Literary Criticism, 1855–1864" in Shattock and Wolff, 109–144. The section concerning *Pinocchi* occurs on 115–16: "This passage from an 1856 review of the Pinochi [sic] of one Percy Jones seems to me to typify the kind of criticism I have been examining ... Percy Jones and Browning [are said to] write 'inverted gibberish'..."

4. Lord Grantley was also associated with the PreRaphaelites. See Roger W. Peattie, *Selected Letters of William Michael Rossetti* (University Park: Penn State University Press, 1990), 69 n33: "*Pinocchi*, published anonymously in 1856, was called by the *Athenaeum* a PreRaphalite book (17 May 1856 p. 613)."

5. Rev. of *Pinocchi, Fraser's* 53 (1856): 438.

6. "Caroline Elizabeth Sarah Sheridan" (http://www.greathead.org/Wonersh 2-o/p194.htm).

7. Peattie, 69 n33.

8. Rev. of *Pinocchi*, 441.

9. [William Scott], "Poetical Nuisances," *Saturday Review* 23 Feb. 1856: 327–328.

10. [W.E. Aytoun], "Poetry of the War," 533. Some scholars have identified this reviewer as E.B. Hamley, but given the extremism of the vocabulary, Aytoun seems the more likely culprit. The poetic reference is to *Pinocchi*, 12.

11. [Norton, Lord Grantley], *Pinocchi* 56, 59–60 (emphasis in the original).

12. [Scott], "Poetical Nuisances," 328.

13. Rev. of *Pinocchi*, 438.

14. [Scott], "Poetical Nuisances" 327.

15. [Oliphant], "Modern Light Literature—Poetry," 127. Other articles were as direct as Oliphant is here; *The Guardian* declared that "*Maud* is a poem in the 'Spasmodic' school of poetry, hardly superior in kind to *The Roman* or *Balder*, or *Festus*" (qtd. in Edgar F. Shannon, Jr., "The Critical Reception of Tennyson's *Maud*," *PMLA* 68 [1953]: 398). For further quotes using this term, see Weinstein, *William Edmondstoune Aytoun*, 178–79.

16. See Trilling, *Matthew Arnold*,

Notes—Chapter 7

136–37 for evidence that "Empedocles" was removed because Arnold felt it suffered for its relation to Spasmodic poetry; "perhaps he had only reiterated the confusion of the methodistic self-contemplation," Trilling notes. After all, Empedocles' self-absorption was such that he committed suicide by leaping into a volcano in a somewhat Spasmodically grand gesture.

17. According to Edgar F. Shannon, Jr., "It has been said—and often repeated—that *Maud* was Tennyson's last poem which mattered.... From the reception of the poem it was apparent that he had misjudged his audience and projected his poetry too deeply into the realms of abnormal psychology, politics, and opinion. Hurt and annoyed, he withdrew from the troublesome nineteenth century to his favorite era, the past, and diffidently began the protracted process of casting in mellifluous splendor the *Idylls of the King* ("The Critical Reception of Tennyson's *Maud*," 414).

18. Joseph J. Collins, "Tennyson and the Spasmodics," *Victorian Newsletter* 43 (1973): 24. Collins considers Buckley, Saintsbury, and Gosse primarily responsible for the blight of the "Spasmodic" epithet on *Maud*. Collins' offended tone again demonstrates how effective Aytoun's anti–Spasmodic campaign was on the progress of criticism, requiring such a defense as late as the 1970s.

19. The sales figure is provided in Christopher Ricks, *The Poems of Tennyson* (Berkeley: University of California Press, 1987), 515, and evidence for its appeal to the general public appears in Shannon, 397 and 399.

20. Gordon N. Ray, *Tennyson Reads Maud* (Vancouver: University of British Columbia, 1968), 18; David Goslee, *Tennyson's Characters: "Strange Faces, Other Minds"* (Iowa City: University of Iowa Press, 1989), 151.

21. Bryant, *The Spasmodic School*, 271 and 271n.

22. [W. E. Aytoun], Rev. of *Maud*, by Alfred Tennyson, *Blackwood's Edinburgh Magazine* 78 (1855): 319, 317.

23. [Aytoun], Rev. of *Maud*, 311–312.

24. [Oliphant], "Modern Light Literature—Poetry," 138.

25. John D. Jump, ed., *Tennyson: The Critical Heritage* (New York: Barnes and Noble, 1967), 335.

26. Jump, 218–19.

27. Jump, 187, 189.

28. [Aytoun], Rev. of *Maud*, 321.

29. Weinstein, 179.

30. M.L. Howe, "Rossetti's Comments on *Maud*," *MLN* 49 (1934): 291–92.

31. Ricks, *The Poems of Tennyson*, 515; see also Jump, 435.

32. William E. Buckler, *The Victorian Imagination: Essays in Aesthetic Exploration* (New York: New York University Press, 1980), 219.

33. Buckler, 214.

34. A. Dwight Culler, "Monodrama and the Dramatic Monologue," *PMLA* 90 (1975): 380.

35. [Aytoun], Rev. of *Maud*, 314–15, 318.

36. [Aytoun], Rev. of *Maud*, 319–320.

37. Tennyson, *Maud*, II.ii.49–77. All references to *Maud* are to part, scene, and line, and refer to the text given in Ricks.

38. Tennyson, *Maud*, I.i.1–4.

39. Tennyson, *Maud*, I.i.16, I.v.98, III.vi.14.

40. Smith, *A Life-Drama*, 7.

41. Jump, 192–93.

42. Jump, 309.

43. Culler, 369–71, 378–79.

44. [Oliphant], "Modern Light Literature," 133.

45. Tennyson, *Maud*, I.iv.149–55.

46. Tennyson, *Maud*, I.xviii.635–38

47. Tennyson, *Maud*, I.x.396–97.

48. D.C. Somervell, "The Reputation of Robert Browning," *Essays and Studies* 15 (1929): 122.

49. C.C. Watkins, "Browning's *Men and Women* and the Spasmodic School," *Journal of English and Germanic Philology* 57 (1958): 58, 57.

50. [Massey], "Poetry—The Spasmodists," 239; Trilling, *Matthew Arnold*, 136.

51. Jerome Thale, "Browning's 'Popularity' and the Spasmodic Poets," *Journal of English and Germanic Philology* 54 (1955): 353. Thale believes that

Notes—Chapter 7

"Popularity" dates from this period and is intended to ridicule the Spasmodics, though his evidence is somewhat sketchy and could as easily be used to imply that, say, the Pre-Raphaelites were Browning's targets. The mention of the poet as a star and the reference to John Keats certainly call to mind the Spasmodics, however.

52. DeLaura, "Robert Browning the Spasmodic," 58.
53. Jump, 194.
54. Weinstein, 187; see also Buckley, *The Victorian Temper*, 62–63 for a discussion of some supposedly "spasmodic" passages in the poem.
55. Boyd Litzinger and Donald Smalley, *Browning: The Critical Heritage* (London: Routledge, 1970), 160.
56. Thale, "Browning's 'Popularity,'" 354.
57. Carl Dawson, *Victorian Noon: English Literature in 1850* (Baltimore: Johns Hopkins University Press, 1979), 94.
58. Thale agrees that "Browning's *Pauline*, with its poet hero and morbid preoccupation with the self, is surely Spasmodic. And his *Paracelsus*, like the Spasmodic works, deals with the development or an ardent young soul" ("Browning's 'Popularity,'" 331). Much has been made of the fact that *Paracelsus* contains a character named "Festus," but this apparent connection between Browning and Bailey has been shown to be a coincidence. See Weinstein, 183–84.
59. William Clyde DeVane, *A Browning Handbook* (New York: Appleton-Century-Crofts, 1955), 74.
60. See, for example, the quote from *The Examiner* in Watkins, 58; also see Litzinger and Smalley, 162–163 and 174.
61. Tennyson's remark is quoted in Somervell, 124, among other places; DeVane relates other anecdotes such as Mrs. Carlyle's infamous remark that she "had read the book through without being able to make out whether Sordello was a man, a city, or a book" and Douglas Jerrold's and Miss Martineau's fears that they had gone mad because they were unable to comprehend it (85). Devane thinks that *Sordello* "ruined" Browning's hitherto "promising reputation.... It took Browning twenty-five years to recover fully from the effect of the poem" (86).
62. [Peter Bayne?], "Balder and the Harbingers," 171; Jump, 361.
63. [Massey], "Poetry—The Spasmodists," 239; [Oliphant], "Modern Light Literature," 137; [Bayne?], "Balder and the Harbingers" 165, 167.
64. Trilling, 33.
65. Somervell, 128.
66. Somervell, 132–33. DeLaura, "Robert Browning the Spasmodic," 60 n14 notes that Browning's poems even served as the basis for the "beginnings of a high-brow cultural audience." The Spasmodics, of course, appealed primarily to middle-class readers.
67. Buckley quotes as evidence that Browning was "driven to renounce his visions for a selfless view of the outside world" a lyric from *Pauline* proclaiming, "I'll look within no more" and lamenting that he has "trusted my own vain self, vague intuition." Even at this early stage in his poetic development, Buckley asserts, Browning is ready to move beyond "the subjective method and the effusive Confessional style" (*The Victorian Temper*, 22–23).
68. W.M. Rossetti, "William Bell Scott and Modern British Poetry," 427.
69. Walker, *The Literature of the Victorian Era*, 527.
70. T. Earle Welby, *The Victorian Romantics 1850–1870* (London: Howe, 1929), 527. See also Kirstie Blair, "Swinburne's Spasms: *Poems and Ballads* and the Spasmodic School," 180–196.
71. Buckley, 214.
72. Buchanan, *A Look Round Literature*, 197.
73. Buckley, 238–39. M.L. Megroz describes Phillips in terms which, again, sound all too familiar: his "music and imagery were entirely pastiche, while the idea, when not borrowed, was trite" (*Modern English Poetry: 1882–1932* [London: Nicholson, 1933], 44).
74. Holbrook Jackson, *The Eighteen Nineties* (1913; New York: Capricorn, 1966), 30.
75. Jackson, 163.

Epilogue

1. Lucasta Miller, *The Brontë Myth* (New York: Anchor, 2005).
2. Martha Westwater, "Sydney Dobell: Sunk without Trace," *Dalhousie Review* 69, no. 3 (Fall 1989): 357–365.
3. Mary Jane W. Scott, "Alexander Smith: Poet of Victorian Scotland," *Studies in Scottish Literature* 14, no. 1 (1979): 98–111, https://scholarcommons.sc.edu/ssl/vol14/iss1/9.
4. Jerome Thale, "Sydney Dobell: A Spasmodic Poet," Ph.D. diss., Northwestern University, 1953.
5. Roger Keith Brookes, "Ebenezer Jones: A Study," MA thesis, University of British Columbia, 1971.
6. Martha Westwater, *The Spasmodic Career of Sydney Dobell* (Lanham, MD, 1992).
7. Simon Berry, *Applauding Thunder: Life, Works, and Critics of Alexander Smith* (Inverness" FTRR, 2013).
8. Natalie M. Houston, "Reading the Victorian Souvenir: Sonnets and Photographs of the Crimean War," *The Yale Journal of Criticism* 14, no. 2 (Fall 2001): 353–383.
9. Richard Cronin, "Alexander Smith and the Poetry of Displacement," *Victorian Poetry* 28, no. 2 (Summer 1990): 129–145.
10. Kirstie Blair, "A Very Poetical Town": Newspaper Poetry and the Working-Class Poet in Victorian Dundee," *Victorian Poetry* 52, no. 1 (Spring 2014): 89–109, 183.
11. For example, the special issue of *Victorian Poetry* (Winter 2004) contains Kirstie Blair's "Spasmodic Affections: Poetry, Pathology, and the Spasmodic Hero" (473–490) and Herbert F. Tucker's "Glandular Omnism and Beyond: The Victorian Spasmodic Epic" (429–450). Another notable article in this physiological vein is Jack Rooney, "Words of Healing": The Literature of Automatic Writing as Treatment and Prescription in the Victorian Age," *Literature and Medicine* 39, no. 1 (Spring 2021): 108–132.

Bibliography

Books, Periodicals, and Monographs: Signed, Unsigned, and Identified

(Authors whose names appear in brackets have been identified by *The Wellesley Index* or by library card catalogues)

"Alexander Smith's Poems." *Blackwood's Edinburgh Magazine* 75 (1854): 346.
Altick, Richard D. *The English Common Reader*. Chicago: University of Chicago Press, 1957.
———. *Writers, Readers, and Occasions: Selected Essays on Victorian Literature and Life*. Columbus: Ohio State University Press, 1989.
"The Anti-Spasmodic School of Poetry." *New Quarterly Review* 7 (1858): 123–35.
Armstrong, Isabel. *Victorian Scrutinies: Reviews of Poetry 1830–1870*. London: Athlone, 1972.
Auden, W.H., ed. *Nineteenth Century Minor Poets*. New York: Delacorte, 1966.
"A.Y." [Alexander MacMillan]. "The 'Quarterly Review' on Mr. Tennyson's 'Maud.'" *Macmillan's* 1 (1859/60): 114–15.
[Aytoun, W.E.]. "Poetry of the War." *Blackwood's Edinburgh Magazine* 77 (1855): 531–35.
———. Rev. of *Firmilian: A Spasmodic Tragedy*, by T. Percy Jones. *Blackwood's Edinburgh Magazine* 75 (May 1854): 533–51.
———. Rev. of *Maud*, by Alfred Tennyson. *Blackwood's Edinburgh Magazine* 78 (1855): 311–21.
———. "Ruskin on Architecture and Painting." *Blackwood's Edinburgh Magazine* 75 (1854): 740–56.
———. "The Two Arnolds." *Blackwood's Edinburgh Magazine* 75 (1854): 303–14.
[Bailey, P.J.]. *Festus: A Poem*. 1839. New York: Knox, 1885.
Batho, Edith and Bonamy Dobree. *The Victorians and After: 1830–1914*. New York: McBride, 1938.
[Bayne, Peter?]. "Balder and the Harbingers." *Tait's Edinburgh Magazine* 21 (1854): 164–71.
———. "The Last Spasm." *Tait's Edinburgh Magazine* 21 (1854): 557–61.
———. Rev. of *Poems*, by Alexander Smith. *Tait's Edinburgh Magazine* 20 (1853): 302–305.
Benedicks, Crystal. *Spasmodic Bodies and Victorian Poetics: Biology, Masculinity, and Modernity in Spasmodic Poetry*. PhD diss., City University of New York, 2005. ProQuest Dissertations Publishing (3169891).
Berry, Simon. *Applauding Thunder: Life, Work, and Critics of Alexander Smith*. Inverness: FTRR, 2013.
Bevington, Merle Mowbray. *The Saturday Review: 1855–1868*. New York: AMS, 1966.
Bigg, John Stanyan. *Night and the Soul: A Dramatic Poem*. London: Groombridge, 1854.

Bibliography

Birley, Robert. *Sunk Without Trace: Some Forgotten Masterpieces Reconsidered.* Westport, CT: Greenwood, 1962.
Black, Greta A. "P.J. Bailey's Debt to Goethe's *Faust* in His *Festus*." *MLR* 28 (1933): 166–75.
Blainey, Ann. *The Farthing Poet.* London: Longmans, 1968.
Blair, Kirstie. "Spasmodic Affections: Poetry, Pathology, and the Spasmodic Hero." *Victorian Poetry* 42, No. 4 (2004): 473–490.
_____. "Swinburne's Spasms: *Poems and Ballads* and the Spasmodic School." *The Yearbook of English Studies* 36, no.2 (2006): 180–196.
Boos, Florence S. "'Spasm' and Class: W.E. Aytoun, George Gilfillan, Sydney Dobell, and Alexander Smith." *Victorian Poetry* 42, No. 4 (2004): 553–584.
Brimley, George. *Essays.* New York: Rudd and Carleton, 1861.
Bristow, Joseph, ed. *The Victorian Poet: Poetics and Persona.* London: Croom Helm, 1987.
Bryant, Hallman B. *The Spasmodic School: A Study of a Victorian Literary Phenomenon.* Ph.D. Diss. Vanderbilt, 1968.
Buchanan, Robert. *A Look Round Literature.* London: Ward and Downey, 1887.
Buchman, Ralf. *Martin F. Tupper and the Victorian Middle Class Mind.* Bern: Verlag A. Francke, 1941.
Buckler, William E. *The Victorian Imagination: Essays in Aesthetic Exploration.* New York: New York University Press, 1980.
Buckley, Jerome. *The Victorian Temper.* Cambridge: Harvard University Press, 1951.
Bulloch, John. *Scottish Notes and Queries,* second series, vol. 3. Aberdeen: Brown, 1902.
Carlyle, Thomas. *On Heroes, Hero-worship and the Heroic in History.* https://www.gutenberg.org/files/1091/1091-h/1091-h.htm.
Chambers, Robert, ed. *Chambers's Cyclopædia of English Literature: A History, Critical and Biographical, of Authors in the English Tongue from the Earliest Times Till the Present Day, with Specimens of Their Writings.* New ed. vol. 3. Philadelphia: J.B. Lippincott, 1910.
Chew, Samuel. *Byron in England: His Fame and After-Fame.* New York: Russell and Russell, 1965.
Collins, Joseph J. "Tennyson and the Spasmodics." *Victorian Newsletter* 43 (1973): 24–28.
Cox, R.G. "Victorian Criticism of Poetry: The Minority Tradition." *Scrutiny* 18 (1951): 2–17.
Crawford, Robert. "Alexander Smith, James Macfarlan, and City Poetry." *Scottish Literary Journal* 12 (1985): 35–52.
Cronin, Richard. "Alexander Smith and the Poetry of Displacement." *Victorian Poetry* 28 (1990): 129–45.
Cronin, Richard, Antony Harrison, and Alison Chapman, eds. *A Companion to Victorian Poetry* New York: Wiley, 2008.
Cross, Nigel. *The Common Writer: Life in Eighteenth-Century Grub Street.* Cambridge: Cambridge University Press, 1985.
Cruse, Amy. *The Victorians and Their Reading.* Boston: Houghton-Mifflin, 1935.
Culler, A. Dwight. "Monodrama and the Dramatic Monologue." *PMLA* 90 (1975): 366–85.
Dalziel, Margaret. *Popular Fiction One Hundred Years Ago.* London: Cohen and West, 1957.
Dawson, Carl. *Victorian Noon: English Literature in 1850.* Baltimore: Johns Hopkins University Press, 1979.
DeLaura, David. "Robert Browning the Spasmodic." *Studies in Browning and His Circle* 2 (1974): 55–60.
DeVane, William Clyde. *A Browning Handbook.* New York: Appleton-Century-Crofts, 1955.

Bibliography

Dobell, Sydney. *Balder: Part the First.* London: Smith and Elder, 1854.
Donnelly, Dorothy F. "Philistine Taste in Victorian Poetry." *Victorian Poetry* 16, no. 1/2 (1978): 100–11.
"Edward Young." *North American Review* 165 (1854): 269–96.
Ehnes, Caley. *Victorian Poetry and the Poetics of the Literary Periodical.* Edinburgh: Edinburgh University Press, 2018.
Ford, George H. *Keats and the Victorians: A Study of his Influence and Rise to Fame, 1821–1895.* Hamden, CT: Archon, 1962.
[Gilfillan, George]. "Alexander Smith's Poems." *The Eclectic Review* ns 6 (1853): 541–53.
_____. *Modern Literature and Literary Men: Being a Second Gallery of Literary Portraits.* New York: Appleton, 1850.
_____. "Recent Poetry." *The Eclectic Review* ns 2 (1851): 447–62.
_____. Rev. of *The Roman,* by Sydney Dobell. *The Eclectic Review* 101 (1850): 672–84.
Goslee, David. *Tennyson's Characters: "Strange Faces, Other Minds."* Iowa City: University of Iowa Press, 1989.
Gosse, Edmund. *Portraits and Sketches.* London: Heinemann, 1912.
_____. *A Short History of Modern English Literature.* New York: Appleton, 1900.
Graff, Gerald. *Professing Literature: An Institutional History.* Chicago: Chicago University Press, 1987.
Gross, John. *The Rise and Fall of the Man of Letters.* London: Weidenfeld, 1969.
[Hamley, E.B.]. "Alexander Smith's Poems." *Blackwood's Edinburgh Magazine* 75 (1854): 345–51.
Harrison, Antony H. "Victorian Culture Wars: Alexander Smith, Arthur Hugh Clough, and Matthew Arnold in 1853." *Victorian Poetry* 42, No. 4 (2004): 509–520.
_____. *Victorian Poets and Romantic Poems: Intertextuality and Ideology.* Charlottesville: University Press of Virginia, 1990.
Hawley, J.C. "Charles Kingsley and Literary Theory of the 1850s." *Victorian Literature and Culture* 19 (1992), 167–88.
Horne, Richard Hengist. *A New Spirit of the Age.* 1844. London: Oxford University Press, 1907.
Houghton, Walter E. *The Victorian Frame of Mind 1830–1870.* New Haven: Yale University Press, 1957.
_____ "Victorian Periodical Literature and the Articulate Classes," *Victorian Studies* 22, No. 4 (1979): 389–412.
Howe, M.L. "Rossetti's Comments on *Maud.*" *MLN* 49 (1934): 290–93.
Hughes Linda K. Alexander Smith and the Bisexual Poetics of "A Life-Drama" *Victorian Poetry* 42, No. 4 (2004): 491–508.
J[olly], E[mily]. *The Life and Letters of Sydney Dobell.* 2 vols. London: Smith and Elder, 1878.
Jackson, Holbrook. *The Eighteen Nineties.* 1913. New York: Capricorn, 1966.
James, Louis. *English Popular Literature 1819–1851.* New York: Columbia University Press, 1976.
Jones, T. Percy [W. E. Aytoun]. *Firmilian: Or, The Student of Badajoz, A Spasmodic Tragedy.* New York: Redfield, 1854.
Jump, John D., ed. *Tennyson: The Critical Heritage.* New York: Barnes and Noble, 1967.
"Keats and His School." *Fraser's Magazine for Town and Country* 38 (1848): 495–502.
[Kingsley, Charles]. "Alexander Smith and Alexander Pope." *Fraser's Magazine for Town and Country* 48 (1853): 452–66.
_____. "Thoughts on Shelley and Byron." *Fraser's* 48 (1853): 568–76.
LaPorte, Charles and Jason R. Rudy. "Editorial Introduction: Spasmodic Poetry and Poetics," *Victorian Poetry* 42, No. 4 (2004): 421–428.
LaPorte Charles. "Spasmodic Poetics and Clough's Apostasies." *Victorian Poetry* 42, No. 4 (2004): 521–536.

Bibliography

Lindsay, Maurice. *History of Scottish Literature*. London: Hale, 1977.
Litzinger, Boyd, and Donald Smalley. *Browning: The Critical Heritage*. London: Routledge, 1970.
Lowry, Howard Foster, ed. *The Letters of Matthew Arnold to Arthur Hugh Clough*. London: Oxford University Press, 1932.
Lunsford, Andrea A. "A Bibliographical Note on William Edmondstoune Aytoun's Manuscript: Lectures on Rhetoric and Belles Lettres." *Rhetoric Society Quarterly* 16 (1986): 327–35.
[Mansfield, Horatio]. Rev. of *Poems,* by Matthew Arnold. *Tait's Edinburgh Magazine* 21 (1854): 59–60.
Marchand, Leslie A. *The Athenaeum: A Mirror of Victorian Culture*. Chapel Hill: University of North Carolina Press, 1941.
Marshall, William, ed. *Lord Byron: Selected Poems and Letters*. Boston: Houghton-Mifflin, 1968.
Marston, John Westland. *Gerald: A Dramatic Poem and Other Poems*. London: Mitchell, 1842.
Mason, Emma. "Rhythmic Numinousness: Sydney Dobell and 'The Church,'" *Victorian Poetry* 42, no. 4 (2004), 537–552.
[Massey, Gerald]. "Poetry—The Spasmodists." *North British Review* 28 (1858): 231–50.
_____. Rev. of *Balder,* by Sydney Dobell. *The Eclectic Review* ns 8 (1854): 424–35.
McKillop, Alan D. "A Victorian Faust." *PMLA* 40 (1925): 743–68.
Megroz, M.L. *Modern English Poetry: 1882–1932*. London: Nicholson, 1933.
Miles, Alfred H., ed. *The Poets and Poetry of the Century*. London: Hutchinson, 1898.
"The Month, The Library, and The Studio." *Chambers' Edinburgh Journal* 25 Feb. 1854: 127.
More, Paul E., ed. *The Complete Poetical Works of Byron*. Boston: Houghton-Mifflin, 1933.
Nichol, John, ed. *The Poetry of Sydney Dobell (Selected)*. London: Scott, 1887.
_____. *Thoughts on Art, Philosophy, and Religion: Selected from the Unpublished Papers of Sydney Dobell*. London: Smith and Elder, 1876.
Nicoll, W. Robertson, and Thomas J. Wise, *Literary Anecdotes of the Nineteenth Century: Contributions Towards a Literary History of the Period*. 2 vols. London: Hodder and Stoughton, 1896.
[Norton, Thomas Brinsley, Lord Grantley]. *Pinocchi*. London: Parker, 1856.
O'Donoghue, Heather. *English Poetry and Old Norse Myth: A History*. London: Oxford University Press, 2014.
[Oliphant, Margaret]. "The Byways of Literature." *Blackwood's Edinburgh Magazine* 84 (1858): 200–16.
_____. "Modern Light Literature—Poetry." *Blackwood's Edinburgh Magazine* 79 (1856): 125–38.
"Our Eighteen-Hundred-and-Fifty-Four Poets." *The Eclectic Review* 9 (1855): 39–44.
"Our Library Table." *Athenaeum* 22 August 1857: 1055–57.
"Our Weekly Gossip." *Athenaeum* 17 Jan. 1857: 84.
Paige, Lori A. "Charlotte Brontë and the Spasmodic School." *Brontë Society Transactions* 21 no. 3 (1994): 63–69.
[Patmore, Coventry]. "New Poets." *Edinburgh Review* 104 (1856): 337–62.
Peattie, Roger W. *Selected Letters of William Michael Rossetti*. University Park: Penn State University Press, 1990.
Perkins, David. "The Construction of 'The Romantic Movement' as a Literary Classification." *Nineteenth-Century Literature* 45 (1990): 129–43.
Peters, Robert L., ed. *Victorians on Literature and Art*. New York: Appleton, 1961.
Pittock, Malcolm. "Dobell, *Balder,* and Post-Romanticism." *Essays in Criticism* 42 (1992): 221–42.

Bibliography

Quiller-Couch, Arthur. *Studies in Literature.* Urbana-Champaign: University of Illinois Press, 1924.
Ray, Gordon N. *Tennyson Reads* Maud. Vancouver: University of British Columbia, 1968.
"Retrospect of the Literature of the Quarter." *New Quarterly Review* 3 (1854): 121–34.
"Retrospect of the Literature of the Quarter IV." *New Quarterly Review* 4 (1855): 1–21.
Rev. of *Balder,* by Sydney Dobell. *Athenaeum* 14 Jan. 1854: 49–50.
―――― *Balder,* by Sydney Dobell. *Chambers' Edinburgh Journal* 8 July 1854: 26–29.
―――― *Balder,* by Sydney Dobell. *The British Quarterly Review* 19 (1854): 570–73.
―――― *Balder,* by Sydney Dobell. *The New Monthly Magazine* 100 (March 1854): 292–96.
―――― *City Poems,* by Alexander Smith. *Athenaeum* 12 Sept. 1857: 1146.
―――― *England in Time of War,* by Sydney Dobell and Alexander Smith. *New Quarterly Review* 5 (1856): 420–23.
―――― *Firmilian,* by "T. Percy Jones." *Athenaeum* 30 Sept. 1854: 1165.
―――― *Firmilian,* by "T. Percy Jones." *New Quarterly Review* 4 (1855): 82–85.
―――― *Night and the Soul,* by John Stanyan Bigg. *Athenaeum* 28 Oct. 1854: 39–40.
―――― *Night and the Soul,* by John Stanyan Bigg. *Dublin University Magazine* 212 (1854): 479–83.
―――― *Pinocchi. Fraser's* 53 (1856): 438–42.
―――― *The Roman,* by Sydney Dobell. *Athenaeum* 13 April 1850: 389–90.
―――― *The Roman,* by Sydney Dobell. *Chambers' Edinburgh Journal* 21 Sept. 1850: 187–89.
―――― *The Roman,* by Sydney Dobell. *The Literary Gazette.* 25 Jan. 1851: 62–63.
Richards, Bernard. *English Poetry of the Victorian Period 1830–1890.* London: Longmans, 1988.
Ricks, Christopher. *The Poems of Tennyson.* 3 vols. Berkeley: University of California Press, 1987.
Riding, Laura, and Robert Graves. *A Pamphlet Against Anthologies.* 1928. New York: AMS, 1970.
Rossetti, W.M. "William Bell Scott and Modern British Poetry." *Macmillan's* 33 (1876): 418–27.
Rudy, Jason R. "Rhythmic Intimacy, Spasmodic Epistemology." *Victorian Poetry* 42, No. 4 (2004): 451–472.
Rutherford, Andrew, ed. *Byron: The Critical Heritage.* London: Routledge, 2013.
Scott, Mary Jane. "Alexander Smith: Poet of Victorian Scotland." *Studies in Scottish Literature* 14 (1979): 98–111.
Scott, P.G. "Alexander Smith's Glasgow Miscellany and Robert Burns." *Studies in Scottish Literature* 16 (1981): 241–42.
[Scott, William]. "Poetical Nuisances." *Saturday Review* 23 Feb. 1856: 327–29.
――――. Rev. of *England in Time of War,* by Sydney Dobell. *Saturday Review* 26 July 1856: 304–305.
Shannon, Edgar F., Jr. "The Critical Reception of Tennyson's *Maud*." *PMLA* 68 (1953): 397–417.
Shattock, Joanne, and Michael Wolff, eds. *The Victorian Periodical Press: Samplings and Soundings.* Toronto: University of Toronto Press, 1982.
Sir Nathaniel [Francis Jacox]. "Literary Leaflets 24, 'Firmilian.'" *The New Monthly Magazine* 102 (1854): 140–47.
Smith, Alexander. "Essayists, Old and New." *North British Review* 37 (1862): 132–69.
――――. "How We Went to Skye." *Blackwood's Edinburgh Magazine* 85 (1859): 155–64.
――――. "In a Skye Bothy," *Macmillan's* 1 (1859/60): 119–29.
――――. *Last Leaves: Sketches and Criticisms.* Edinburgh: Nimmo, 1869.
――――. "Novels and Novelists of the Day." *North British Review* 38 (1863): 168–90.
――――. *Poems.* 1853. Boston: Ticknor and Fields, 1855.
――――. "Rambles Round Glasgow." *Blackwood's Edinburgh Magazine* 83 (1858): 467–83.

Bibliography

[Smith, William Henry]. "Festus." *Blackwood's Edinburgh Magazine* 67 (1850): 415–30.
Somervell, D.C. "The Reputation of Robert Browning." *Essays and Studies* 15 (1929): 122–38.
"The Spasmodic Drama." *Dublin University Magazine* 44 (1854): 488–92.
Thale, Jerome. "Browning's 'Popularity' and the Spasmodic Poets." *Journal of English and Germanic Philology* 54 (1955): 348–54.
_____. *Sydney Dobell: A Spasmodic Poet.* Ph.D. Diss. Northwestern University, 1953.
Tillotson, Geoffrey. *Criticism and the Nineteenth Century.* Hamden, CT: Archon, 1967.
Trilling, Lionel. *Matthew Arnold.* 1939. New York: Meridian, 1955.
[Troup, George]. "Poets and Poetry," *Tait's Edinburgh Magazine* 15 (1848): 549–60.
Tucker, Herbert F. "Glandular Omnism and Beyond: The Victorian Spasmodic Epic." *Victorian Poetry* 42, No. 4 (2004): 429–450.
Tupper, Martin Farquhar. *Proverbial Philosophy: A Book of Thoughts and Arguments, Originally Treated.* New York: Wiley, 1846.
Vinson, James, ed. *Great Writers of the English Language: Poets.* New York: St. Martins, 1979.
Walker, Hugh. *The Age of Tennyson.* London: Bell, 1914.
_____. *The Literature of the Victorian Era.* Cambridge: Cambridge University Press, 1910.
"The War." *The Athenaeum* 13 Jan. 1855: 45–47.
Ward, Sir A.W. and A.R. Waller, *The Cambridge History of English Literature.* 15 vols. New York: Putnam, 1917.
Watkins, C.C. "Browning's *Men and Women* and the Spasmodic School." *Journal of English and Germanic Philology* 57 (1958): 57–59.
Watson, Nick J. "Muscular Christianity in the Modern Age," *Sport and Spirituality.* London: Taylor and Francis, 2007.
Weinstein, Mark A. *William Edmundstoune Aytoun and the Spasmodic Controversy.* New Haven: Yale University Press, 1969.
Welby, T. Earle. *The Victorian Romantics 1850–1870.* London: Howe, 1929.
Westwater, Martha. *The Spasmodic Career of Sydney Dobell.* New York: University Press of America, 1992.
Weygandt, Cornelius. *The Time of Tennyson: English Victorian Poetry as it Affected America.* New York: Appleton, 1936.
Willett, Mischa. "'Fading Crimean Flowers': Spasmodic *Sonnets on the War.*" *Victoriographies* 8 no. 2 (2018), 135–150.
Wimsatt, William K., and Cleanth Brooks. *Literary Criticism.* New York: Knopf, 1959.
"Z." "The Last New Poet." *Athenaeum* 3 Jan. 1857: 16–18.
_____. "The Last New Poet." *Athenaeum* 10 Jan. 1857: 52.

Anthologies Containing Spasmodic Poems and Excerpts

Adams, W. Davenport, ed. *Dictionary of English Literature.* New York: Cassell, 1880.
Douglas, George. *The Book of Scottish Poetry.* New York: Baker, 1953.
Gray, Donald J., ed. *Victorian Literature: Poetry.* New York: Macmillan, 1976.
Hayward, John, ed. *The Oxford Book of Nineteenth-Century Verse.* Oxford: Clarendon, 1964.
Lewis, D.B. Wyndham, and Charles Lee. *The Stuffed Owl: An Anthology of Bad Verse.* London: Dent, 1948.
Lindsay, Maurice, and R. Mackie, eds. *A Book of Scottish Verse.* New York: St. Martin's, 1983.
MacDiarmid, Hugh, ed. *The Golden Treasury of Scottish Poetry.* New York: Macmillan, 1941.

Bibliography

Messenger, N.P. and J.R. Watson, eds. *Victorian Poetry*. Totowa, New Jersey: Dent, 1974.
Miles, Alfred H., ed. *Poets and Poetry of the Nineteenth Century*. London: Routledge, 1907.
Mitchell, Dugald, ed. *The Book of Highland Verse*. London: Nutt, 1912.
Quiller-Couch, Arthur, ed. *The Oxford Book of Victorian Verse*. Oxford: Clarendon, 1913.
Stedman, Edmund Clarence, ed. *A Victorian Anthology 1837–1895*. Boston: Houghton-Mifflin, 1895.
Stevenson, Burton Egbert. *Home Book of Verse, American and English*. New York: Holt, 1912.
Ward, Thomas Humphrey, ed. *The English Poets: Selections*. London: Macmillan, 1881.
Willmott, Rev. Robert A., ed. *The Poets of the Nineteenth Century*. New York: Harper, 1857.
Wilson, James Grant, ed. *The Poets and Poetry of Scotland*. London: Blackie, N.D.

Index

agnosticism 34, 64, 120, 125
alienation 65, 97, 102, 116
Altick, Richard D. 30–32
American poets and the Spasmodics 6
anarchy 53, 159
anthologies 24–27, 98
anti–Classical trends 37, 38
anti–Romantic sentiment 24, 42, 91, 121, 126, 137, 142, 161
anti–Spasmodic backlash 4, 56, 75, 88, 91, 98, 100, 126, 137, 151, 165
Apollodorus [George Gilfillan] 17, 27, 131, 132, 140, 144
aristocracy, British 42, 62, 88, 148, 150, 152
Arnold, Edwin 127
Arnold, Matthew: "Balder Dead" 105; and Browning 163–164; and Classical standards for literature 11, 16, 27, 45, 109, 141, 142, 146; and Clough 15–16, 30, 88, 98; critical influence 4, 25, 118, 126, 170–171; "Dover Beach" 8; 853 Preface 2–3, 16, 17, 23, 126, 134, 140; "Empedocles on Etna" 126, 151; "Haworth Churchyard" 43; misogyny 14; pessimism 7; "Poems" 51, 88; and social issues 104; and social class prejudice 5, 12, 16, 24, 27, 40, 89, 95
atheism 147, 148, 154
The Athenaeum 13, 37, 43, 48, 51, 85, 97, 118, 141, 142, 144, 162
Auden, W.H. 26
Aytoun, William Edmondstoune (W.E.): anti–Romantic views 40, 69, 129, 138–139; critical legacy 19, 128, 134, 142, 149; "Firmilian" (article) 17, 127, 130; *Firmilian* (book) 5, 57, 72, 80, 98, 123, 134, 137–139; and Gilfillan 106, 132, 140; as parodist 17, 128; relationship with Alexander Smith 132; reviews of Spasmodic poems 143, 156, 162

Bagehot, Walter 154
Bailey, P.J.: and the Browniings 161, 163; as the first Spasmodic 7, 12, 18, 42, 51, 120, 146; and *Gerald* 78, 81; popularity of *Festus* 32, 34, 44, 47, 50, 55–60, 63, 75, 110,

152; Romantic elements in *Festus* 60–62, 64–66, 80, 96, 137; social class 29; stylistic elements of *Festus* 29, 54, 65, 67–69, 72–74, 79, 87
Balder see Dobell, Sydney
ballads 73, 104, 128
Barrett-Browning, Elizabeth: admiration for Horne 74–75; admiration for Smith 87; *Aurora Leigh* 4, 16, 162–163
Bartleby the Scrivener 88
Baudelaire, Charles 148
Bayne, Peter 89, 93
Bigg, John Stanyan (J.S.): death 54, 165; identified as a Spasmodic 12, 19, 29, 51, 54, 100, 144; *Night and the Soul* 119–123, 141; social class 29
Birley, Robert 55
bisexuality 6
Blackwood's Edinburgh Magazine 32, 83, 125–126, 129, 133, 143
Blair, Kirstie 21
Brontë, Anne 169
Brontë, Branwell 169
Brontë, Charlotte 4, 13–14, 43, 54, 71, 101, 116, 169
Brontë, Emily 13, 14, 19, 43, 169
Browning, Elizabeth Barrett *see* Barrett-Browning, Elizabeth
Browning, Robert: admiration for Horne 74; admiration for Tupper 34; associated with Spasmodic poets 8, 19, 20, 79, 161, 163–166; attitude toward Romantic poets 41, 45; critical attitude toward 53, 55, 74, 151, 161; *Men and Women* 151, 162; poetic technique 116, 156; *Sordello* 163, 164, 195
Buchanan, Robert 100, 101, 146, 167
Buckley, Jerome 2–3, 5, 19, 78, 95, 111, 166, 170–171
Buckler, William 156
Burns, Robert 11, 41, 73, 84, 142
Byron, Lord (George Gordon): "Cain" 60, 61, 68, 69, 71; critics' attitude toward 1, 41–45, 52; influence on *Maud* 152, 159; influence on Spasmodic poetry 3, 8, 19,

Index

34, 59–62, 68–69, 73, 88–89, 111, 116, 136, 148; *Manfred* 19, 23, 41–42, 60, 69, 90, 102, 113; Spasmodic poets' adulation of 11, 12, 29, 57, 102, 143, 155; Victorian attitudes toward 4, 16, 20–23, 40, 145

Calvinism 56, 59
Cambridge Apostles 41, 45
canon, literary 4, 5, 8, 24, 25, 37, 53, 123, 146, 163, 170, 172
Carlyle, Thomas: attitude toward Byron 22, 41–43, 49; "Goethe's Works" 20; "Heroes and Hero Worship" 77; influence on Spasmodics 3, 5, 7, 59, 77, 85, 89, 96; *Sartor Resartus* 41, 132
Catholicism 132
Chambers' Cyclopaedia of English Literature 54, 55
Chambers' Edinburgh Journal 103–105, 141
Christianity 21, 33, 49, 50, 93, 107, 117
Clough, Arthur Hugh 2, 4, 11, 15–16, 30, 45, 54, 56, 88–89, 95, 98, 109
Cockney School 22, 36, 45, 126
Coleridge, Samuel Taylor 21, 23, 41, 45, 48, 49, 111
Cronin, Richard 85, 97
Culler, A. Dwight 156, 159
culture-at-home publications 30

Decadents 6, 21, 148, 167, 168
Dickinson, Emily 6
Dobell, Sydney: *Balder* 39, 90, 93, 105–117, 124; and the Brontë sisters 13–14, 43; and Byron 23, 42, 44; critical reception 24, 35, 118, 141–146, 149, 166, 170; early life 12–13, 29, 100–102; *England in Time of War* 18, 117, 130, 144; relationship with Alexander Smith 7, 98; relationship with George Gilfillan 12, 45, 47, 49–51, 58, 62, 104, 125; *The Roman* 39, 48, 56, 97, 102–10; *Sonnets on the War* 75, 98, 104, 147, 155, 171
Doctor Faustus see Marlowe, Christopher
dogmatism 7, 33–35, 38, 46, 79
dramatic monologue 103, 107, 156, 163
Dublin University Magazine 120, 123, 140
Duck, Stephen 32

Edinburgh Review 41, 43
Edwin of Deira see Smith, Alexander
Elizabethan literature 79, 146, 156
"Empedocles on Etna" *see* Arnold, Matthew
evangelism 29, 49, 56, 62, 93, 102, 105

Faust see Goethe
feminism 6, 19, 162, 163, 169, 171
Festus see Bailey, P.J.

Firmilian see Aytoun, W.E.
French Revolution 36
Freudian criticism 114

Garnett, Richard 13
Gaskell, Elizabeth 14
gender issues 5, 14, 21, 34, 101, 171
Gifford, William 85, 140, 149
Gilfillan, George: death 18; early life 11, 29; as literary critic 11–14, 17, 23, 24, 28, 47–52, 98, 101, 122, 130, 134, 142; relationship with Alexander Smith 12, 14, 58, 85, 98; relationship with Sydney Dobell 15, 58, 104, 105, 108, 131; as Spasmodic mentor 12, 14–16, 45, 56, 84, 86–87, 102, 120, 125–127, 132; *see also* Apollodorus
Goethe, Johann Wolfgang von 3, 20, 22, 41–43, 58–62, 68, 70–72, 135, 159
Gosse, Edmund 45, 54, 62, 74
Gothic novels 6, 15, 31, 32, 38, 102, 106, 110, 111, 114, 124, 126, 132, 147, 159
Grantley, Lord (Thomas Brinsley Norton): *Pinocchi* 147–151

Hazlitt, William 22
Heathcliff 14, 19, 101, 113; *see also* Brontë, Emily
Homer 109, 133
homosexuality 15, 87
Hopkins, Gerard Manley 123, 154
Horne, Richard Hengist (Orion): and the Brownings 20, 74, 75; as an early Spasmodic 19, 20, 58, 59, 74–75, 80; "A New Spirit of the Age" 47, 79–80, 96, 161, 163; *Orion* 74–75
Houghton, Walter 30, 38
Hughes, Linda 15
hypocrisy in Victorian society 8, 35, 42, 109

Idylls of the King see Tennyson, Alfred Lord 152
industrialization 12, 23, 64, 88, 99
infanticide 16, 31, 63, 113, 124, 136

Jeffrey 36, 149
Jolly, Emily 102, 114
Jones, Ebenezer 19, 22, 29, 171
Jones, T. Percy *see* Aytoun, William Edmondstoune (W.E.)

Keats, John: critical views of 4, 19, 21–23, 36–37, 40–45, 49, 73, 74, 85, 86, 126, 140, 158, 163; "Endymion" 132; Smith accused of plagiarizing from 97; Spasmodic emulation of 3, 23, 38, 48, 73, 90–92, 102, 119, 125, 142, 145, 151
Kingsley, Charles 20, 21, 36, 37, 42, 43, 46, 48, 95, 125, 168

206

Index

"Kubla Khan" *see* Coleridge, Samuel Taylor

liberalism 56, 102, 126, 162
libertinism 22, 137, 154
A Life-Drama see Smith, Alexander
Lockhart, John Gibson 36

Macaulay, Thomas Babington 50, 103
Mammonism 81
Manfred see Byron, Lord (George Gordon)
Marlowe, Christopher 59, 60, 68, 71, 139
Marston, John Westland (J.W.): critical views of 20, 79–80, 100, 163; education 29; *Gerald* 18, 19, 63, 77–84, 90, 92, 93, 96, 100, 112, 118–121, 137
Massey, Gerald 12, 19, 22, 29, 32, 125, 135, 161
Maud see Tennyson, Alfred Lord
McKillop, Alan D. 65, 170
melodrama 20, 31, 32, 34, 78, 79, 90, 104, 110, 124, 128, 134, 147, 167
Miller, Lucasta 169
Milton, John 55, 60, 64, 65, 80, 102, 111, 167, 183
misogyny 12, 14, 36
monodrama 156, 159, 161
mythology 66, 74, 105, 113

narcissism 16, 65, 88, 128, 163
National Magazine 19, 88
National Review 144
neo–Romantics 1, 11, 20, 39, 64, 99, 116, 142, 145, 152, 161, 163
New Monthly Magazine 117, 125
Norton, Caroline Elizabeth 148

Oliphant, Margaret 125, 145, 146, 151–154, 159, 164
Orientalism 15, 87, 139
Oxbridge 30, 170
Oxford Brotherhood 161
Oxonians 41
"Ozymandias" *see* Shelley, Percy Bysshe

paganism 66
The Palladium 13, 131
Patmore, Coventry 27, 145, 164
penny-bloods *see* penny dreadfuls
penny dreadfuls 27, 30–32, 124
Philip von Artevelde 43, 59
Phillips, Stephen 167
Philistinism 51, 78, 100, 168
Pinocchi see Grantley, Lord (Thomas Brinsley Sheridan)
Pre-Raphaelites 7, 8, 78, 90, 115, 133, 134, 148, 166, 167

Quiller-Couch, Arthur 25

Radcliffe, Ann 102, 116
Ragg, Thomas 34
The Roman see Dobell, Sydney
Romantic poets 21, 36, 37, 43, 54, 60, 84, 145, 166
Romanticism 7, 8, 21, 22, 27, 32, 35, 41, 62, 78, 101, 124, 144, 152, 165, 166
Rossetti, Dante Gabriel 7, 58, 87, 100, 104, 110, 155, 161, 166
Rossetti, William Michael 58
Rousseau, Jean-Jacques 159
Ruthven, Lord 19

sadism 159
Saintsbury, George 41
Satan *see* Milton, John
satire 34, 42, 114, 123, 132, 134
Scott, Sir Walter 20, 97, 153, 170
Shakespeare 20, 77, 133, 162
Shelley, Percy Bysshe: critical views of 1, 3, 20–23, 40–41, 74, 158; "Hymn to Intellectual Beauty" 70; influence on Spasmodic poetry 23, 50, 59, 97, 102, 119, 125; "Ozymandias" 66; political views 15, 53, 62, 96; Victorian attitudes toward 4, 36, 45, 49, 142
Sheridan, Richard Brinsley 148
Smith, Alexander: accused of plagiarism 97, 118; *City Poems* 151; critical views of 5–7, 8, 16, 23, 25, 35, 117, 124–127, 135, 141–144, 148, 170; death 18, 54, 165; *A Life-Drama* 69, 70, 77, 80–103, 111, 112, 121; novels 18; parodied in *Firmilian* 129, 132; popularity of 15, 30, 32, 34, 46–47, 51; relationship with Dobell 7, 98, 118; relationship with Gilfillan 12, 14, 45, 51, 58, 85, 98; *Sonnets on the War* 18, 70, 75, 98, 104, 147, 148, 155, 171; working-class origins 14, 19, 29, 149
Sordello see Browning, Robert
Sturgeon, Theodore 5
Swinburne, Algernon Charles 4, 6, 8, 24, 41–43, 58, 166

Tait's 89, 102, 124, 125, 140, 141
Taylor, Henry 43, 44, 49, 59
Tennyson, Alfred Lord: admiration for *Festus* 47, 55, 56; association with the Spasmodics 2, 4, 6, 8, 21, 25, 151, 164, 167; critical views of 23, 45, 50, 53, 74, 87, 145; *Idylls of the King* 152; *Maud* 152–161, 164, 166; meeting with Dobell 44; satirized in *Firmilian* 132
Thackeray, William Makepeace 14, 56, 143
Thale, Jerome 105, 114, 119, 171
Thompson, Samuel 101

207

Index

Trilling, Lionel 2, 3, 5, 99, 161, 170, 171
Tupper, Martin Farquhar 33, 34, 63, 64, 67

Unitarianism 56, 101
Universalism 56, 62, 66, 68, 184
University of Edinburgh 18, 98, 128
University of Glasgow 11, 57
Utilitarianism 46

Victoria, Queen 54
Victorianism 2, 6, 8, 35

Walker, Hugh 57, 63, 65–67, 114, 166
Weinstein, Mark A. 4, 27, 132, 162, 170, 171
Welby, T. Earle 24, 166

Westwater, Martha 100
Weygandt, Cornelius 56, 62
Whitman, Walt 6
Wilde, Oscar 21, 90, 118, 148, 168
Wordsworth, William: critical views 37, 40, 41, 43, 145; death 21; "Expostulation and Reply" 91; influence on the Spasmodics 23, 91, 145; "The Recluse" 152; Victorian attitudes toward 32, 36, 42, 45, 48, 49
working-class poets 5, 12, 17, 22, 24, 29, 32, 36, 45, 84, 86, 97, 98, 126, 129, 149, 171

Yendys, Sydney *see* Dobell, Sydney

www.ingramcontent.com/pod-product-compliance
Lightning Source LLC
Chambersburg PA
CBHW032043300426
44117CB00009B/1178